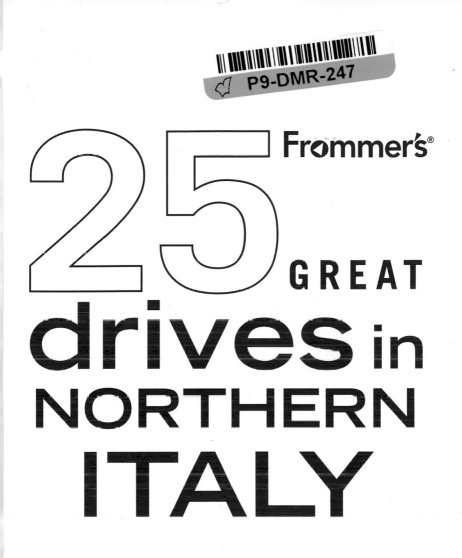

Frommer's®

25 GREAT
drives in
NORTHERN
ITALY

WILEY

Wiley Publishing, Inc.

Touring Club Italiano
Chairman: Roberto Ruozi
Touring Editore
Managing director : Armando Peres
General manager: Marco Ausenda
Assistant general manager: Renato Salvetti
Editorial director: Michele D'Innella
Head of guidebooks: Anna Ferrari-Bravo
Editing: Cinzia Rando
Editorial production and layout: Studio editoriale Selmi
Written by: Marina Tagliaferri
Translated by: Barbara Fisher
Picture research : Rossella Barresi
Maps: Graffito-Cusano Milanino; Revised maps: Sergio Seveso

Revised fifth edition published 2010
Revised fourth edition published 2008
Revised third edition published 2006
Revised second edition published 2004
First published 2002

© 2002, 2004, 2006, 2008, 2010 Touring Editore
Management and editorial offices: Corso Italia 10, Milano

© Concept and design: AA Media Limited

This Best Drives guidebook was produced by Touring Club Italiano in agreement with AA Media Limited, owner of the 'Best Drives' series

© English translation: AA Media Limited 2002, 2004, 2006, 2008, 2010

The contents of this publication are believed correct at the time of printing. Nevertheless, the publishers cannot accept responsibility for errors or omissions or for changes in details given in this guide or for the consequences of any reliance on the information provided by the same. Assessments of attractions and so forth are based upon the author's own experience and, therefore, descriptions given in this guide necessarily contain an element of subjective opinion which may not reflect the publisher's opinion or dictate a reader's own experience on another occasion.

Published by AA Publishing

Published in the United States by
Wiley Publishing, Inc.
111 River Street, Hoboken, NJ 07030

Find us online at Frommers.com

Frommer's is a registered trademark of Arthur Frommer.
Used under license.

ISBN 978-0-470-56025-9

Photolitho and photocomposition: Emmegi Multimedia, Milan
Printed and bound by : G. Canale & C. S.p.a., Torino, Italy

A04153

CONTENTS

ABOUT THIS BOOK

This book is not only a practical touring guide for the independent traveller, but is also invaluable for those who would like to know more about the Italian Lakes. It is divided into six geographical regions, with town visits and itineraries included for each one. Specific city tours are featured for Como, Bergamo, Brescia, Verona and Venice. Each tour has details of the most interesting places to visit en route. Boxes catering for special interests follow some of the main entries – for those whose interest is in history or walking or those who have children. There are also boxes which highlight scenic stretches of road and which give details of the natural environment, local traditions and gastronomy. Special features cover the lake resorts' holiday tradition, the lakes' geological origin, food and wine, and flora. The simple route directions are accompanied by an easy-to-use map at the beginning of each tour, along with a chart showing how far it is from one town to the next in kilometres and miles. This can help you decide where to take a break and stop overnight. (All distances quoted are approximate.) Before setting off it is advisable to check with the information centre listed at the start of the tour for recommendations on where to break your journey, and for additional information on what to see and do, and when best to visit.

This symbol on the maps represents other attractions seen along the routes, often mentioned in the panels.

Tour Information
See pages 168–176 for the addresses, telephone numbers and opening times of the attractions mentioned in the tours, including the telephone numbers of tourist information centres.
General information on boat services on the lakes and in Venice is on pages 158–159, along with general information on motoring in Italy.

Accommodation and restaurants
Pages 160–167 list hotels, farm holiday centres and camping sites situated at the point of departure or along the route of each tour.
Also listed are restaurants where you may like to stop for a meal. There are, of course, other possibilities to be found along the way.

Credit Cards
All principal credit cards are accepted by most establishments, but not petrol stations.

Currency
The unit of currency in Italy is the Euro (€). Euro bank notes are in denominations of €5, €10, €20, €50, €100, €200 and €500; coins are in denominations of 1, 2, 5, 10, 20 and 50 cents, and €1 and €2.

Customs Regulations
Items for personal or professional use may be brought into Italy free of charge, but take receipts for valuable articles to avoid paying duty on them. Travellers' allowances for Italy are the same as other EU countries. Check current guidelines.

Electricity
The current is 220 volts AC, 50 cycles, with two round-pin plugs. British, Australian or New Zealand appliances normally requiring a slightly higher voltage will work. Visitors from North America with appliances requiring 100/120 volts, and not fitted for dual voltage, will require a voltage transformer.

Emergency Telephone Numbers
Police tel: 112. Ambulance tel: 113. Fire tel: 115.

Entry Regulations
The only document necessary for UK, Irish, Commonwealth and US citizens is a valid passport for any stay of up to three months. Officially visitors from other EU countries need only a national identity card to enter Italy, but in practice you will need a passport.
However, passport and visa requirements are subject to change, so you should check prior to your visit.

Health
Health insurance is recommended, but visitors from EU countries are entitled to health services as available to Italians. This means obtaining, prior to departure, the relevant documentation (EHIC – European Health Insurance Card).
The high cost of treatment makes insurance essential if you are a non-EU citizen. Keep all bills for medical treatment and medicines to claim back later.

Post Offices
Post offices are generally open 8–1.30/2 Mon–Fri; to 11.45am on Sat. On the last day of the month offices close at noon. Times vary from place to place.

Public Holidays
1 January – New Year's Day
6 January – Epiphany
Easter Monday
25 April – Liberation Day (1945)
1 May – Labour Day
2 June – Proclamation of Republic (celebrated on following Saturday)
15 August – Ferragosto (Assumption)
1 November – All Saints
8 December – Immaculate Conception
25–26 December – Christmas.

Roads
The Italian pre-Alpine lake region, spread over Piedmont,

Lombardy, Veneto and Trentino-Alto Adige, is served by an extensive road network. The main axis is the A4, which runs from Turin via Novara, Milan, Bergamo, Brescia, Verona, Vicenza and Padua to Mestre, Venice and Trieste.

Main roads and motorways branch off the A4 to the lakeshores: the A26 from Genoa to Arona; the SS229 and SS32 from Novara to lakes Orta and Maggiore respectively; the A8 from Milan to Lake Maggiore and Varese; the A9 to Como, Chiasso and Lugano; the SS36 and SS342d to Lecco; the SS510 from Brescia to Lake Iseo; the SS572 from Desenzano and Peschiera and then 45 bis and SS249 Gardesana Occidentale and Orientale respectively; the A22 Brenner motorway from Verona to Trento.

Dual carriageways and motorways are used to cover certain approaches more quickly

Cadenabbia on Lake Como

or to speed up the return journey, but tours generally use A roads and sometimes secondary roads. Those skirting the lakes suffer from heavy traffic, especially at weekends, during holiday periods (July and August in particular) and on the main lakes (Maggiore and Garda).

Parking in the cities (Como, Bergamo, Brescia, Verona) is a problem. Some suggestions are given in the text and on the maps; others can be obtained from the tourist information offices. Venice poses its own peculiar problems.

Telephones

Most phone booths on streets and in bars, tobacco shops and restaurants take coins or a phone card *(una scheda telefonica)*, bought from post offices, stores or bars. Tear the corner off the card before use.

To call abroad, dial 00, then the country code, followed by the city code and number. The prefix for the UK is 0044; for

Eire 00353; for the US and Canada 001; for Australia 0061.

Free phone numbers *(numeri verde)* usually begin with 800 and national call rate numbers begin with 848 or 199. Hotels tend to overcharge for long-distance and international calls, so it is best to make calls from public phones, using telephone cards.

Rates are lowest on Sunday and between 10pm and 8am weekdays and Saturday.

Tourist Offices

The Italian State Tourist Office (ENIT) is represented in the following:
Australia: – Level 26, 44 Market Street, Sydney NSW 2000 (tel: 02 9262 1666).
Canada: Suite 907, 175 Bloor Street East, Toronto M4W 3R8 (tel: 416/925-4882).
UK: 1 Princes Street, London W1B 2AY (tel: 020 7408-1254).
US: Suite 1565, 630 Fifth Avenue, New York NY 10111 (tel: 212/245-5618).

LAKE MAGGIORE

Lake Maggiore, or Verbano as it is also known, is the second largest lake in Italy (after Lake Garda) and the most westerly pre-Alpine lake, created over several millennia as glaciers slowly melted. With a surface area of 212sq km (80 square miles), it forms part of a complex hydrographic system that also includes the nearby lakes of Orta, by comparison in size a mere splash of water, and the curiously shaped Lugano. There are several small islands – the three Borromean islands (Bella, Madre, Pescatori) in the centre of the gulf of the same name; the islet of San Giovanni, opposite Pallanza; and the isles that are home to the Cànnero castles, built in the 12th century. The lake's shores lie in Lombardy (in the province of Varese), Piedmont (in the provinces of Novara and Verbano-Cusio-Ossola), and the northern section lies in Switzerland. Its central position and an extensive road and motorway network make the lake easily accessible from the main northern Italian cities.

Thanks to its splendid position and the trade routes of the Ticino river and canals to the centre of the Po plain, right up to Milan and Pavia, Lake Maggiore has long been a major transport and trade link between northern Italy and central Europe. As a result, this territory was fortified with strongholds and castles (such as those of Angera and Arona, positioned to defend the lower lake), which still mark the landscape.

The splendid villas, lush gardens, grand hotels and art nouveau mansions built between the 18th and 20th centuries along its shores, especially between Arona, Stresa and Intra, have made the lake universally renowned. This was the era when, thanks to its mild climate and delightful resorts, Lake Maggiore became a firm favourite of the Lombard aristocracy and an obligatory stop on the Grand Tour so popular with foreign travellers.

Fishing on Lake Maggiore, near the Cànnero castles

Tour 1

This itinerary winds around the Borromean Gulf, the lake's geographical centre and a great tourist attraction, stopping in some of the best-known towns such as Stresa and Pallanza and visiting villas and splendid gardens. The starting point is Stresa, the scene of aristocratic society life in the early 1900s, where you can visit the gardens of Villa Pallavicino. A short boat trip will take you to the Borromean islands, one of the most famous and romantic places on the lake. Again, Isola Bella and Isola Madre feature gardens of extraordinary beauty. A detour leads inland to Lake Mergozzo and the Val Grande National Park, one of Italy's major wilderness zones. You then return to the lake, at Intra and Pallanza, to visit the world-famous botanical gardens of Villa Taranto.

Tour 2

This scenic route visits the southernmost part of the lake and its hinterland, the green Vergante plateau, dotted with tiny villages. From Arona to Stresa the lakeside road offers superb views of the opposite shore. You then climb inland along quiet roads that give sweeping – and sometimes spectacular – views of Lake Maggiore and the nearby lakes of Monate and Varese. This is an ideal spot for tranquil nature walks. Last comes a visit to the Lagoni di Mercurago Regional Park.

Tour 3

The scenery takes on a different character on this tour, which explores the northernmost part of Lake Maggiore. Here the gentle Mediterranean views give way to a harsher landscape, with mountains descending to the water and increasingly fewer villages perched on the rocks. The route passes through the lovely Val Vigezzo (known for its Alpine scenery and painted houses) and Centovalli, to reach

Locarno, in Switzerland, on the northernmost tip of the lake, before returning on the east coast to Laveno, and the ferry back to Verbania.

Tour 4

The journey starts at Stresa and leads to Lake Orta, the most romantic of all the pre-Alpine lakes, passing the Mottarone massif for incomparable views of the Verbano and Cusio areas. After a visit to the Sacro Monte (sacred mountain) of Varallo, a 16th-century masterpiece of art and devotion, it returns to Stresa, skirting Lake Orta from the north.

The Sanctuary of Santa Caterina del Sasso, above Lake Maggiore

Tour 5

The final tour in this region explores the east shore of Lake Maggiore and its hinterland. The first part winds through a gentle, hilly landscape with such fascinating attractions as the Sacro Monte (sacred mountain) religious complex at Varese. The second part follows the lakeshore and includes a visit to some of its most famous monuments, such as the Sanctuary of Santa Caterina del Sasso and the Rocca di Angera.

The Borromean
Gulf

This romantic visit to the heart of Lake Maggiore, from Stresa to Pallanza, explores the Borromean Gulf – the lake's geographic centre and a great tourist attraction – with its spectacular villas and splendid gardens showing superb seasonal displays of flowers. A short boat trip takes you to the lake's three 'pearls', the Borromean islands.

ITINERARY		
STRESA	▶	**Isole Borromee**
		(by boat)
STRESA	▶	**Baveno (4km-2½m)**
BAVENO	▶	**Feriolo (5km-3m)**
FERIOLO	▶	**Mergozzo**
		(10km-6m)
MERGOZZO	▶	**Cicogna (22km-14m)**
CICOGNA	▶	**Intra (16km-10m)**
INTRA	▶	**Pallanza (4km-2½m)**
PALLANZA	▶	**Stresa (16km-10m)**

1 DAY • 77KM • 48 MILES

ⓘ Stresa

Stresa and Pallanza sit at either end of the Borromean Gulf, the heart of Lake Maggiore. Stresa became famous in the 19th century when it was 'discovered' by travellers undertaking the Grand Tour of Europe. In Italy the Tour retraced the steps of the poet Lord Byron (1788–1824) and the novelist Stendhal (1783–1842), who were among the first to succumb to the charm of the pre-Alpine lakes. During the pre-World War I belle époque era, the town – which had in the meantime

acquired grand hotels, sports clubs, a casino and splendid villas set in well-tended gardens – rivalled Monte Carlo and the Lido di Venezia for society life. Its success was assured by the construction, in the early 1900s, of the Simplon railway, which made it easy to reach from countries on the other side of the Alps. Elegant, exclusive and snobbish, it became – partly thanks to the excellent climate – a favourite destination of the

A peacock displays its spectacular tail in the gardens of Isola Bella

Stresa viewed from the cable-car that climbs to Mottarone

European aristocracy and upper classes. Much of that glorious past lives on today in Stresa, which remains one of the lake's main holiday resorts and the venue for congresses and major cultural events, such as the 'Music Weeks' of late summer.

Dominated by the heights of Mottarone (1,491m/4,891 feet), the town has a beautiful lakeside promenade with delightful views of the Borromean islands and is an irresistible place for a

FOR CHILDREN

Llamas, kangaroos, zebras, flamingos and many more exotic mammals and birds are among the main attractions of the Villa Pallavicino park in Stresa. The animals live free in large restricted areas, where children can observe them at close range. There is also a playground for the very young, and older children (and adults) can visit the fine botanical gardens. For a relaxing day close to nature the complex also offers picnic areas, a restaurant and a bar.

stroll. The lakeside is lined with grand hotels and elegant residences, among which is the noteworthy 18th-century Villa Ducale, where the Italian philosopher Antonio Rosmini died in 1855. It's now the home of the Rosmini International Study Centre.

The town centre is a pedestrian zone given over to shopping and good dining. A cable-car climbs to Mottarone, which can also be reached by car on a toll road (see Tour 4).

On the edge of the town, towards Belgirate, stands the 19th-century Villa Pallavicino, surrounded by a 20-hectare (49-acre) park and an excellent

example of an 'English garden', created in the 1800s on the shore of the lake.

i Piazza Marconi 16

▶ *Take a boat from the jetty in Piazza Marconi or Carciano to Isola Bella, and from here to Isola Pescatori and Isola Madre.*

2 Isole Borromee
In the Middle Ages these islands housed military garrisons and monasteries, but they were transformed in the 18th century by the illustrious Borromeo family of Milan, who turned Isola Bella into an island-palace,

Isola Pescatori into a rural island and Isola Madre into an island-garden. The three small Borromean islands, only open to the public from late March to late October, are still among the most delightful places on the lake and receive a constant flow of visitors. In years past they were favoured by intellectuals and VIPs, from the Italian conductor Arturo Toscanini to writers Ernest Hemingway and George Bernard Shaw, and the British Royal Family.

First comes Isola Bella, named after Isabella d'Adda, the wife of Count Carlo III Borromeo, who deserves the credit for having – in 1632 –

begun work on the grandiose palace that still occupies most of the island. The main impetus for the project came, however, from his son, Vitaliano Borromeo, who commissioned the leading architects and artists of the time to create the palace and its spectacular gardens. Once completed, this massive undertaking was to give the island the appearance of a ship, representing the glories of the Borromeo family, with a bow formed by the steps and gardens. Actually the original plans were never carried out; work continued for decades, and the northern façade was not completed until 1959. The palace, with its sumptuous interiors, contains works of art dating from several periods, including a number of precious 17th-century Flemish tapestries. The lower rooms are extremely

Left: an aerial view of Isola Bella, almost entirely occupied by the 17th-century Palazzo Borromeo
Below: the palace gardens

unusual and resemble a grotto encrusted with stones, tufa, shells and marble, an ideal place of refuge from the overbearing summer heat. The palace leads out on to one of the most spectacular Italian gardens of the baroque period. Spread out over ten terraces at differing levels and adorned with statues and

FOR HISTORY BUFFS

Lake Maggiore has many reminders of the presence of the Borromeo family, loyal to the lords of Milan, who, in the mid-15th century, appointed the Borromeos to be responsible for the area's defence against Switzerland. The family reinforced the defences erected around the lake by the Visconti family, enlarging and strengthening the twin castles of Arona and Angera, which controlled the southern basin. Their name is linked with the lake's discovery as a holiday resort. They chose the three islands in the centre of the lake – Bella, Madre and Pescatori – as the sites for their elegant summer residences, embellishing them with splendid gardens. The gulf between Stresa and Pallanza and the three islands (still owned by the family) continues to bear the family name.

fountains, they are dominated by a huge statue of a unicorn, the symbol of the Borromeo family. An entrance fee is charged to visit the palace and gardens. Next to the monumental complex is a small village with shops, bars and restaurants.

From Isola Bella you move on to Isola Pescatori (Fishermen's Island), so called because it was formerly the largest fishing village on the lake. Today its inhabitants (about 100) concentrate on tourism and have managed to preserve intact the island's charm, simplicity, unhurried pace of life and vernacular architecture.

Last comes Isola Madre, the largest and perhaps the most fascinating of the three, with its impressive Borromean palace and, above all, a splendid botanical garden, renowned for its spring flowering of azaleas, camellias and rhododendrons. The palace exhibits period furnishings, livery collections, chinaware, puppets and an 18th-century theatre (admission charge). If you wish you can take a boat direct from Pallanza (see page 14) without stopping at the other two islands.

▶ *Follow the lake on the **SS33** to Baveno.*

Detail of one of the frescoes depicting the life of St John in the baptistery of Baveno

3 Baveno

In the 1800s Baveno, like nearby Stresa, was a particularly fashionable holiday resort, as is still demonstrated by its elegant villas. Illustrious guests here have included Queen Victoria and the German Emperor Frederick III, who both stayed in Villa Henfrey (now Villa Branca). Of particular note is Villa Fedora, owned in the early 20th century by the composer Umberto Giordano, who wrote *Fedora* and *Andrea Chenier*. The lakeside offers a privileged view of Isola Pescatori and an interesting feature of the village is the Romanesque complex comprising the parish church of SS Gervasio e Protasio and an octagonal baptistery. The name of Baveno is linked to that of the prized pink granite quarried in the area and used for public and

A hiker scans the 'sea of clouds' covering Val Grande

private buildings, such as the Galleria Vittorio Emanuele in Milan and St Peter's Basilica in Rome.

ⓘ *Piazza Dante Alighieri 14*

▶ *Continue along the lakeside on the SS33 to Feriolo.*

4 Feriolo
Feriolo overlooks a small gulf which was a transit station in ancient times, *Forum Iulii*, for Roman troops heading for the Alps. Subsequently it became the location for the processing and embarkation of its prized local marble. Although now discovered by tourism, it still has the sleepy air of a fishing village.

▶ *Continue on the SS33 to Gravellona Toce; just past it you will see a sign on the left for Mergozzo.*

5 Mergozzo
Mergozzo is a small resort that gives its name to the adjacent lake. Surrounded by green woods, this tiny sheet of water was once part of Lake Maggiore but has now been separated from it by the alluvial deposits of the River Toce. Motorboats have been banned here for years and its crystal-clear water is ideal for swimmers. It's a

SCENIC ROUTES

As you climb Monte Orfano, which separates the Toce Plain from Lake Mergozzo, the view gradually opens over the Borromean Gulf, sweeping to the opposite shore of Lake Maggiore. The best views are on the lower stretch of the journey before the road enters a wood. Leave the car near the church of San Giovanni, in the centre of a tiny village, and continue on foot to the top. The stone church is of medieval origin and is an interesting example of Romanesque architecture, with a nave and high transept.

traditional village with stone houses huddled together, steep streets, a square with an ancient elm tree, the Romanesque oratory of Santa Maria and an antiquarium housing archaeological finds as well as exhibits illustrating the ancient stone, marble and granite work that flourished in the area.

▶ *Follow the lakeside to Fondo Toce and the signs for the climb towards Val Grande.*

6 Cicogna
The village of Cicogna is the starting point for a walk in the Val Grande National Park,

which, with an area of 12,000 hectares (29,651 acres), is the second largest park in Piedmont after Gran Paradiso. It has dozens of paths and is Italy's largest wild area and one of the main wilderness zones on the peninsula. After being exploited in past centuries by woodcutters, herdsmen and charcoal-burners, the valley was abandoned and is now almost totally uninhabited. Nature has taken over again and dense forests have covered the former mule tracks. Countless animals, from eagles to chamois, now live here in total freedom. The World Wilderness Association has described it as 'the only European nature area to integrally conserve its original environmental characteristics'.

▶ *Descend by the same road following the signs via San Bernardino Verbano to Intra.*

7 Intra
With nearby Pallanza, Suna and other small centres, Intra forms the municipality of Verbania, capital of the province of Verbano-Cusio-Ossola, which was established in 1995. Intra became a major textile centre in the 18th and 19th centuries thanks to the abundance of water supplied by the San Bernardino and San Giovanni streams, and remains one of the lake's principal trade centres.

As a result, it has a more urban appearance than its neighbours. The area of greatest interest to visitors is the lakeside with the pleasant Piazza Ranzoni, behind which lies an old centre featuring fine 17th- and 18th-century mansions and the Basilica de San Vittore, with its distinctive copper dome. A renowned and picturesque market is held on

The 19th-century Villa Taranto at Pallanza, famous for its gardens

Saturdays, where you can buy goods of all kinds.

i *Piazza Flaim*

▶ *Skirt the lake following Via Vittorio Veneto until you come to Pallanza.*

8 Pallanza
Pallanza's gardens are among the most spectacular and flower-filled on the lake. This is one of the best-known resorts on Lake Maggiore, and is extremely popular with foreign visitors. The town is Roman in origin; in the Middle Ages it was protected by a castle and was granted the right to hold a major market. In following centuries it continued to maintain its independence, and was the only town on the lake that was never subdued by the Borromeo family. Pallanza's present appearance, with its splendidly verdant gardens, is more recent, dating from the 17th to the 19th centuries. The most distinctive area starts in Piazza Garibaldi, on the lakeside, and climbs up Via Ruga, the main street of the old town centre, lined with

porticoed houses, churches and mansions. As well as the gardens of Villa Taranto, where the extraordinary wealth of plant species has encouraged local gardeners to seek out rare flowers and plants, there are particularly delightful grounds at Villa San Remigio, on the highest point of the Castagnola headland. Here the eclectic displays feature a succession of Italian flowerbeds and terraces, woods and English gardens.

Off the lakeshore, on the islet of San Giovanni is the former site of an ancient castle, where the Borromeo family built a palace in the 17th century. For many years the conductor Arturo Toscanini sought refuge in this solitary place.

i *Corso Zanitello 6/8; Viale delle Magnolie 1*

▶ *Return to Stresa along the lakeshore via Fondotoce and Feriolo.*

Lower Verbano
& Vergante

This itinerary visits Lake Maggiore, its hinterland and the Vergante
plateau, with its green woods and scattering of small villages that
offer spectacular views of the lake and beyond to the nearby
lakes of Monate and Varese. Lining the shore are holiday resorts,
popular since the 18th century and home to splendid villas
surrounded by large parks.

1 DAY • 50KM • 31 MILES

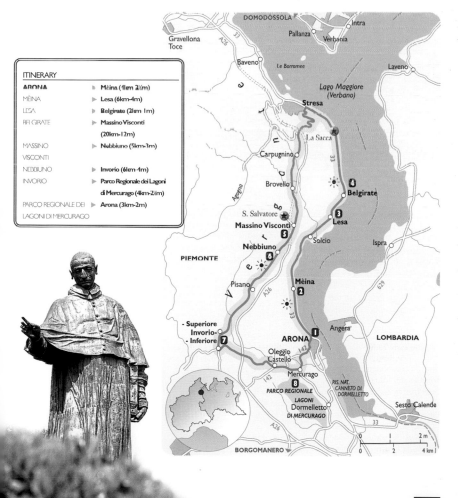

ITINERARY

ARONA	▸ Mèina (11km-7m)
MÈINA	▸ Lesa (6km-4m)
LESA	▸ Belgirate (2km-1m)
BELGIRATE	▸ Massino Visconti
	(20km-12m)
MASSINO	▸ Nebbiuno (5km-3m)
VISCONTI	
NEBBIUNO	
INVORIO	▸ Invorio (6km-4m)
	▸ Parco Regionale dei Lagoni
	di Mercurago (4km-2½m)
PARCO REGIONALE DEI	▸ Arona (3km-2m)
LAGONI DI MERCURAGO	

❶ Arona

With more than 16,000 inhabitants, Arona is the largest municipality on the southern shore of Lake Maggiore. It marks the start of the Riviera – which ends at Stresa – chosen by the Lombard aristocracy from the 18th century onwards as a favourite holiday location. Thanks to its strategic position, guarding the lower lake, the town has been a centre of trade since ancient times. It was once protected by a mighty

created between 1614 and 1698 for Carlo's nephew, Cardinal Federico Borromeo, who intended to build a Sacro Monte, or holy acropolis (similar to the nearby ones of Orta and Varese) as a further tribute. The work was never completed: only two chapels and the church of San Carlo were actually built. After Napoleon destroyed Arona's stronghold, the room where Carlo was born was reconstructed with some of its original furnishings, adjacent to this

Antiques fair in Arona

stronghold, the Rocca, whose ruins can still be seen atop the hill that dominates the centre. Built by the Visconti family in the 13th century, and enlarged by the Borromeos, it provided an excellent defensive point for the lake's entire southern basin, together with Angera on the opposite shore. It was dismantled in the early 1800s by Napoleon, and is now surrounded by a public park. In 1538 Carlo Borromeo was born there; a colossal copper statue dedicated to the saint can be seen from a distance on a mound about 2km (1 mile) from the town. This tireless church-builder and scourge of heretics was made archbishop of Milan in 1564, and became a leading figure of the Counter-Reformation. Standing 35m (115 feet) high, the statue was

church. His statue, popularly known as San Carlone, contains a narrow staircase that climbs to the head; its reinforced internal masonry uses exactly the same

technique employed for the Statue of Liberty in New York.

Arona has a well-preserved old centre with a charming atmosphere. Overlooking Piazza del Popolo are the church of Santa Maria di Loreto (begun in the 15th century and completed in the 17th), the Broletto (town hall) and sections of an old portico. Of note among the religious buildings are the Benedictine churches of SS Martiri Graziano and Felino, and the Collegiate of Santa Maria Nascente. The Archaeological Museum houses important finds dating from prehistoric times.

i *Piazzale Duca d'Aosta*

▶ *Follow the SS33 towards Stresa to Mèina.*

❷ Mèina

This ancient settlement, the first to be established in the area, dates from the Bronze Age (2nd millennium BC). In the 15th century it was the feudal possession of the Visconti family and, subsequently, the Borromeos. In the 18th and 19th centuries, like nearby Arona, Mèina became a highly popular resort and the Lombard and Piedmontese nobility and upper classes built luxurious summer residences here. Numerous villas can still be admired (mostly from the outside as they are private property). The most famous is Villa Faraggiana, whose neo-classical façade is clearly visible from the main road. It was built in 1855 for Senator Raffaello Faraggiana and now belongs to the nuns of the order of the Franciscan Sisters of Bergamo. Other fine residences include Villa Favorita, which combines neo-classical with art nouveau, the neo-Palladian Villa Eden, the 17th-century Palazzina Savoiroux, Villa Bonomi in eclectic style, and Palazzo Bedone, dating from the mid-18th century.

▶ Follow the shore on the same road to Lesa.

3 Lesa
Lesa's most illustrious guest was Italian novelist Alessandro Manzoni (1785–1873), who spent long periods at Villa Stampa, owned by the family of his second wife, Teresa Stampa, whom he married in 1840. The austere, neo-classical villa, in a peaceful location on the lakeshore, is now open to visitors and displays period furnishings and the writer's documents. As well as other villas set in large lush gardens, the village also features the remains of a fortified medieval enclosure, built by the nuns of

Neo-classical Villa Faraggiana on the lakeside at Mèina

The lakeside port of Belgirate

San Salvatore in Pavia, to which
the area once belonged.

▶ *Proceed along the* **SS33**
to Belgirate.

4 Belgirate
With its mild climate and sunny
position, Belgirate owes its name
to the fact that it stands where
the shoreline turns to the west
(*bel* – lovely; *girare* – turn),
approaching the Borromean
Gulf. The old centre, set on a
slight slope, is a maze of narrow
streets flanked by old buildings
with small porticoes and loggias.
A short distance away, in a
scenic position on a hill, is the
Romanesque church of Santa
Maria, extended in the 15th
century and featuring 16th-
century frescoes by the school of
Lombard painter Bernardino
Luini. Small as it is, Belgirate
has for centuries been a

favourite with scholars.
Illustrious past guests include
the French novelist Henri
Stendhal (1783–1842), who was
apparently inspired by these
locations to write some pages of
his masterpiece *The Charterhouse
of Parma*. Poets and writers were
lured to Belgirate at the turn of
the 20th century by Milanese
publisher Enrico Treves, whose
elegant villa was frequented
by Verga, Edmondo de Amicis
and Gabriele d'Annunzio,
among others.

[i] *Via Mazzini 12–14*

▶ *Continue along the lake to
Stresa (see Tour 1) and from
here turn inland on the
Vergante plateau, following
the signs for Massino Visconti.*

5 Massino Visconti
This small village, 465m (1,525
feet) above sea level, is one of
Vergante's main centres. Its
name comes from the noble
Visconti family who obtained
the territory around the year
1000 and later, at the end of the
13th century, became lords of
Milan and much of northern
Italy. Some parts of the Castello
Visconti, the family's summer
residence, have survived in the
old centre, though much altered
over the centuries. Among its
monuments is the Romanesque

church of San Michele, with an
unusual leaning bell tower and
frescoes dating from the 14th
and 15th centuries.

[i] *Via Ing Viotti*

▶ *Continue along the provincial
road that crosses Vergante
to Nebbiuno.*

6 Nebbiuno
Peaceful Nebbiuno forms a sort
of balcony on Lake Maggiore,
and is today a peaceful summer
resort, with splendid views of
Lake Maggiore and the nearby
lakes of Monate and Varese.
The ideal starting point for

Lower **Verbano** & Vergante

Above: Lagoni di Mercurago Regional Park
Below: exploring the park on horseback

walks on the mountains behind (Cornaggia and Torriggia), Nebbiuno has in recent years specialised in growing flowers, selling them in Italy and abroad.

▶ *Continue on the same road to Invorio.*

🔘 Invorio
A castle once stood here but all that remains is a tall stone tower that used to control the access routes to the Vergante plateau. Today Invorio is a small resort, the ideal place to spend a few peaceful hours wandering around the gardens.

BACK TO NATURE

Although dotted with small villages, the Vergante plateau is a partly wild habitat. Its dense woods and meadows are crossed by a system of paths, ideal for walks of varying lengths that lead to scenic views of the lake. The plateau runs parallel to the lakeshore from Arona to Baveno and does not rise above 500m (1,640 feet).

▶ *Descend from the plateau following the signs for Arona. Before reaching it, after Oleggio Castello, take the road on the right to the Lagoni di Mercurago.*

🔘 Parco Regionale dei Lagoni di Mercurago
Extending over 444 hectares (1,097 acres), the park comprises the Lagoni di Mercurago and surrounding pools, as well as heaths, woods and, at the top on the hill, grazing land where thoroughbred horses are reared. These stud farms have produced one of Italy's most famous racehorse dynasties, the Dormello Olgiata breed, which has sired many champions in its time. The park has a route approximately 15km (9 miles) long, which takes five hours to cover completely, but those with less time can just walk a few sections that lead to the animals and marsh birds. As well as its nature, the area is of interest for its history – or rather its prehistory, as finds have shown that it was already inhabited in the Bronze Age.

▶ *Return to Arona on the SS142.*

FOR CHILDREN

The Lagoni di Mercurago Regional Park can be visited on horseback, and numerous stables in the area organise guided excursions. For cycling enthusiasts, young and old, the park has 20km (12 miles) of dirt track to explore.

Upper Verbano

1/2 DAYS • 135KM • 84 MILES

The lake narrows in the upper Verbano area; the villages become fewer, the mountains slope down to the water and the shores become more rugged. This itinerary also explores inland treasures such as the unspoiled Val Vigezzo, the 'valley of painters'. The route leads to Locarno, in Switzerland, on the northernmost tip of the lake, before turning back on the east coast to Laveno.

ITINERARY	
VERBANIA	▶ **Cànnero Riviera** (13km-8m)
CÀNNERO RIVIERA	▶ **Cannobio** (7km-4½m)
CANNOBIO	▶ **Santa Maria Maggiore** (30km-18½m)
SANTA MARIA MAGGIORE	▶ **Locarno** (32km-20m)
LOCARNO	▶ **Luino** (36km-22½m)
LUINO	▶ **Verbania** (17km-10½m)

ⓘ *Viale delle Magnolie 1, Pallanza;
Corso Zanitello 6/8, Verbania*

▶ *Follow the* **SS34** *northbound
along the lake.*

🚩 Cànnero Riviera

Cànnero has rightly earned itself
the title 'Riviera' for the mild
climate that has allowed lemon

and olive trees and a lush, typically Mediterranean flora to
acclimatise here. This has
produced the remarkable
contrast with the chestnut
groves immediately inland that
gives the village its special
charm. Its symbol is the camellia, to which an international
show is dedicated every year.
But the mild climate alone is not
all that has attracted visitors
since the 19th century. Opposite
the village are two small islets
bearing the ruins of castles, one
of the lake's major tourist attractions. Originally known as the
Malpaga castles, they were built
between 1100 and 1400 by the
Mazzarditi, a family who
terrorised the local population.
In 1414, to put an end to their
forays, Duke Filippo Maria
Visconti had the manors razed to
the ground and on their ashes
the Borromeos – the new local
lords – built the Vitaliana stronghold to defend the lake
against Swiss incur-
sions. Although
now in ruins,
the castles –

The Sacro Monte (holy
mountain) of Ghiffa, on the
western upper lakeshore

which can be reached by boat –
have a wonderfully romantic
atmosphere. Those who
succumbed to their charm
include Massimo d'Azeglio
(1798–1866), politician and
scholar, who had a villa built at
Cànnero, where he retreated
to write his best-known work,
I miei ricordi (*My Memories*).

ⓘ *Via Roma 37*

▶ *Continue along the* **SS34** *to
Cannobio.*

🚩 Cannobio

This is the last Italian town
before the Swiss border.
Probably founded in Roman
times, where Val Cannobina
opened on to the lake, it was

Slate roofs and bell towers in Val Vigezzo

an important medieval centre of transit and trade, as is evident in the central Palazzo della Ragione, built in the late 13th century and subsequently enlarged, and the Romanesque tower of the Comune (town hall). The Collegiate of San Vittore dates from the mid-18th century, but the sanctuary of the Pietà is older, built in the early 16th century and extended in 1571 by San Carlo Borromeo. Today Cannobio, with its modern sports facilities that include a swimming pool and a sailing club, is a popular holiday resort. Its attractions include the Orrido di Santa Anna, a narrow rocky gorge reached after

climbing for 2km (1 mile) up Val Cannobina towards Traffiume. The swirling waters of the Cannobino stream, which flows through it, are crossed by two bridges, one of Romanesque origin and the other constructed in the 19th century. Adding to the charm of this location is the austere façade of the church of Santa Anna, built in the 17th century on the edge of the precipice.

i *Via A Giovanola 25*

▶ *Take the SS631 Val Cannobina road to Santa Maria Maggiore.*

❸ Santa Maria Maggiore

Santa Maria Maggiore is the main centre in Val Vigezzo, an alpine valley with the unusual distinction of being the birthplace of generations of artists. Of the seven schools of painting that existed in the 19th century in the 'valley of painters' just one remains, the well-known and highly respected Rossetti Valentini school of Santa Maria Maggiore. In summer it organises courses of painting and sculpture for beginners. The picture gallery annexed to the institute houses works by the valley's leading artists, including

Carlo Giuseppe, Enrico Cavalli, Camillo Besana and Carlo Fornara. The houses in the village (and the other centres in the valley in general) have been influenced by this age-old artistic tradition. Built in stone, they are embellished with imaginative decorations, particularly around the windows and doors.

An interesting testimony to the past is the curious Chimney-sweep Museum, which uses tools and pictures to tell the story of an old skill practised by generations of valley dwellers from the 17th century onwards.

Sweeps left the valley to work
all over Europe, conversing with
each other in a secret jargon
incomprehensible to outsiders.

☐ *Piazza Risorgimento 10*

▶ *Continue along the SS337 to
the border with Switzerland.
After crossing this take the
Centovalli road to Locarno.*

4 Locarno (Switzerland)
The cosmopolitan town of
Locarno is situated on the northernmost tip of Lake Maggiore.
Its temperate climate, hotels and
environs have made it a famous
holiday resort. The centre of this
town is the bustling Piazza
Grande, which in summer
becomes the stage for the
International Film Festival, one
of the most important European
events of the area. The old
centre climbs up the lower
slopes of the mountain that
dominates the town.

Monuments of note include
the 18th-century church of San
Antonio, the church of Santa
Maria in Selva, with fine 15th-
century frescoes, and the castle
begun in the 14th century, now
home to the Archaeological
Museum. A cable-car climbs
to the Madonna del Sasso, a
sanctuary founded in the 15th
century and rebuilt in the
17th century in a splendid
scenic position.

☐ *Largo Zorzi*

▶ *Follow the lake to the east
shore and cross back into*

*Italy. Continue along the
lakeshore on the SS629 to
Luino.*

5 Luino
Luino, another centre founded
in the Roman era, is the main
tourist resort on the north
Lombard shore of the lake, with
good hotels and modern sports
facilities. A forerunner of
modern tourism, it was linked in
1885 with Ponte Tresa, on Lake
Lugano, via a narrow-gauge
railway serving the flow of visitors from across the Alps. This
memory lives on in the monumental railway station and the
Locomozioni festival, which in
early summer relives the splendours of the past and the history
of railway transport.

The oldest part of the town
is on the side of the mountain.
Here you can visit the parish
church of San Pietro, decorated
with 15th-century frescoes
attributed to Bernardino Luini
(who came from Luino). On the
lakeside is the 15th-century
church of the Madonna del
Carmine with several frescoes
also attributed to Luini. The
Porto Vecchio (port), designed at

Spinnakers fill with wind during a
sailing regatta off Luino

the time of Napoleon and
completed in the Habsburg
period, marks the beginning of
the Contrada dei Mercanti, a
busy shopping thoroughfare.
Every Wednesday the streets
and squares come alive with
colourful market stalls at one of
the most popular markets on the
lake, dating from the 16th
century and now an historic
institution for Luino.

☐ *Via Piero Chiara 1*

▶ *Follow the road to Laveno,
where you take the ferry back
to Verbania.*

THE HOLIDAY TRADITION

With their mild climate and beautiful, varied scenery, the pre-Alpine lakes have for centuries been among the best-known and most popular holiday resorts in Italy. Over the years villas, parks and – from the mid-19th century – grand hotels have appeared on its shores and still dot the landscape, constituting an attraction in themselves.

From the Borromeos to Stendhal

Lake Maggiore was chosen in the 17th century by the Borromeo family (who erected sumptuous palaces on Isola Bella and Isola Madre) as a place of amusement and delight; then, in the 18th century, it became a favourite holiday destination of the Lombard nobility, who built villas set in extensive parks here. Subsequently the European upper classes flocked here to spend long periods in the luxurious grand hotels. They were gradually joined by poets and scholarly travellers, and the lake became one of the most exclusive holiday destinations on the continent. Intellectuals and crowned heads were particularly bewitched by the Borromean islands. They also appealed to orchestra conductor Arturo Toscanini, who came to

Italian poet Gabriele d'Annunzio at the Vittoriale in the Gardone Riviera

Isola Pescatori in the company of artists and literati such as Ernest Hemingway, George Bernard Shaw, the Emperor of Japan and the British Royal Family. Novelist Alessandro Manzoni spent long periods at Lesa, and Stresa, which rivalled Monte Carlo for its belle époque society lifestyle, drew philosopher Antonio Rosmini and Elizabeth of Saxony, Duchess of Genoa. Belgirate was much loved by the French novelist Henri Stendhal.

Love and holidays

The secluded and romantic Lake Orta enchanted German philosopher Friedrich Nietzsche, who fell in love with Lou Salomé on its shores. In the mid-18th century, Lake Lugano, with its Alpine scenery, and Lake Varese, with Monte Rosa as a backdrop, became obligatory stops on the 'Grand Tour'.

Lombard villas

Lake Como has a long tradition as a holiday destination. As early as 1493, Maximilian of Habsburg chose Bellagio as the venue for a great ball to celebrate his marriage to Bianca Maria Sforza. Between the 16th and 19th centuries, the noble Lombard families built impressive villas on its shores, especially along the west shore and on the Bellagio headland, usually staying there from March to September. Today, with their gardens opened to the public, these still constitute one of the lake's major tourist attractions. Other residences of note are Villa Serbelloni and Villa Melzi d'Eryl at Bellagio, Villa Carlotta at Tremezzo and Villa Balbianello, near Lenno.

The delights of Garda

Lake Garda boasts the singular distinction of having been loved not only by the nobility of Brescia, who started building

Display case in the Manzoni room in Villa Stampa at Lesa

24

their holiday homes here in the 17th century, and the brilliant representatives of the belle époque, who made the Gardone Riviera one of the international capitals of the rich, but also by poets and writers of all eras. It was popular with the Roman poets Virgil and Catullus, and later with Dante Alighieri (who described it in *Canto XX* of his *Inferno*),

Ugo Foscolo, Goethe, James Joyce, Gabriele d'Annunzio and Ezra Pound. The first to fall for its charms was Catullus (born in Verona in the 1st century BC), whose family had a villa at Sirmione. Over the centuries he managed to convey the appeal of Sirmione to Ezra Pound, who in one of his letters to James Joyce, wrote: 'Here I am at home...I would like you to

the lake's splendours that he spent the last 17 years of his life in Villa Cargnacco di Gardone.

Between Iseo and Franciacorta

Lake Iseo, with its austere charm, was also well known and visited over the past centuries. Its many celebrated guests include English scholar Lady

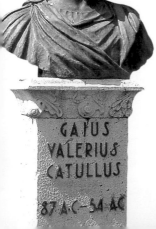

Above: the remains of the grand Roman villa at Sirmione
Left: bust of Catullus

GAIUS
VALERIUS
CATULLUS
87 AC–54 AC

spend a week here with me...the place is worth a day's train journey. You have a guarantee from Catullus and me.' Many other non-Italian writers have been enchanted by the lake's atmosphere – the German lyrical poet Heinrich Heine, Lord Byron, Henri Stendhal, D H Lawrence and Franz Kafka (who stayed at Desenzano and Malcesine between 1909 and 1913). Gabriele d'Annunzio (1863–1938) was so taken with

Mary Montagu, Madame de Sévigné, Madame de Stäel and the writer George Sand, who stayed here at length to forget her unhappy love affair with the poet Alfred de Musset. In September 1895 – three years before her assassination – the Empress Elizabeth of Austria also visited. Writers Ezra Pound and James Joyce, and in more recent times photographer Henri Cartier-Bresson and film director Luchino Visconti, also stayed between the lake and Franciacorta, in the gentle hills of the hinterland where the nobility of Brescia built their country homes.

Lake Maggiore to Lake Orta

1/2 DAYS • 150KM • 93 MILES

This tour leads from Lake Maggiore to Cusio via Mottarone, the 'mountain of the two lakes'. Lake Orta and the Isle of San Giulio act as a prelude to the masterpieces of art and devotion of the Sacro Monti (holy mounts) of Orta San Giulio and Varallo.

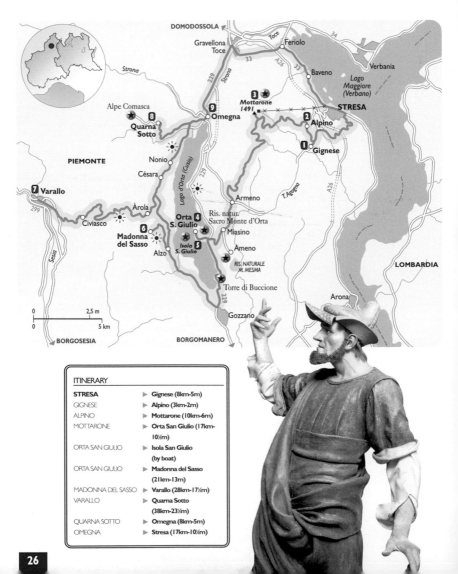

ITINERARY

STRESA	▶	**Gignese (8km-5m)**
GIGNESE	▶	Alpino (3km-2m)
ALPINO	▶	Mottarone (10km-6m)
MOTTARONE	▶	Orta San Giulio (17km-10½m)
ORTA SAN GIULIO	▶	Isola San Giulio (by boat)
ORTA SAN GIULIO	▶	Madonna del Sasso (21km-13m)
MADONNA DEL SASSO	▶	Varallo (28km-17½m)
VARALLO	▶	Quarna Sotto (38km-23½m)
QUARNA SOTTO	▶	Omegna (8km-5m)
OMEGNA	▶	Stresa (17km-10½m)

i Via Canonica 3, Stresa

▶ *From Stresa, climb Mottarone following signs for Gignese.*

❶ Gignese

Set in a beautifully scenic position, Gignese is a small village on the Vergante plateau, renowned for its unusual Umbrella and Parasol Museum. This is dedicated to one of the principal past activities of its inhabitants (and the local population in general), who

Above: a painting in the Umbrella Museum at Gignese
Below: the peaks of Mottarone

---

are known in Italy and beyond the Alps as strolling umbrella-sellers. On display are dozens upon dozens of specimens in the most original and imaginative designs of all epochs and from all countries.

i Via Per Nocco 2

▶ *Continue to Alpino.*

❷ Alpino

Alpino is a quiet holiday resort 768m (2,519 feet) above sea level. Known for the nearby golf courses, it is the ideal holiday spot for those wishing to spend time walking and practising sports while surrounded by nature and tranquillity.

▶ *Continue towards Mottarone (the last section is on a private toll road).*

FOR CHILDREN

Children (and adults) can see mountain flowers and shrubs close up, learn their names and start to distinguish them from each other at Alpinia, a lovely botanical garden with approximately 2,000 specimens of alpine flora and medicinal plants, set in a splendidly scenic position at Alpino, overlooking Lake Maggiore.

---

❸ Mottarone

At 1,491m (4,891 feet) above sea level, Mottarone is Stresa's 'mountain', a venue for Sunday excursions and winter ski trips (when there is sufficient snow, which is not every year). It can be reached by car or in about 20 minutes using the cable-car that departs from Lido di Stresa (see Tour 1). From the top the view is truly unique, sweeping over lakes Maggiore and Orta (hence its reputation as 'the mountain of the two lakes'), the Po valley and the Alps, including Monte Rosa and Mischabel (in Switzerland).

▶ *Descend towards Lake Orta via Armeno, Miasino and Legro to Orta San Giulio.*

❹ Orta San Giulio

Set on a green headland projecting from the west shore of the lake, Orta San Giulio is a pearl of art and history best visited on foot after leaving your car in one of the car parks dotted around the old centre. It was put on the tourist map in the late 18th century by English travellers, who were enthralled by the deep turquoise waters of the lake (one of the most romantic in Italy), by its lush nature and by its art treasures. It has attracted poets, writers and scholars such as the French novelist Honoré de

Balzac and the German philosopher Friedrich Nietzsche. In 1882, during a walk on the holy mount, Nietzsche fell hopelessly (and unrequitedly) in love with his travelling companion, the Russian poetess Lou Salomé. When he published his masterpiece, *Thus Spake Zarathustra*, he dated it 'Von Orta an' ('from Orta on').

The village, seat of the Lord of San Giulio since the 13th century, slopes down to the lake opposite the Isola San Giulio. The oldest part dates from the Middle Ages and has Romanesque fortified houses, but it was in Renaissance and baroque times that the village assumed its present appearance, marked by handsome mansions, courtyards and Italian-style gardens. At the centre of the village is Piazza Mario Motta, surrounded on three sides by houses with large ground-floor arches and open on the fourth towards the lake. Here is the Palazzo della Comunità (1582), where the 'Council of the Riviera' was once based and justice administered. An external staircase links the large ground-floor portico with the single room on the *piano nobile* (main floor) and the façade is decorated with the arms of the local bishop-counts. Also dating from the 16th century is the parish church of the Assunta, at the top of Via della Motta. Beside this a road leads (about half an hour on foot) to the Sacro Monte, Orta's artistic jewel. Built between the late 16th and the early 17th century (although the last chapel dates

from 1785) on a hill that dominates the village, the Sacro Monte is one of Italy's best-known sanctuaries. This religious complex is named after St Francis and consists of 21 chapels surrounded by woods. It was created as part of a project devised by the Capuchin father Cleto de Castelletto Ticino, to tell worshippers the story of St Francis of Assisi and encourage them to meditate and pray. There are 375 life-size terracotta statues, many realistic and expressive, and more than 900

frescoes in the chapels, depicting stories from the life of the saint. The spiral route was designed to link the buildings closely with nature, leaving part of the woods intact and planting trees and bushes such as box-tree and laurel along the paths to guide visitors and provide shaded resting places along the way. Originally there was no view of the lake, so that the pilgrims would not be distracted from prayer. Today, however, some of the chapels and the courtyard of the church of San Nicolao, at

Above: Orta San Giulio
Opposite: windsurfing on Lake Orta

the end of the route, open on to lovely views of Cusio.

[i] *Via Bossi 11*

▶ *From Piazza Motta in Orta San Giulio, take the ferry to Isola San Giulio.*

🖸 Isola San Giulio

After a 10-minute crossing you come to the Isola San Giulio, a realm of silence. Since time immemorial this has been the religious heart of the lake, visited by pilgrims and wayfarers, and it is still home to an enclosed convent.

The church, which is very old, is reached by climbing a covered flight of steps. According to legend, San Giulio himself founded it in the 4th

The sanctuary of the Madonna del Sasso, dominating the west shore of Lake Orta

RECOMMENDED WALK

The medieval Torre di Buccione (Buccione Tower), which rises on a hill on the eastern shore of the lake, close to Gozzano, is considered the symbol of Cusio. It is reached in about 15 minutes along a branch of the provincial Gozzano-Miasino road. The walk is pleasant and, from the highest points, the view superb. The tower was formerly part of a castle built in the early 13th century and owned by the bishop of Novara. Now it is the centrepiece of the Buccione Tower Hill special nature reserve.

▶ *Descend to Alzo again on the same road. Then follow the signs for Césara to the left and from here to Varallo via Àrola and Civiasco.*

century; it was rebuilt in the 9th century and repeatedly adapted and enlarged, and is now decorated with 18th-century frescoes. The precious medieval pulpit, sculpted in black marble around the 11th century, is a masterpiece of northern Italian Romanesque art.

San Giulio is buried in the crypt; his tomb has been venerated for centuries. Around the church are the bishop's palace,

the female Benedictine abbey Mater Ecclesiae and a number of buildings constructed between the 16th and 19th centuries. The small island (just 700m/2,300 feet in perimeter) is visited by following the only road that runs around it.

▶ *Take the ferry back to Orta San Giulio and follow the lakeshore to Gozzano; here, return along the west shore of the lake and at Alzo climb inland to the Madonna del Sasso.*

6 Madonna del Sasso

Made up of several small hamlets, sitting 700m (2,300 feet) above sea level in the lake's western hinterland, the village of Madonna del Sasso takes its name from the large 18th-century sanctuary built on a rock sheer above the lake. Its white profile can be seen from a distance and the view from the courtyard is unequalled. Inside, it features a complex painted cycle by Lorenzo Peracino (1710–98) and a monumental 16th-century organ.

7 Varallo

Varallo, the main town of Valsesia, is famous for its Sacro Monte (holy mountain), which dominates it from the top of a rocky spur. This is the oldest and most important Sacro Monte, which served as a model for the others built in the 15th century on in Piedmont and Lombardy. It was conceived in 1478 by Bernardo Caimi, who wanted to create a miniature Holy Land, reproducing the principal sanctuaries of Palestine to inspire the faith of the valley's inhabitants. The complex, built over three centuries, is made up of 45 chapels, more than 800 statues and 4,000 paintings, which together narrate the story of the life of Jesus. Famous architects, including Benedetto Alfieri, and painters and sculptors such as Gaudenzio Ferrari, Giovanni d'Errico, Morazzone and Pellegrino Tibaldi, worked on its construction from the 15th to the 18th century. It is divided into two areas. The lower area,

SPECIAL TO...

The Calderara Foundation at Vacciago (a hamlet near Armeno) shows about 350 works of contemporary art by leading European and non-European artists, focusing in particular on the international avant-garde movements of the 1950s and 1960s. The collection is arranged in the 17th-century studio-home of the painter Antonio Calderara (1903–78), who was associated with the most significant representatives of the 20th-century international art scene.

on the hill slope, is designed as a large garden, with paths that lead visitors to the various chapels. The first illustrates the story of Adam and Eve, while the other 18 tell the story of the life of Jesus before his entry into Jerusalem. The upper area, at the top of the hill, is entered through the Golden Gate and is intended to be a symbolic reconstruction of the city of Jerusalem, with the Temple and Tribunal squares, the centres of religious and political life respectively. Here the chapels tell stories from the life of Jesus when he was in Jerusalem. This presentation as a 'town' is what distinguishes the Sacro Monte of Varallo from all other similar religious complexes.

Also distinctive is the old town centre, mainly late medieval and Renaissance, where you can visit the 15th-century church of the Madonna delle Grazie and the Picture

The Ecce Homo chapels of Varallo's Sacro Monte with its many statues

Gallery (which includes works by Gaudenzio Ferrari and Tanzio da Varallo, both from Valsesia). The Collegiate of San Gaudenzio, an 18th-century conversion of a 13th-century church, stands spectacularly on a rock.

[i] *Via Regaldi 4*

▶ *Return by the same road to Césara and continue to the north of the lake via Nonio. Turn left for Quarna Sotto.*

8 Quarna Sotto

Quarna Sotto stands 809m (2,654 feet) above sea level on the mountain that dominates Omegna. Its inhabitants used to be known for making wind instruments, which from the mid-19th century were exported all over the world. Not surprisingly, the village has a museum displaying old and new instruments and prototypes, and illustrating the traditional methods of production. The museum has a folk section featuring reconstructions of rooms in old houses

SCENIC ROUTES

From Cusio Sotto, an asphalted road leads to Alpe Comasca, 1,230m (4,035 feet) above sea level. Here the sunny meadows at the foot of Monte Mazzuccone afford an exceptional view of Lake Orta and the Lower Novarese area.

and collections that illustrate what life was like for the local peasant in days gone by.

▶ *Return to the lake on the same road towards Omegna.*

9 Omegna

Omegna lies on Lake Orta's northern shore and is its historical capital and main town. Set on the Nigoglia River, it is known as the home of the leading Italian manufacturers of small household appliances and goods. These goods are sold directly in factory shops, which have now become a local tourist attraction. The old part of the town centre is concentrated around Piazza XXIV Aprile, overlooking the lake and backed by the fishing quarter. Continuing along Via Cavallotti, you come to the 10th-century Collegiate of Sant'Ambrogio, with a Romanesque bell tower 70m (230 feet) high and a baroque interior rich in works of art.

The Rodari Park is a former industrial site converted for cultural and social use, and now home to the Foundation-Forum Museum of Crafts and Industry. This active cultural centre has an auditorium, exhibition rooms and a museum which records the history of local household goods production, with a particular eye to the important relationship between designers and applied technology.

[i] *Piazza XXIV Aprile 17*

▶ *Return to Stresa following the SS229 to Gravellona Toce, then on the lakeside road to Feriolo and Baveno.*

From Varese
to Lake Maggiore

1 DAY • 105KM • 65 MILES On its journey from the holy mountain of Varese, a religious complex of 17th-century origin, to the Rocca di Angera, which dominates the southern part of Lake Maggiore, this tour takes in the Sanctuary of Santa Caterina del Sasso, built on a precipice above the lake and one of its most evocative locations.

i *Via Carrobbio 2, Varese*

▶ *Leave Varese on Viale Aguggiari and follow the signs for the Sacro Monte. After passing Sant'Ambrogio Olona you will come to the church of Immacolata, where the Sacro Monte (holy mountain) starts.*

❶ Sacro Monte

The Sacro Monte is a holy way that winds for 2km (1 mile) to the sanctuary of Santa Maria del Monte. Like the other 20 or so that can still be visited in northern Italy and Switzerland, its route – which rises steeply by 300m (984 feet) – is flanked by

SPECIAL TO

Sant'Ambrogio, the elegant residential suburb of Varese set at the foot of the Sacro Monte, is the home of the archaeological museum of the Castiglioni brothers, explorers from Varese. Containing rare objects from ancient Egypt and Africa, it also features reconstructions of Tuareg camps and scenes of ancient battles. The collection is kept in an annexe of the Villa Toeplitz, a sumptuous late 19th-century residence with a scenic terrace and a tower for astronomical observation. The villa has a park featuring stone fountains and clever tricks of perspective worked into its design.

Above: frescoes on the Sacro Monte
Right: the Campo dei Fiori astronomical observatory

chapels. In this case there are 14, decorated with frescoes and statues portraying the Mysteries of the Rosary and the Via Crucis (Way of the Cross). The religious complex was begun in 1604 by local architect Giuseppe Bernasconi. Today it is also embellished with a fresco by Renato Guttuso, one of the founders of Italian realism, who painted *The Flight into Egypt* in the third chapel in 1983.

BACK TO NATURE

The Campo dei Fiori mountain area – a ridge of mountains north of Varese – has been designated a regional park, and stretches over 5,400 hectares (13,343 acres). There are numerous paths, indicated on notice boards. Situated on top of the mountain, 1,226m (4,022 feet) above sea level, are the two domes of the Schiaparelli astronomical observatory, open (to groups) for observation of the night sky.

FOR HISTORY BUFFS

The starting point of the tour, Varese, boasts ancient origins. Apparently its name comes from the Latin *vallium exitus*, or 'exit from the valleys', indicating its position (385m/1,263 feet above sea level) at the foot of the Sacro Monte and mounts Tre Croci and Campo dei Fiori. A commercial town since the Middle Ages, it was a major silk trading centre between the 17th and 19th centuries, where industry included paper and silk mills. It became a holiday destination in the mid-18th century.

Over the centuries a small village called Santa Maria del Monte has grown up around the sanctuary; access is via the church courtyard, on foot from the Sacro Monte, or by car along the road that climbs up Monte Tre Croci (Via Campo dei Fiori). As well as exploring its medieval walls, arches and stones, you can

The grounds of Villa della Porta Bozzolo at Casalzuigno

visit the Baroffio Museum, which displays religious objects and the art collection of its founder, Baron Baroffio, and Villa Pogliaghi, built at the end of the 19th century by the sculptor Ludovico Pogliaghi to house his eclectic collections of antiquities and Oriental art.

▶ *Return to Sant'Ambrogio Olona and follow the provincial road that winds through the bottom of the valley along the River Olona. After Rasa di Varese descend towards Valcuvia and, after passing Brinzio, at Rancio turn towards Laveno. After a few kilometres you will see the turning on the right for Casalzuigno.*

2 Casalzuigno
Still visible close to the village are the remains of ancient water mills along the Marianna stream, but the main attraction here is Villa della Porta Bozzolo, a rare example in these parts of a manor house and farm. Built in the 17th century by Carlo Girolamo della Porta, it was extended early in the following century and is now owned by the municipal authorities. Only the park is open to visitors but

it is none the less interesting to observe the grand overall structure and perspective with a long approach drive, monumental entrance, descending stone terraces and large sloping lawn ending with a fountain. A second drive climbs through the woods to the top of the hill and the church of Santa Maria Assunta, originally built as the villa's chapel and later serving as the village parish church.

▶ *Continue along the same road to Arcumeggia.*

RECOMMENDED WALK

Called the '3V: Via Verde Varesina', this is a well-signposted scenic route along easy paths, suitable for all, that leads, in ten stages, to Lake Maggiore. It starts at Pogliana, about 10km (6 miles) north of Varese (on the road to Porto Ceresio), and ends near the Forcora Pass, in the upper Luino area. Along the way, you can visit tiny villages and sample local dishes and produce such as honey, cold meats and cheeses.

❸ Arcumeggia

Due to its strategic position halfway along the valley, Arcumeggia already had a garrison in Roman times. Today the village is renowned because, since the 1950s, it has gradually been turned into a large open-air art gallery. Artists such as Remo Brindisi, Aligi Sassu and Ernesto Treccani have drawn large, brightly coloured frescoes on the outside walls of the houses and this tradition has continued ever since. To see them, leave your car in the church courtyard and follow the route indicated on a notice board. Your visit should also include the 14 stations of the Via Crucis (Way of the Cross) painted by various contemporary masters.

▶ *Descend by the same road towards Lake Maggiore to Porto Valtravaglia.*

❹ Porto Valtravaglia

Overlooking Lake Maggiore, Porto Valtravaglia has a small lakeside area popular for strolls. Behind this is the old part of the village with the 17th-century Oratory of San Rocco and the parish church of the Assunta, featuring fine frescoes dating

Leisure craft in Laveno harbour

from the 16th and 17th centuries

▶ *Continue southbound on the SS629 following the lake.*

❺ Laveno

It is said that the town is named after a Roman general, Titus Labienus, who fought a critical battle here. Laveno sits in the deepest and most protected natural inlet on the east shore of the lake, and has therefore always played an important role as a port. It became home to numerous types of industry,

including pottery. Its history is told in the Civic Chinaware Collection on display in the 16th-century Palazzo Perabò, in the hamlet of Cerro. From Laveno you can take a car ferry to Intra, on the east shore.

ⅰ *Palazzo Municipale, Piazza Italia*

▶ *Continue along the SS629 and at the junction for*

The houses and coastline of Porto Valtravaglia

Leggiuno take a detour right that leads in about 1 km (½ mile) to a car park. Leave the car and descend on foot to the Sanctuary of Santa Caterina del Sasso (it takes approximately 10 minutes).

⑥ Santuario di Santa Caterina del Sasso

This is one of the best-known locations on the lake. The sanctuary is set on a rock sheer above the water in a delightful scenic spot with a sweeping view of the opposite shore, the Borromeo Gulf and Mottarone. It is made up of a number of buildings constructed in various periods, but according to legend was founded in the 12th century by a merchant who devoted himself to penitence and prayer in thanks for having been saved from a tempest.

The first community of monks to live here was Dominican. Initially there were three chapels, dedicated to Santa Caterina, the Madonna and San Nicola di Bari, and in the early 14th century these were joined together with a single façade, seen today. Inside

Above: the lakeside at Ispra, green with woods and gardens
Right: the crenellated enclosure of the Rocca di Angera

are works of art created mainly between the 15th and 17th centuries; of particular note are the frescoes in the chapter house. Suppressed by the Austrians in the 19th century, the convent was brought back to life by the Dominicans, who settled here again in 1986.

▶ *Return along the same road to Leggiuno and then turn right on to the SS629 for Ispra.*

⑦ Ispra

Ispra, the home of the European Union Euratom Nuclear Studies Centre, is dominated by the remains of an ancient medieval stronghold that is reached on foot. In the town, the parish church of San Martino has 17th-century frescoes, and 19th-century villas adorn the lakeshore with their spectacular gardens.

▶ *Continue on the SS629 to Angera.*

8 Angera

Overshadowed by the impressive Borromeo *rocca* (castle), the towers and battlements of which dominate not only the town but the entire southern basin of the lake, Angera dates from ancient times. It was first a prehistoric settlement, then an important Roman centre, and in the Middle Ages became the seat of a county that extended its control over much of Lake Maggiore. The stronghold – built, with its twin in Arona on the opposite shore, to guard the southern basin of the lake – was erected in the 13th century and repeatedly extended until the 17th century. It consists of four blocks arranged around a central courtyard, enclosed by a mighty

crenellated wall. Historically and artistically the most interesting part is the Visconti wing, constructed in the late 13th century for Ottone Visconti. The Hall of Justice presents a fine cycle of frescoes by 14th-century Lombard masters, among the best examples of northern Italian secular medieval painting. In 1449 the castle – which offers a splendid view of the lake – passed to the Borromeo family, who still own it. In the centre of Angera is the Civic Archaeological Museum, which houses prehistoric and Roman displays.

i *Piazza Garibaldi 10*

▶ *Return to Varese on the SS629 to Sesto Calende and then on the provincial road via Vergiate, Mornago and Azzate.*

THE LAKES OF VARESE & LAKE LUGANO

The town of Varese and its four lakes lie at the point where several pre-Alpine valleys open on to the Po plain. Although quite small, this area is one of considerable environmental and historic complexity, full of places of interest and tourist attractions. The system of lakes stretching west of the town was formed over thousands of years, as the depressions created when the Ice-Age glaciers gradually filled. The largest is Lake Varese, once joined to nearby Lake Comabbio, and the smallest is Lake Biandronno. The fourth lake, Monate, forms part of the Lake Maggiore basin. Surrounding them are marshy areas, such as the Brabbia marsh, most of which were reclaimed decades ago.

Prehistoric settlements grew up on the shores of these lakes, and left their legacies in the many items found during excavations, and the more substantial remains of lake-villages. The area has been inhabited ever since. Small towns and castles appeared and, later, villas were built as visitors saw the benefits of the mild climate, lovely scenery and varied environments. The lakes were popular as holiday destinations from the 18th century on, and today's tourists can still enjoy the charm of grand aristocratic villas surrounded by spectacular gardens, 19th-century town houses and art nouveau mansions.

Lake Varese with Monte Rosa in the background illuminated by the sunrise

South of Varese stretches Valle Olona, a major centre of activity during the Middle Ages, which has preserved many interesting and unique medieval and Renaissance monuments in its main towns of Castiglione Olona, Torba and Castelseprio.

Wedged between Lake Maggiore and Lake Como, Lake Lugano – also known as Lake Ceresio – is surrounded by a range of mountains giving an unmistakable character to the landscape. Situated 270m (886 feet) above sea level, more than two-thirds of Lugano lies in Switzerland. The section of shore between Porto Ceresio and Ponte Tresa, the eastern arm, including Porlezza and the Campione d'Italia enclave, belong to Italy. The shores are linked by boats that sail from Lugano to Porlezza and Porto Ceresio in Italy.

Tour 6

This tour visits the four lakes around Varese and Valle Olona. Some of the areas along the route are densely inhabited and busy with industrial developments – but much of the natural environment is still unspoiled and the scenery has lost none of the charm that has attracted numerous travellers since the 18th century. In those days, one of the best-loved views in northern Italy was of Lake Varese surrounded by the pre-Alps and Monte Rosa. In Valle Olona, some areas of the landscape are still wild in parts.

The tour takes you to the beautiful village of Castiglione Olona, a Renaissance 'island' of Tuscan art in Lombardy; there are also visits to the 8th-century monastic complex of Torba and the Castelseprio archaeological site, with rare early medieval frescoes in the church of Santa Maria Foris Portas.

Then come the lakes – first Comabbio and the adjoining Ticino Regional Park, followed by a stop at Lake Monate (suspended between the plain and the peaks of the pre-Alps), then partially drained Lake Biandronno, and Lake Varese, with the romantic Virginia island at its centre.

Tour 7

Winding its way between Italy and Switzerland, this tour explores Lake Lugano and its environs, crossing the national borders several times with ease (remember to bring your passport with you). Checks are sometimes made at the border but these are usually quite quick (there are no particular baggage restrictions for tourists). Drivers must have a driving licence, a national sticker on the car and third-party insurance with the appropriate international green card.

The first part of the route visits the southwest shore of the lake, between Porto Ceresio and

The scenery around Lake Monate, seen from Cadrezzate

Ponte Tresa, in the province of Varese. This section of Lake Varese is the least developed for visitors, but it offers fine scenic views. You then enter Switzerland to reach Lugano, after stopping in the traditional village of Morcote. After wandering around Lugano (it shares its name with the lake), where visiting exhibitions and shopping are some of the highlights, you continue along the lakeshore and cross the border again to the picturesque Valsolda, enclosed between the waters of Lake Varese and the mountains behind it. Then there's a climb up the Val d'Intelvi, which, along with its side valleys, links Lake Lugano and Lake Como. Old villages bear witness to the skill of the valley's builders, who have, since the Middle Ages, been in demand in Italy and all over Europe. After a visit to Campione d'Italia (an Italian enclave on Swiss territory, popular for its casino), there's an easy return journey to Como on the motorway.

A gazebo in the Scherrer di Morcote Park, on Lake Lugano

The Lakes of Varese

1 DAY • 85KM • 53 MILES

The Olona valley is a treasure house of medieval and Renaissance art, preserved in the towns of Castiglione Olona, Torba and Castelseprio. From here the tour moves on to the lakes around Varese – Lake Comabbio, Lake Monate, tiny Lake Biandronno and Lake Varese, complete with Virginia island.

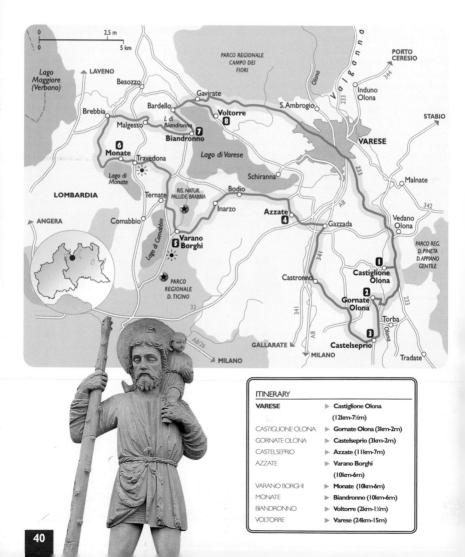

ITINERARY		
VARESE	▶	**Castiglione Olona** (12km-7½m)
CASTIGLIONE OLONA	▶	**Gornate Olona** (3km-2m)
GORNATE OLONA	▶	**Castelseprio** (3km-2m)
CASTELSEPRIO	▶	**Azzate** (11km-7m)
AZZATE	▶	**Varano Borghi** (10km-6m)
VARANO BORGHI	▶	**Monate** (10km-6m)
MONATE	▶	**Biandronno** (10km-6m)
BIANDRONNO	▶	**Voltorre** (2km-1½m)
VOLTORRE	▶	**Varese** (24km-15m)

i *Via Carrobbio 2, Varese*

▶ *Take the SS233 to the turning on the right for Castiglione Olona.*

❶ Castiglione Olona

Its Renaissance appearance and unified style have given this village its reputation as an 'island' of Tuscany in Lombardy. The person responsible for its importance was Cardinal Branda Castiglioni (1350–1443), a Papal nuncio who, between 1430 and 1440, almost completely rebuilt the existing village to designs based on fashionable Tuscan Renaissance models applied by the great Filippo Brunelleschi (1377–1446).

Spread across two hills above the Olona river, the village still maintains its striking appearance, marked by the presence of prestigious and somewhat incongruous monuments and mansions– unexpected in such a small village. The most notable buildings stand on the northern hill and form a splendidly homogeneous historical grouping, with the Collegiate and Baptistery constructed on the site of a castle that once guarded the river passage. Inside are precious frescoes of the Tuscan school, executed mostly by Masolino da Panicale between 1428 and 1435 and considered

The Benedictine Torba monastery, at Gornate Olona

The Baptism of Jesus by Masolino da Panicale in the baptistery of Castiglione

among his greatest works. Other frescoes can be seen in Palazzo Branda Castiglione, the 14th century home of the Cardinal. Opposite this is the church of Villa (1430–41) – its square plan, dome and grey stone edging on white plaster were clearly influenced by contemporary monuments built in Florence by Brunelleschi. Some suggest that the maestro had a direct hand in the work, helped by Masolino.

Of lesser interest is the south hill, with the 19th-century Monteruzzo castle, Clerici home and Doro courtyard featuring 15th-century frescoes of the Lombard school.

i *Via Cardinale Branda 14*

▶ *Follow the signs for Gornate Olona.*

❷ Gornate Olona

This small *comune* in Valle Olona also teems with medieval buildings – in particular the monastic complex of Torba, somewhat isolated on the road to Busto Arsizio. The history of the monastery is bound to that of nearby Castelseprio, to which it was once linked by a long wall (some sections have been excavated). Composed of a number of buildings, including

outhouses, it was founded in the 5th to 6th centuries as a military garrison and converted into a monastery in the 8th century. This was probably when the frescoes were painted to decorate the mighty square tower (one of the cornerstones of the early outpost); the church, transformed in Romanesque times, was probably of the same period. The complex was restored in the 1980s and – along with Villa della Porta Bozzolo at Casalzuigno and Villa Menafoglio Litta Panzo at Biumo and Biumo Superiore – is owned by the FAI (Italian Environmental Fund).

▶ *Follow the signs to Castelseprio.*

🎱 Castelseprio

In earlier times this was the capital of a vast territory stretching from Val d'Intelvi to Milan; now it is one of the most interesting archaeological sites in Lombardy. Its churches were razed to the ground in 1287 by Ottone Visconti, and all that remains of the early medieval village are sections of walls, foundations and several other ruins. Because of its strategic position on a plateau, the town was fortified with a citadel in the

early 5th century. It gradually grew in importance, and by the 8th century, under Desiderio, last king of the Lombards, it was minting its own gold coin, and holding markets and a tribunal. Evidence of that period and the centuries immediately following can be seen on the site in the remains of the Basilica of San Giovanni (5th–7th century), the baptistery and the Romanesque church of San Paolo (10th–12th century). The most important building stands on the hillock opposite the enclosure: the church of Santa Maria Foris Portas, the origin and date of which (fixed between the late 5th and early 11th centuries) is still a subject of debate. It has an unusual plan (rectangular, with three apses arranged as a trefoil, preceded by an atrium) and extremely valuable frescoes, a virtually unique northern Italian example of the passage from classical to Byzantine and medieval art. They were probably executed by an Oriental artist between the 7th and 8th centuries (or, according to some scholars, between the 9th and 10th), and depict episodes from the life of Mary and the infant Jesus.

▶ *Head northwards towards Castronno, where you take the SS341 to the turning on the left for Azzate.*

🎲 Azzate

Set in a beautifully scenic position on the south shore of Lake Varese, ancient Azzate is about 10km (6 miles) from the provincial capital. The most significant buildings in its small centre are the Romanesque Palazzo Pretorio, which incorporated

parts of existing Roman buildings, and Villa Castellani Benizzi, now the Town Hall, a Renaissance palace refashioned in baroque style.

ⓘ *Via Castellani 1*

▶ *Go to Varano Borghi via Bodio and Inarzo.*

🎯 Varano Borghi

This is the main centre on Lake Comabbio, the southernmost lake in Varese and once joined to Lake Varese (the area between the two lakes dried to form the Brabbia marsh). Despite the intense industrialisation that has principally affected the eastern lakeshore, the landscape is still largely untouched, and there are many interesting views. Varano Borghi owes its name to the fact that, in the early 1900s, the Borghi family built a model

Visiting the archaeological site of Castelseprio

Age civilisations (5th–1st millennium BC); some of the finds are on display in a small museum (open in summer, usually at weekends), but most are in the Villa Mirabello Civic Museum in Varese. Remains of lake-settlements, together with utensils, furnishings and jewellery, have also been found elsewhere on the shore of Lake Varese.

▶ *Follow the signs for Gavirate and divert to Voltorre.*

8 Voltorre

Standing on the north shore of Lake Varese, Voltorre is the setting for a small architectural masterpiece – the cloister of the Romanesque church of San Michele, once part of the abbey belonging to Cluniac monks, who reclaimed some of the surrounding territory between the 12th and the 15th century. Three sides of the cloister were built in the 12th century; the fourth dates from the 14th century. Voltorre is a hamlet of nearby Gavirate, the largest town on the lake, renowned for its pipe-makers (celebrated in an unusual museum) and for

village here to house the workers of the fabric and yarn factory.

▶ *Skirt Lake Comabbio north wards and then follow the signs for Travedona and Monate.*

6 Monate

Overlooking the lake of the same name, Monate is a small rural village of stone-walled houses. The church of Santa Maria della Neve dates from the second half of the 14th century and has an 18th-century bell tower. Subterranean springs, fed by Lake Monate, have attracted people since ancient times, as is demonstrated by the remains of

pile-dwellings and prehistoric settlements uncovered during excavations.

▶ *Follow the signs for Brebbia, where you turn right for Malgesso and Biandronno.*

7 Biandronno

Situated between the small lake of the same name (now mostly dried up) and Lake Varese, Biandronno is a peaceful village set in delightful surroundings. From here you can take a boat to Virginia Island, or the Isolino, as it is known locally – a charming water haven with ancient trees and remains. Excavations begun in the mid-19th century brought to light evidence of neolithic, aenolithic and Bronze

Voltorre's famous biscuits

biscuits known as *brutti ma buon* (roughly translated as 'ugly but nice').

▶ *Return to Varese via Gavirate and the SS233. Alternatively, follow the lake to the south, then turn left for Varese.*

RECOMMENDED WALKS

The south shore of Lake Comabbio forms part of Lombardy's Ticino Natural Park, which lies partly in the province of Varese, along the Ticino river from Lake Maggiore to the point where it flows into the Po. The park has countless walks (and carriage rides) with natural, artistic and historical appeal.

FOR CHILDREN

Schiranna, the 'lido' of Varese, has a large public park with a playground and miniature railway. There is also a swimming pool near by (admission fee).

Lake
Lugano

Travel from Italy to Switzerland (Svizzera) and back along the shores of Lake Lugano, amid splendid mountain and lake scenery as well as traditional lakeside villages.

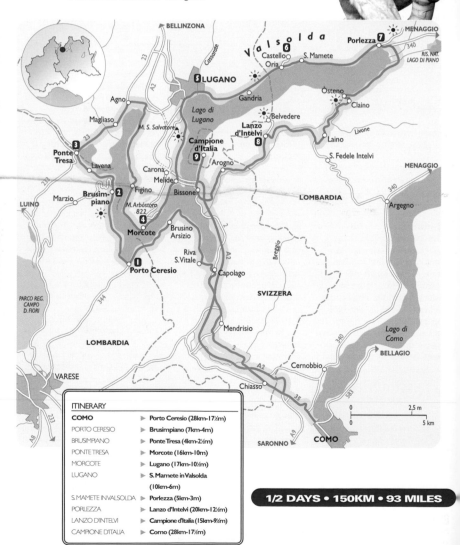

ITINERARY		
COMO	▶	**Porto Ceresio (28km-17½m)**
PORTO CERESIO	▶	**Brusimpiano (7km-4m)**
BRUSIMPIANO	▶	**Ponte Tresa (4km-2½m)**
PONTE TRESA	▶	**Morcote (16km-10m)**
MORCOTE	▶	**Lugano (17km-10½m)**
LUGANO	▶	**S. Mamete in Valsolda**
		(10km-6m)
S. MAMETE IN VALSOLDA	▶	**Porlezza (5km-3m)**
PORLEZZA	▶	**Lanzo d'Intelvi (20km-12½m)**
LANZO D'INTELVI	▶	**Campione d'Italia (15km-9½m)**
CAMPIONE D'ITALIA	▶	**Como (28km-17½m)**

1/2 DAYS • 150KM • 93 MILES

▶ *Leave Como on the **SS35** northbound and cross the border at Chiasso. Continue on the **A2** following the signs for Lugano. At the head of the lake, turn left on to the road that skirts the lake to reach Porto Ceresio.*

❶ Porto Ceresio
This is the main town on the Varese side of Lake Lugano. Navigazione Lago boats to Switzerland berth at the lakeside, with its lovely view of the Swiss shore and the village of Morcote opposite. The hamlet of Ca' del Monte also has fine views of the lake.

▶ *Follow the lake to Brusimpiano.*

❷ Brusimpiano
Brusimpiano's long history as a tranquil holiday resort is still reflected in its centre. Italian patriot Giuseppe Garibaldi (1807–82) sailed from these shores when he took refuge in Switzerland. A lovely scenic road climbs from the village to Marzio and a spectacular view of the lake.

▶ *Follow the lake.*

❸ Ponte Tresa
In the middle of a small gulf, at the westernmost point of Lake Lugano, the Tresa river, which marks the border with Switzerland, flows into the lake. Ponte Tresa has developed at this point in recent decades, basing its economy on commercial and tourist traffic through the customs crossing. The nearby village of Lavena – formerly the home of a priory – is full of character, and stands on a scenic headland.

▶ *Continue on the **SS23** and at Agno take the lakeside road southbound to Morcote.*

❹ Morcote
Set on the tip of the large peninsula that extends into Lake Lugano, opposite Porto Ceresio, Morcote is dominated by a medieval castle. The distinctive old centre has a picturesque lakeside with its maze of alleyways, cobbled streets and old town houses. Worth a visit are the 14th-century Torre del Capitano and the 15th-century Palazzo Paleari.

On the edge of the village lie the Scherrer Park, with tropical trees and fanciful architecture inspired by oriental buildings, and the sanctuary of Santa Maria del Sasso, approached by an 18th-century flight of 400 steps and decorated with 16th-century frescoes.

▶ *Continue along the lake and climb to Lugano.*

❺ Lugano (Switzerland)
Lugano is the principal city of the Swiss canton of Ticino. Overlooking the northwestern shore of its lake, it boasts a mild

The charming village of Morcote

climate and Mediterranean vegetation, rich art collections and luxury shops. It is the home of banks and banking institutions and serves as a major cultural and financial centre – one of the leading financial markets in Switzerland, in fact, after Zurich and Geneva. The heart of the city is Piazza della Riforma, where the Palazzo Civico, built in the mid-19th century as the seat of cantonal government, now functions as the city hall. Around the square are elegant streets full of art galleries and boutiques: on

---

FOR CHILDREN

Magliaso, near Ponte Tresa, is the setting for the Al Maglio Zoo, the only one in the canton of Ticino, with more than 100 animals from all over the world.

TOUR 7 — **Lake** Lugano

SPECIAL TO...

Lugano's Museum of Extra-European Culture – one of the richest and most interesting in Europe – exhibits art and religious pieces, particularly wooden sculptures, from Oceania, the Malay Archipelago, New Guinea and western sub-Saharan Africa.

---

elegant tree-lined waterside street with a lovely view of the lake and surrounding mountains), and the city park, where Villa Ciani houses the Museum of Fine Arts and the Cantonal Museum of Natural History. Continuing towards the village of Gandria, you can visit Villa Favorita, which shows a small part of Baron Von Thyssen's acclaimed art collection (now transferred to Madrid).

church remain of the old castle after which it was named.

▶ *Continue along the lake to Porlezza.*

7 Porlezza

In the Middle Ages Porlezza was the northern capital of Lake Lugano and an important parish of the diocese of Milan. Its transformation to an industrial town with spinning mills and

one side is Piazza Rezzonico, Via Nassa (a temple of luxury shopping) and Piazza Bernardino Luini, with the Franciscan church of Santa Maria degli Angeli; on the other, Via Canova with the Cantonal Museum of Art (holding major temporary exhibitions and a contemporary art collection), Riva Altobelli (an

---

FOR HISTORY BUFFS

Valsolda provides the setting for the works of Antonio Fogazzaro (1841–1911), one of Italy's leading 19th-century writers. His masterpiece *The Little World of the Past* (1895) is set in San Mamete and Oria – the latter also being the setting of Villa Fogazzaro Roi, where the writer spent long periods of his life.

---

i | *Palazzo Civico, Riva Albertolli*

▶ *Follow the lakeside to the border with Italy and cross it to enter Valsolda.*

6 Valsolda

Fewer than 2,500 people live in this small valley, now a *comune* (municipality) extending as far as Porlezza. Bordered to the north by high mountains and to the south by Lake Lugano, it is dotted with small villages. San Mamete is the municipal seat and, since time immemorial, the valley's main civic centre. Its historic Palazzo Pretorio is where the Magnificent Sovereign Council of the Valley used to sit.

The loveliest place in the valley is Castello, a fortified village in a dominant position on a rocky spur. Only ruins and the

Sweeping view of the lake and Lugano from Lanzo d'Intelvi

glassworks came later in the 18th century, which explains why the old centre is a mixture of 17th-century porticoed buildings, disused sites and modern constructions. A cluster of old houses with great character huddles on the lakeside. From Porlezza, the SS340 leads to Menàggio on Lake Como (see page 66).

BACK TO NATURE

From Porlezza, climb Val Cavargna along a scenic road that winds through majestic mountains, woods and meadows in an unspoiled and, in places, untamed landscape.

▶ Skirt the bottom of the lake to Claino, then take the road to Laino, and from here follow the signs to Lanzo d'Intelvi.

8 Lanzo d'Intelvi

Lanzo d'Intelvi is the main centre in the valley of the same name, set among splendid greenery. Sitting about 900m (2,950 feet) above sea level, at the centre of a sunny plateau, it has an interesting old centre and

▶ Follow signs to Arogno and Bissone; from here skirt the lake up to Campione d'Italia.

9 Campione d'Italia

This is an Italian enclave entirely surrounded by Swiss territory, with special status that includes exemption from custom duties. Campione d'Italia is principally known and visited for its casino (one of four in Italy). Opposite this is

area and beyond. A spectacular flight of steps climbs from the lake to the Santuario della Madonna dei Ghirli (Madonna of the Swallows). Built in the 14th century but much altered since, the church features fine late Gothic and Renaissance frescoes under the right-hand portico and inside. Shopping streets, restaurants, bars and night spots enliven the area around the casino.

the parish church of San Siro, altered in the 19th century but of much older origin. From here you can reach the other small villages in the valley (such as San Fedele d'Intelvi), where ancient architecture is embell-ished with frescoes and wrought-iron, wood and stone finishes. The master builders, stonecut-ters and stucco-workers of the valley were renowned through-out Europe, especially during the 17th and 18th centuries.

i *Palazzo Comunale*

RECOMMENDED WALK

From Lanzo d'Intelvi, a delightful 20-minute walk takes you to the Belvedere, with exceptional views of Lake Lugano.

---

the Civic Gallery, devoted to the famous Maestri Campione (Masters of Campione) – local stonecutters, sculptors and engravers who in the 14th and 15th centuries, embellished churches and mansions in northern Italy and the Alpine

▶ Return to Como, skirting the lake and taking the main road or the **A2** motorway, a total distance of 28km (17.5 miles).

At the roulette table of the Campione d'Italia Casino

LAKE COMO

Lake Como, also known as Lake Lario, lies at the centre of the Italian lake system, the third largest after Garda and Maggiore, and the deepest, at 414m (1,358 feet). It's divided into three arms – Como (Lario) to the southwest, Lecco to the southeast and Colico to the north. In the generally mild climate, Mediterranean and exotic plants flourish on the shores and in the villa gardens. The River Adda is both its tributary and its outlet to the sea, and it has just one island, Comacina.

A ring of mountains frames the lake. The highest, Monte Legnone (2,609m/8,560 feet), towers above Colico. Beautiful peaks also form a backdrop to the harsher east shore, including the Grigne range and the Corni di Canzo, sloping down to the water to form inlets and bays. The principal towns on this shore are Lecco, Varenna and Bellano. Gentler and more Mediterranean – and more popular with tourists – is the west shore, leading to Como. From the 18th century this was a favourite holiday ground of the Lombard nobility, who built spectacular villas here, surrounded by large gardens. The most famous of these resorts, including Cernobbio and Menàggio, are found in this area.

One of the Riva refuge huts, at the foot of Monte Grignone, on the east shore of Lake Lecco

The coast road retraces an ancient Roman route – the Regina road – and passes a succession of villas, parks and typically characteristic villages. For centuries people have travelled through this land en route from the Po Plain to the transalpine countries, but the lake towns also harboured a rich artistic life, and have a particularly impressive heritage of Romanesque monuments built by the 'Como masters', who, during the Middle Ages, carried their architectural influence right across Europe.

An unusual and delightful way to visit Lario is to use the frequent boat services that link the shores and provide views of all the towns, villas and gardens that are scattered along the shoreline. To admire the local scenery from above, climb to the high ground surrounding the lake, using the Como-Brunate or Argegno-Pigra cableways.

Tour 8

This tour explores Como, sitting at the tip of the lake named after it. It visits the pleasant old centre, once enclosed within a ring of walls which are now for the most part lost. Here you can take in the Duomo, the Broletto (former town hall), the Basilica of San Fedele, the civic museums and picture gallery. The route also takes you to the church of Sant' Abbondio, a masterpiece of Romanesque architecture.

Tour 9

From Como this tour sets off to explore lower Lario. The first section visits its best-known stretch along the SS340 coast road that winds past villas and gardens. Leave your car at Sala Comacina and take a boat to the isle of Comacina, famous for its important early medieval archaeological ruins, mostly still unexplored. Back on the coast, stop at Tremezzo to visit the gardens and art collections of Villa Carlotta, one of the lake's most famous attractions. Then take a ferry across the lake to Varenna. The tour continues along the east coast to Lecco and Civate, where, high above the village, the church of San Pietro is a masterpiece of Lombard Romanesque style, and Erba, a traditional destination for Milanese days out.

Canoeing on Lake Segrino

Tour 10

Starting from Milan you wind your way between Lake Como and Brianza, the undulating and densely populated strip of high plain that encircles the city to the north. Since the 1700s this has been a holiday destination for the Milanese nobility, and it was a hotbed of early Lombard entrepreneurs. The first stop is Lecco, which gives its name to the eastern arm of the lake. Here, follow in the footsteps of writer Alessandro Manzoni (who spent his youth here) and the characters in his novel *The Betrothed*. You then move into the heart of Lario and the enchanting Bellagio peninsula, one of the loveliest and best-

The small headland on which Menàggio stands

known places in Brianza, returning towards Milan through Valassina (with interesting views of the lake) and Brianza, which, despite its industrial and residential sprawl, still has places of special charm. The last stop is the town of Monza, where you can visit the Duomo and its artistic treasures, and the gardens of Villa Reale, including the famous motor-racing circuit.

Tour 11

This tour follows the east shore of the lake from Lecco to Varenna, where you can take the car ferry to the opposite shore at Menàggio, an old-fashioned village set against a backdrop of high mountains. From here you can skirt the north lakeshore. Scenic attractions – such as a stop at the Pian di Spagna and Lake Mezzola nature reserve – are combined with historic and artistic highlights. A visit to some of the major monuments of Lombard Romanesque art includes the church of Santa Maria del Tiglio at Gravedona and the Abbey of Piona. The route returns to Lecco via Valsàssina – a green valley dominated by the Grigne mountain range.

TOUR
8

Como

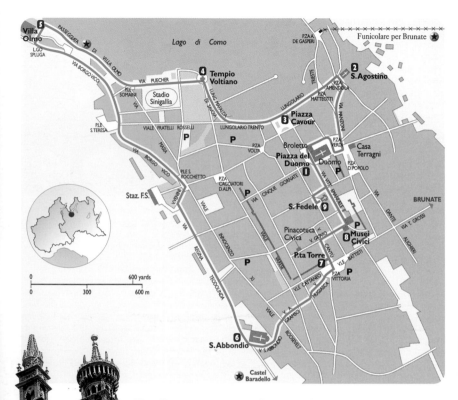

The fine monuments of this 'walled city', including the Duomo, the Broletto, the Basilica of San Fedele and Porta Torre, are combined on this tour with trips to the lakeside, a stroll through the city streets and a visit to the museums. In contrast, Sant'Abbondio, a masterpiece of Lombard Romanesque architecture, evokes the skills of Como's old masters.

1 DAY

i *Piazza Cavour 17*

❶ Piazza del Duomo

Piazza del Duomo, the heart of the old city centre, is now almost entirely pedestrianised, with old monuments rubbing shoulders with shops, boutiques and restaurants. On this square stand some of the city's most important monuments, starting with the Broletto, the former court of justice. Built together with the adjacent tower in 1215, it has a distinctive striped white, grey and red marble façade.

Beside it stands the Duomo (cathedral), begun in 1396 and extended several times before 1740, when the construction of the dome marked its completion. The Renaissance Gothic façade is enlivened by a rose window, sculptures by the Rodari brothers dating from the 15th and 16th centuries and statues of the Latin writers Pliny the Elder and Pliny the Younger (1st century AD, from Como) flanking the doorway. Inside, precious works of art include nine late-16th-century tapestries; a 16th-century wooden ancona by Giovan Angelo da Maiano, depicting stories from the life of Sant'Abbondio, patron

FOR HISTORY BUFFS

Como's centre is still called the 'walled city' although most of the walls that surrounded it in the 12th century – rebuilt after their destruction by Milan in 1127 – have now disappeared. The streets in this old quarter, arranged in chequerboard fashion, reproducing the ancient Roman road layout, are lined with ancient buildings, forming a distinctive townscape in the middle of modern Como.

saint of the city; and the altarpiece of San Gerolamo, a masterpiece by Bernardino Luini (*c*1480–1532).

▶ *Go to Piazza Verdi and Piazza del Popolo and then along Via Manzoni to Piazza Amendola and Sant'Agostino.*

❷ Chiesa di Sant'Agostino

In Piazza del Popolo, facing the apse of the cathedral, is the former Casa del Fascio, built between 1932 and 1936 by Giuseppe Terragni, the greatest Italian rationalist architect,

Above: relaxing on the Como lakeside
Below: frescoes in the apse of the basilica of Sant'Abbondio

and considered one of his most important works.

The church of Sant'Agostino was founded in the 14th century by the Hermits of St Augustine; it was altered in the 18th century and returned to its original form by recent restoration work. Once the religious centre of the village of Colognola (known today as Borgo Sant'Agostino), on the road to Bellagio, it contains a cycle of paintings depicting stories from the life of the Virgin Mary, by Morazzone (1573–1626).

▶ *Take Via Crespi and continue to follow the lakeshore on Lungolario Trieste.*

century on the site of an old port, which silted up in 1871; the landing stage of the Navigazione Lago di Como ferry service is also here.

▶ *Continue along Lungolario Trento and Lungolago Mafalda di Savoia.*

④ Tempio Voltiano
A pleasant stroll along the lake takes you to the public gardens and, where they meet the lake, the Tempio Voltiano, a neo-classical building constructed in 1927 to celebrate the centenary of the death of Alessandro Volta (1745–1827). Volta invented the battery and discovered methane gas. Inside are memorabilia and

belongs to the municipal authorities and is used as a venue for exhibitions, conferences and international gatherings.

▶ *From Largo Spluga take Via Borgo Vico to Piazzale San Rocchetto, where you continue along Via Venini, Via Regina Teodolinda and Via Sant'Abbondio.*

⑥ Basilica di Sant'Abbondio
Dedicated to Sant'Abbondio, the fourth bishop of Como and patron saint of the city, the basilica is a masterpiece of Lombard Romanesque architecture. Built between 1050 and 1085, it is the oldest of Como's three great Romanesque churches (the others are San Giacomo and San Fedele). It also has the best-maintained original features, the work of the 'Como masters' – bricklayers, carpenters and stone-cutters who were much in demand all over northern Italy and in the canton of

> **FOR CHILDREN**
>
> The public gardens near the Tempio Voltiano are a green haven where children can play in the open air; attractions include a playground, roundabouts and crazy golf.

The spectacular view of Como from Brunate

the instruments and apparatus invented and used by him.

▶ *Follow the lakeside along Via Puecher, Piazzale Somaini and the Villa Olmo promenade.*

⑤ Villa Olmo
Set in the centre of a large public park (with a lido, restaurant and tennis club), Villa Olmo was built in the late 18th century and extended in the 19th century. The imposing neo-classical building now

The Tempio Voltiano displays many of Alessandro Volta's scientific instruments and documents

③ Piazza Cavour
Overlooking the lake, this square is a busy meeting-place for Como inhabitants. Built in the late 19th

> **SCENIC ROUTES**
>
> A steep road climbs from Via Grossi in Como to Brunate, a fashionable belle époque resort, which commands a spectacular view of the lake and city. The village can also be reached in about ten minutes on a cableway, inaugurated in 1894 to link Piazza De Gaspari with the mountain behind it.

RECOMMENDED WALK

A beautiful stroll leads to Castel Baradello, which has exceptional views of the city and Brianza. Part of the ring of walls and the tower are all that remain of the castle, rebuilt in 1158 by Barbarossa and dismantled in the 16th century by the Spanish. It is reached by car along the street of the same name (entered from Via Rimoldi); after about 1.5km (1 mile), continue on foot for a quarter of an hour.

Ticino for their building and decorative skills. The basilica has five aisles, apse towers and a long presbytery and, in the apse, an important cycle of 14th-century frescoes depicting the life and times of Jesus.

▶ *Continue along Via Gramsci, Via Rossa and Via Mugiasca to Piazza Vittoria.*

7 Porta Torre
Built in 1192 at the end of the road from Milan, the great Torre gate formed part of the ring of walls constructed with the aid of Barbarossa – and is today its most important remaining part. The other two surviving towers are the San Vitale tower, on the southeast corner of the walls, and the Porta Nuova tower, on the southwest corner.

▶ *Take Via Cantù and Via Giovio to Via Vittorio Emanuele II.*

8 Civic museums
Como's civic museums are housed in Palazzo Giovio and Palazzo Olginati, built between the 16th and 19th centuries, and divided into two sections. The Town Museum displays archaeological and historical artefacts that illustrate the history of Como and the surrounding area; the Giuseppe Garibaldi Museum of the Risorgimento

Sculptural detail on the façade of the basilica of San Fedele

features historical memorabilia and 19th-century objets d'art.

▶ *Proceed along Via Vittorio Emanuele II to San Fedele.*

9 Basilica di San Fedele
The city's first cathedral, the Basilica of San Fedele, has an unusual and complex structure – the result of combining a basilica layout (with a nave and two aisles) with a quite different German design. Although the chronological development of the building is not yet fully understood, the church must have taken its basic form by the 12th century. The oldest part is the apse, with a doorway flanked by figures of monsters. The façade dates from the early 20th century. In front of the basilica is the Piazza San Fedele, built on the site of the Roman forum and flanked by porticoed houses.

The Torre gate or tower of Porta Vittorio in Como

SPECIAL TO...
Housed in the 17th-century Palazzo Volpi, the Pinacoteca (Civic Picture Gallery) shows 17th-century Lombard paintings, 14th-century frescoes and sculptures and a collection of 20th-century pictures. Two other interesting museums in the city are devoted to silk-manufacturing, for which Como is famous the world over – the Silk Museum and the Fondazione Ratti Textile Museum.

The town market was held here until the 1800s.

▶ *Return to Piazza del Duomo along Via Vittorio Emanuele.*

ORIGIN OF THE LAKES

The Italian lake region – which extends from Piedmont to Veneto – marks the boundary between the Alps and the Po Plain, and has provided a link between these two worlds for many centuries. The lake waters, and the rivers and canals connected to them, provided a transit route for goods and travellers between northern Italy and the transalpine states, as well as a channel for the communication of ideas, arts and culture. Their history has often been turbulent, with numerous confrontations and clashes between rival powers along their shores. But their origin goes back millions of years before humans arrived to exploit them. The ice that once covered the Alps and the Po Plain retreated and the pre-Alpine lakes featured in this guide were created as the cavities hollowed out by the mighty glaciers began to fill up.

Mountain depressions

There was a time when scholars believed that the deep furrows excavated in the pre-Alpine crust were fiords of the distant Po sea. Nowadays they tend to date their origins to a much earlier period, when tremors occurred in the tectonic plates.

Their backdrop today is formed of the peaks of the Alps (from Monte Rosa to the Giudicarie mountains), and they are crowned by the pre-Alps, whose sometimes rugged heights descend to the lake waters. Around the lakes is a cordon of hills farmed and inhabited since prehistoric times. The alternation in the pre-Alpine area of rocks of very different consistencies accounts for the picturesque contrast between plains, pillars, pinnacles and sometimes sheer rock faces (such as the Grigne mountains beside Lake Como or Monte Resegone to the west of Lake Lecco).

Where ancient glaciers used to lie

The westernmost pre-Alpine basin is little Lake Orta, which, with Lake Maggiore (the second largest lake in Italy) and Lake Lugano, forms part of a single complex hydrographic system. At its centre is Lake Como, the deepest pre-Alpine lake in Italy – 410m (1,345 feet) – and indeed one of the deepest in Europe. Its distinctive

upturned Y shape clearly reveals its glacial origin: it formed when a glacier descending southwards encountered the massif of the Larian peninsula and split into two arms. The area between lakes Maggiore and Como is dotted with the smaller lakes of Varese, Commabio and Monate, and other tiny water expanses – Brianza's lakes, Pusiano,

Lake Pusiano has a small island named after the cypress tree that grows on it

small lakes, some reduced to peat bogs.

The Grigne mountain range

Above: Lake Varese's shoreline

Annone and Alserio – lie south of Lake Como. Further east is Lake Iseo, which occupies a hollow excavated in ancient times by a glacier that descended from Val Camònica; skirting it to the south are the fertile morainic hills of Franciacorta. The easternmost and largest Italian pre-Alpine lake is Garda. Its waters occupy an extensive basin formed by large ranges, arranged in five semi-circles that slope down to the lake and interspersed with

Gorges and kettles

Many spectacular geological phenomena, bearing witness to the remote past, can be seen around the pre-Alpine lakes: the Santa Anna gorge on Lake Maggiore in Val Cannobina; the Bellano gorge on Lake Como; the Zone earth pillars near Lake Iseo; the Varone falls at Riva on Lake Garda; the 'giants' kettles' of Nago and the moraines of Dro – huge boulders that slid down to the valley thousands of years ago in the largest landslide of the alpine range, covering a vast surface area of 14.5sq km (6 square miles).

Lower
Lario

The west shore of Lake Como winds along the old Via Regina in an uninterrupted succession of parks and villas. The high points of the tour are the gardens and art collections of Villa

Carlotta at Tremezzo, the lake ferry crossing and the picturesque

1 DAY • 90KM • 56 MILES   village of Varenna.

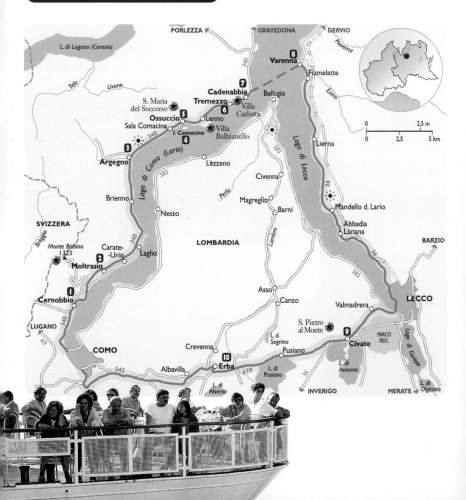

i Piazza Cavour 17, Como

▶ *Skirt the lake following the SS340 to Cernobbio.*

1 Cernobbio

Cernobbio has always been a holiday destination, as is evident in the exclusive villas built here between the 15th and 18th centuries, such as Villa Pizzo and Villa Erba. The most outstanding is mid-16th-century Villa d'Este. Once the residence of the wife of King George IV of England, it was turned into a luxury hotel in 1873, and remains one of Europe's most exclusive hotels.

i Via Regina 33/b

▶ *Continue to Moltrasio.*

2 Moltrasio

This pretty village was once famous for the grey stone in its quarries which was used in buildings all over the lake shores. The fine 18th-century Villa Passalacqua is occasionally open for concerts.

▶ *Drive along the SS340 to Argegno.*

3 Argegno

A stretch of fairly wild coastline leads to Argegno, passing through the village of Brienno, perched on the rugged lakeshore. Argegno lies at the mouth of the delightful Val d'Intelvi, which is also accessible from Lake Lugano. In the village – where a medieval bridge crosses the Telo stream – you can visit the 18th-century sanctuary of Santa Anna and climb by cableway to the tiny village of Pigra, commanding a splendid view of the lake.

i Via Cacciatori delle Alpi 42

▶ *Take the SS340 and continue to Sala Comacina, where you take a boat to Isola Comacina.*

SCENIC ROUTE

A scenic route about 17km (10.5 miles) long climbs from Cernobbio to Monte Bisbino (1,325m/4,347 feet) and offers a sweeping view of the lake, Como and the mountains around it.

The shores of Isola Comacina, with a view of Ossuccio

RECOMMENDED WALK

The Via dei Monti Lariani, a popular local hike, winds from Cernobbio to Sorico, in the upper lake area. Passing at an average 1,000m (3,281 feet) above sea level, the 125km (78-mile) route crosses Val d'Intelvi, Val Menaggio and the valleys of the upper lake. It can be followed in sections picked up from various villages along the way; several mountain refuge huts provide refreshments.

---

4 Isola Comacina

Isola Comacina, 600m (660 yards) long and 200m (220 yards) wide, is the only island on Lake Como. It was fortified by the Romans and Byzantines and in the Middle Ages became an influential political and military centre. After siding with Milan in the ten-year war between Milan and Como, it was ravaged in 1169 by the people of Como. Its inhabitants took refuge at

Varenna, and the island fell into ruin. Not until the 1950s were excavations begun and the slow, laborious process of uncovering its ancient remains got underway. The only intact building is the baroque Oratory of San Giovanni, flanked by the ruins of the basilica of Sant'Eufemia and a baptistery. Further on are the ruins of other churches and buildings.

SPECIAL TO...

On the tip of the wooded Dosso di Lavedo headland (near Lenno), Villa Balbianello is an 18th-century 'place of delight' created by Cardinal Durini. Its loggia, overlooking the lake, the harbour and the vast park make it one of the loveliest villas on the lake. It can be reached by motorboat from Sala Comacina.

Above: the delights of Villa Balbianello, near Lenno
Left: the ruins of the Romanesque basilica of Sant'Eufemia on Isola Comacina

enchanting setting, overlooking the central lake basin, and to visit Villa Carlotta, one of the most famous and spectacular 18th-century residences on the lake. The villa is surrounded by

FOR HISTORY BUFFS

From Ossuccio climb through interesting scenery to the Sanctuary of Santa Maria del Soccorso, made up of 14 chapels dedicated to the Mysteries of the Rosary. It was built between 1635 and 1714 above a sheer gorge cut by the Perlana river. At the very top is a small church erected in 1537. The harmonious blend of devotion, art and nature make this a rural version of the Sacro Monte sanctuaries built from the 16th century in various other parts of the Duchy of Milan.

▶ *Return to Sala Comacina by ferry and proceed along the SS340 to Ossuccio.*

5 Ossuccio

This village is divided into two parts – Spurano (where you can visit the 11th-century church of SS Giacomo e Filippo, with its distinctive bellcote on the façade); and Ospedaletto with the church of Santa Maria Maddalena featuring a Romanesque bell tower that culminates in an unusual late-Gothic belfry – one of the lake's best-known images.

▶ *Follow the SS340 to Tremezzo.*

6 Tremezzo

Tremezzo is a popular destination with Italians and foreigners alike, who flock to enjoy its splendid gardens – partly Italian, with terraces and steps, and partly English. They're especially stunning in spring, when the azaleas and rhododendrons are in flower, creating one of the finest sights in Europe. Villa Carlotta is named after Princess Charlotte of Prussia, who received it as a gift from her mother, Marianna, when she married Prince George of Saxe-Meiningen. In the neo-classical interior, a museum houses sculptures by Antonio Canova and Bertel Thorvaldsen, paintings by Francesco Hayez and many other works of art, furnishings and items of worked gold.

ℹ️ *Via Regina 3*

▶ *Continue to Cadenabbia.*

7 Cadenabbia
With its 19th-century villas and hotels, Cadenabbia is a quiet resort in a scenic position overlooking the lake. A car ferry departs from here to cross the lake to Varenna, on the eastern shore; the trip offers splendid views of the lake.

ℹ️ *Via Statale Regina 1*

▶ *Take the ferry to Varenna.*

8 Varenna
Varenna is an attractive fishing village, set on a headland at the foot of the last Grigne mountain spurs. One of the best preserved locations on Lake Como, it features old houses, beautiful views and a delightful lakeside promenade. The narrow streets and steps of the old centre converge on a square, where you

can find the 14th-century church of San Giorgio (with frescoes on the façade and inside), the 17th-century church of Santa Maria delle Grazie and the medieval church of San Giovanni Battista, one of the oldest on the lake. South of the village are spectacular holiday homes such as Villa Cipressi, a 16th-century architectural complex with buildings and

gardens; and Villa Monastero, a former convent, converted in the 17th century into a noble villa.

ℹ️ *Piazza Venini 1*

▶ *Follow the SS36 as it descends along the lakeshore towards Lecco; beyond the town, drive in the direction of Como to Civate.*

9 Civate
Ancient Civate is the point of departure for San Pietro al Monte (about an hour up a steep mule track), one of the major Lombard Romanesque complexes. The basilica stands on a shelf of Monte Cornizzolo, 662m (2,172 feet) above sea level, with a spectacular view. Probably founded in the Lombard era, its present form dates from the 11th century. Inside, treasures include a precious ciborium (canopied shrine) above the altar (11th century) and rare frescoes and stuccowork of the 11th and 12th centuries. From the village, it's a short distance to Lake Annone and the village of the same name, which also has a golf course.

▶ *Follow the SS639 to the right for Erba and Como.*

10 Erba
Erba has been a bustling holiday resort since the 18th century and lies between the mountain slopes of Vallassina and lakes Pusiano and Alserio. In the early 20th century (when the Milan–Asso railway was built) it

The oratory of San Benedetto, at San Pietro al Monte, Civate

became a traditional day's outing for the Milanese; today, it's a large industrial centre. The oldest part of the town is centred around Piazza Vittorio Veneto and the Romanesque church of Sant'Eufemia. In the hamlet of Crevenna, you can visit the Archaeological Museum, which exhibits finds dating from the palaeolithic period and material from Roman necropolises.

▶ *Return on the SS639 to Como.*

The Lakes
& Hills of Brianza

Starting with a walk in the footsteps of a writer at Lecco, this tour continues to Bellagio, with its splendid villas and spectacular gardens overlooking the lake. From Vallsàssina it proceeds to Brianza, with its art treasures and gentle landscape dotted with villas, and ends in Monza, whose attractions include the famous motor-racing circuit.

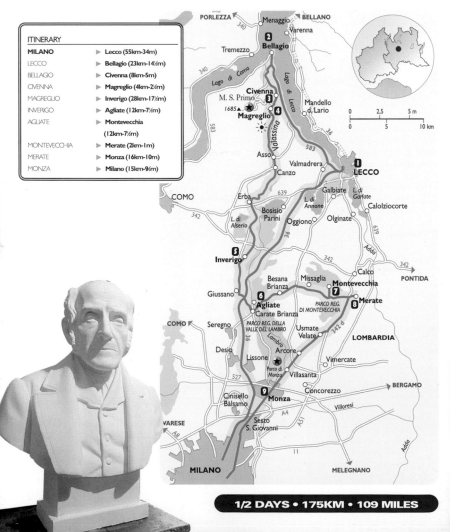

1/2 DAYS • 175KM • 109 MILES

i Via Marconi 1, Milan

▶ *Travel to Lecco on the **SS36**.*

❶ Lecco

Lecco, which gives its name to the eastern arm of Lake Como, sits at the point where the River Adda flows out of the lake. Between the Byzantine period and the era of the *comune*, it was the strategic headquarters of a garrison controlling the passage between the plain and the Alpine lands. Heavily industrialised from the 19th century onwards (mainly steel and metal), it still has a small historic centre, around which the modern town has grown in a somewhat disorderly way. Alessandro Manzoni (1785–1873) set his novel *The Betrothed* in this area (see panel above), and a visit to Lecco inevitably follows in the footsteps of the writer and his book.

You can take a Manzoni tour which starts at Villa Manzoni (Via Guanella 1), where the writer spent his infancy and adolescence; today it is the home of the Manzoni Museum, with manuscripts, books and memorabilia. The ground floor still has the original furnishings.

FOR HISTORY BUFFS

Alessandro Manzoni immortalised Lecco, his home, in *The Betrothed*, a masterpiece of Italian literature and an 'epic story of the humble' in which a love story between two peasants, Renzo and Lucia, is set against the historical backdrop of the Spanish occupation of the 17th century. Sir Walter Scott described the novel as the greatest book ever written.

The second stop is the square named after the writer, with a monument to him at its centre. Inaugurated in 1891, the statue portrays Manzoni seated in meditation, and rests on a plinth decorated with three high reliefs (depicting Lucia's kidnap, the death of Don Rodrigo and the marriage between Renzo and Lucia – all scenes from the novel). Popular tradition identifies the local districts of Acquate and Olate as the homes of

Right: the centre of Lecco
Below: a sailing regatta on Lake Lecco

Renzo and Lucia. At Olate, the house presumed to be that of Lucia is a typical local rural home, and the church of SS Vitale e Valeria is said to be the parish church of Don Abbondio. Don Rodrigo's mansion, on the Zucco headland, was built in the late 16th century by the Arrigoni family (rivals of the Manzonis). It was almost entirely rebuilt in 1938 and no longer corresponds to Manzoni's description. At Acquate the chapel of Via Croce is said to be the place where Don Abbondio and the desperados met.

The Azzone Visconti bridge, which crosses the River Adda as it flows from the lake, is known to locals as the Ponte Grande. Built in the mid-14th century,

A fisherman at sunset on the Lecco lakeside

18th-century Villa Giulia has a large garden sloping down to the lake, and Villa Trivulzio and Villa Trotti were built in the 18th century and extended in the 19th. The appealing town centre has a busy central street where stepped alleys converge. It's worth spending some time at the 12th-century basilica of San Giacomo, much altered in the baroque period.

Bellagio is connected to the lake's main centres by boat.

⌐i⌐ *Piazza Mazzini*

and much altered since, it was of strategic importance during the period of Manzoni's novel, due to the proximity of the Venetian border and the presence of a garrison. The place most closely linked to Manzoni in Lecco (and the only one explicitly named in *The Betrothed*) is Pescarenico, on the section of the River Adda between the two lakes of Lecco and Garlate, which still has the appearance of a fishing village. Only the cloister and some cells remain of Don Cristoforo's Capuchin convent. Other locations in the book are found outside Lecco: to the south, above Lake Garlate, the fort that dominates Chiuso is thought to be the stronghold of the Unnamed. Built on the border between the Duchy of Milan and the Republic of Venice, it was destroyed and abandoned after the League of Cambrai war (1509).

Other noteworthy buildings in Lecco include the Visconti tower in Piazza XX Settembre (which houses the Museum of the Risorgimento and the Resistance), the 19th-century Town Hall, Palazzo Belgioioso (now the Civic Museum) and the basilica of San Nicolò, now the town cathedral.

⌐i⌐ *Via N Sauro 6*

▶ *Follow the SS583 along the lake to Bellagio.*

❷ Bellagio

Set in a splendid position at the tip of the 'Larian triangle', where two arms of the lake converge, Bellagio is one of the best known and most popular resorts in the area. The lake cast its spell on Roman writer and orator Pliny the Younger

---

SPECIAL TO...

Outside town, at the top of the tree-lined elevation that forms Bellagio point, stands the 18th-century Villa Serbelloni (today a first-class hotel, one of the loveliest places to stay in the vicinity). Surrounding it is a huge park (guided visits) with grottoes, Italian gardens, the remains of medieval walls and – at the tip of the headland – the ruins of fortifications and a Romanesque church.

(1st century AD), who, according to popular legend, had a villa built here (on the site of today's Villa Serbelloni). It also worked its magic on the aristocracy of Lombardy, who created an Italian Versailles here in the 18th and 19th centuries. Bellagio is still famous for its villas. Villa Melzi d'Eryl was built in the 19th century in neo-classical style; its lush gardens are dotted with ancient statues and are particularly impressive in spring, when the azaleas flower. The

SCENIC ROUTE

Near Magreglio the church of the Madonna del Ghisallo, dedicated to the patron saint of cyclists, displays bicycles and trophies. From the Ghisallo Pass, a scenic mountain road leads to Piano Rancio and from here to the Monte San Primo Park, which has exceptional views of the lake and plain.

▶ *Follow the signs to Civenna.*

3 Civenna

This small, peaceful resort occupies a scenic position with views of the Grigne mountains. Visit the 17th-century Sanctuary of the Madonna di Somaguggio, with its portico and soaring bell tower.

▶ *Continue along the same road to Magreglio.*

4 Magreglio

The little agricultural village of Magreglio has an interesting parish church dedicated to Santa Marta, reconstructed at the end of the 16th century and extended and decorated in the 1800s. This is the heart of Valassina, a small picturesque valley lying within the Larian triangle and crossed by the Lambro river, which rises here on the slopes of Monte San Primo (the valley is named after the village of Asso). Its inhabitants once worked mainly in farming and the silk industry, but tourism, principally in the winter, has now become an important part of the local economy

▶ *Continue to Canzo, where you follow the signs for Erba. Drive*

The cypresses, gardens and blue lake at Villa Serbelloni, in Bellagio

RECOMMENDED WALK

Peaceful nature walks are marked out along signed paths in the Montevecchia and Curone Valley Regional Nature Park – 2,200 hectares (5,436 acres) of chestnut, oak and birch woods and natural springs.

on to Monoguzzo and take the SS342 towards Bergamo. After approximately 4km (2.5 miles) you will see the sign for Inverigo on the right.

5 Inverigo

Clinging to the gentle slopes of a hill overlooking the Lambro valley, this is one of the loveliest villages in Brianza. From the 17th-century parish church a cobbled way climbs the hill to the 17th-century Villa Crivelli, once home to one of Milan's

The apse of the church of SS Pietro e Paolo in Agliate

most influential aristocratic families. Here you can admire the Viale dei Cipressi, a 2km (1-mile) route and one of the most famous views in Brianza. Not far from the centre is the Rotonda, a neo-classical villa built by Luigi Cagnola in 1831.

▶ *Continue along the same road to Giussano and here follow the signs to Agliate.*

6 Agliate

An important Romanesque monument is tucked away in this quiet hamlet. The basilica of SS Pietro e Paolo was built in the late 10th century and altered at the end of the 19th century, and contains the remains of an ancient fresco cycle. Alongside it stands the baptistery, of the same period, with 11th- to 15th-century frescoes in very poor condition and the remains of the old font.

▶ *Head for Besana and Missaglia, beyond which you turn right to climb to Montevecchia.*

7 Montevecchia

Montevecchia hill (479m/1,571 feet), in the nature park of the same name, is a favourite weekend venue for the inhabitants of Milan and Brianza, who are

Monza's neo-classical Villa Reale, by Giuseppe Piermarini

drawn by the many country trattorias serving good, wholesome food, including the tasty cheeses made by local producers. At the top of the hill, a small village clusters around the 17th-century sanctuary of the Beata Vergine del Carmelo and a *Via Crucis* (Way of the Cross).

▶ *Return to the crossroads and follow the signs to Merate.*

8 Merate
Merate is the home of one of the most spectacular villas of the 18th-century Milanese nobility – Villa Belgioioso. Probably of 15th-century origin, it was given its present form by the Belgioso family in the 1700s, when the

The Monza race circuit

great park was also created. The village, splendidly positioned on the hills of eastern Brianza, is also known for its astronomical observatory.

▶ *Follow the **SS342d** southbound to Usmate Velate and from here via Arcore to Monza.*

9 Monza
The unofficial capital of Brianza also provides a link between the region and the Milanese hinterland. This town of about 120,000 inhabitants is surrounded by extensive, heavily industrialised suburbs, but has an interesting old centre. Two squares form the historic heart: Piazza Roma, with the 13th-century Arengario (town hall), completely rebuilt in the early 20th century; and Piazza Duomo, overlooked by an imposing Gothic Duomo (cathedral) with a fine marble façade

by Matteo da Campione (1396). Inside, the chapel of Theodelinda, adorned with frescoes by members of the Zavattari family (1444), houses the 'iron crown', a priceless piece of medieval goldwork that, according to tradition, belonged to the 7th-century Lombard queen Theodelinda. Its name reflects the legend that it was forged with a nail from the cross of Jesus; and its national historical significance derives from its use to crown the kings of Italy from the Middle Ages to the Napoleonic era. Also of great value is the cathedral treasure, which includes early medieval goldsmithery; in particular, a mother hen with seven gilded silver chicks.

[i] *Piazza Carducci 1*

▶ *Return to Milan.*

BACK TO NATURE

On the northernmost outskirts of Monza stands the neo-classical Villa Reale, whose enormous park, spread over 7,325,000sq m (78,845,640 square feet), is one of the largest enclosed green spaces in Europe. Several avenues cross the park, which also contains a hippodrome, polo and golf courses and the famous Monza motor-racing circuit.

Upper Lario
& Valsàssina

After the unusual views offered by the ferry crossing from Varenna to Menàggio, the route circles the entire upper Lario basin, exploring its scenic beauty and treasures of Romanesque art, such as the church of Santa Maria del Tiglio at Gravedona and the Piona Abbey. Return through the lush Valsàssina.

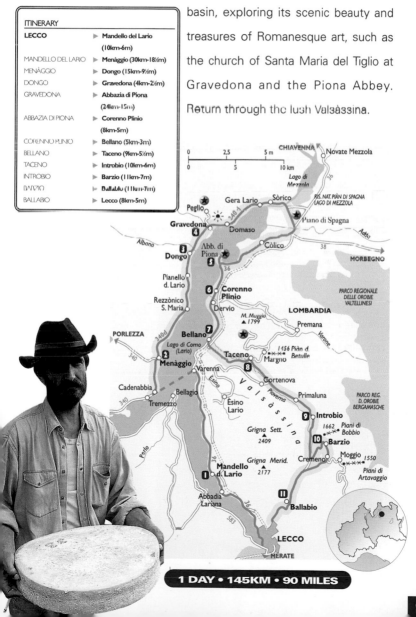

1 DAY • 145KM • 90 MILES

i *Via N Sauro 6, Lecco*

▶ *Follow the SS36, skirting the lake to Mandello del Lario.*

1 Mandello del Lario

Dominated by the Grigne mountains (popular with climbers and mountaineers, with a good network of refuge huts), Mandello del Lario is one of the major centres on the eastern shore of Lake Como. It's also known for its mechanical industries, particularly Guzzi, the famous motorcycle manufacturer, whose history museum attracts thousands of motorcycling enthusiasts every year. The oldest part of the village, on the lakeside, has preserved its medieval appearance with narrow streets, towers and porticoed houses.

On the outskirts of the village, the Oratory of San Rocco has 15th-century frescoes, and the Sanctuary of the Beata Vergine del Fiume is part of a complex including the chapels of a *Via Crucis* (Way of the Cross).

▶ *Continue to Varenna and take the ferry to Cadenabbia. From here follow the lake north on the SS340 to Menàggio.*

2 Menàggio

Generally considered the metropolis of the central lake area, Menàggio is one of the best-equipped sports and tourist centres and one of the liveliest and most popular with young people.

Monte Grigna, north of Lecco

RECOMMENDED WALK

Those wishing to trek in the mountains around the north of the lake can use the Alta Via del Lario, a route that winds from Menàggio to Gera Lario, following high ground along the Swiss border. The itinerary, which can be followed in sections, presents varying degrees of difficulty and requires training and good equipment. Along the way are refuge huts where trekkers can spend the night.

Among other attractions, it has a harbour, an 18-hole golf course, a rock-climbing training ground, riding stables and a dense network of trekking paths. Sitting at the point where the road to Lake Lugano skirts Lake Como, it has a long tourist tradition, having been first discovered by the British, who found it easy to reach from nearby Switzerland. Its lakeside promenade is lined with grand hotels and art nouveau villas, and the old centre has porticoed

houses and interesting monuments, such as the parish church of San Stefano (originally Romanesque, but restored in baroque style), and the 17th-century churches of San Carlo and San Rocco. In the upper part of the town are the remains of a medieval castle.

i *Piazza Garibaldi 8*

▶ *Continue along the SS340d to Dongo.*

3 Dongo

Along with Gravedona and Sòrico, Dongo was one of the principal medieval civil and religious centres of Upper Lario. It now supports metal and steel industries, but has an elegant lakeside area and the Romanesque church of Santa Maria di Martinico, much altered over the years. On the edge of the old centre is the baroque sanctuary of the Madonna delle Lacrime.

▶ *Proceed along the SS340d to Gravedona.*

4 Gravedona

Lying at the heart of a gulf, protected to the north by mountains, Gravedona is a Roman

FOR HISTORY BUFFS

After the fall of Fascism, Benito Mussolini was stopped at Dongo as he tried to flee to Switzerland disguised as a German soldier. Partisans recognised the former dictator and after a summary trial he was shot, along with other Fascists, on the morning of 28 April, 1945, in the hamlet of Giuliano di Mezzegra.

town, and was the main centre in this area during the Middle Ages. It still serves as the region's 'mini-capital'. The major surviving traces of its past are the church of Santa Maria del Tiglio (the most important Romanesque construction in Upper Lario, with black and

The Larian Boat Museum

di Spagna head for the east shore. Approximately 5km (3 miles) after Còlico, take the turning on the right to Abbazia di Piona.

5 Abbazia di Piona

Founded by the Cluniac order in the 11th to 12th century, Piona Abbey is one of Lario's best known monuments – both for its position and for its artistic and historic importance. It was abandoned for hundreds of years, but underwent restoration from the 19th century onwards. The abbey stands at the tip of the Olgiasca peninsula, which extends into the lake opposite Gravedona to create a delightful gulf known as Lake Piona. The complex includes the ruins of a Romanesque church, the church of San Nicolò, with its 18th-century bell tower, and a splendid Romanesque-Gothic cloister with an irregular plan (1252–7), featuring column capitals sculpted with fantastic and naturalistic motifs.

▶ *Return to the SS36 and follow it towards Lecco to Corenno Plinio.*

6 Corenno Plinio

Perched on a rocky spur that extends into the lake, Corenno

Piona Abbey, dominated by its tall 18th-century bell tower

white facing and a high bell tower above the entrance), the church of San Vincenzo, with a crypt decorated with medieval frescoes, and the imposing Palazzo Gallio, dating from the late 16th century. Dominating the village is the 15th-century church of Santa Maria delle Grazie, which contains a vast cycle of frescoes by 16th-century Lombard painters.

▶ *Continue along the SS340d to the bottom of the lake; after passing Sòrico and Piano*

Plinio is a picturesque little village that has survived with its medieval structure intact. The 14th-century castle-enclosure is formed from a ring of walls and two towers to protect the points

The flower-filled meadows along the Val Biandino Trail

of access. On the lovely main square stands the parish church of San Tommaso di Canterbury (Thomas Becket), decorated with 14th- to 17th-century frescoes. Set against its exterior are the three burial arches of the Counts Andreani, feudal lords of the village from 1271 onwards,

Overlooking the Bellano Gorge

and elegant examples of aristocratic 14th-century tombs.

▶ *Follow the same road to Bellano.*

7 Bellano

In the 19th century this was a busy industrial centre specialising in the production of yarn and fabrics; today, Bellano is an elegant holiday resort, with streets leading from its old centre to the lakeside. The manufacturing industry was established here to exploit the hydraulic power generated by the waters of the Pioverna River, which descends from Valsàssina and falls precipitously behind the village in a famous *orrido* (gorge) before flowing into the lake. A walkway crosses the gorge, which can be visited from May to November, during the day or in the evening, when it is illuminated by a play of lights. The waterfall is reached via the Cantoni cotton mill, an interesting 19th-century industrial complex built on the site of a 13th-century convent.

The oldest part of Bellano is clustered about Piazza San Giorgio, where the church of San Giorgio stands. Built around the

middle of the 14th century by the Maestri Campione (Masters of Campione; see page 47), it has a striped façade of dark and light stone, and contains some valuable paintings of the 15th and 16th centuries.

▶ *Travel inland towards Taceno.*

8 Taceno

Taceno is the first stop on the section of the tour that winds through Valsàssina, once known for its iron-working and famous today for its cheeses. Valsàssina is the largest of the eastern valleys in Lario, crossed by the Pioverna river and bordered to the west by the Grigne mountains and to the east by the last offshoots of the Bergamascan pre-Alps.

Thanks to the exploitation of the waters of the Maladiga torrent, Taceno once had several metalworking forges, and it still has an old 'donkey's head' hammer, the only surviving example in Valsàssina. From Taceno take the lovely road through typically Alpine scenery of small rural hamlets, featuring houses with characteristic slate

Skiing on immaculate white snow on the Piani di Bobbio

roofs, to climb Monte Muggio or up to Margno, where a cableway travels to 1,456m (4,777 feet), and Pian delle Betulle (skiing in winter, good summer walking).

▶ *Continue to Introbio.*

9 Introbio

This popular holiday resort is also the main dairy-producing centre of the area. At the heart of the village – formerly the most important in the valley – a mighty 11th- to 12th-century square tower is all that remains of the system of strongholds that once blocked both sides of the valley. More recent is the parish church of Sant'Antonio Abate, built at the end of the 19th century. The 13th-century church of San Michele, on a rise on the edge of the village, has votive frescoes inside.

▶ *Continue along the same road to the turning on the left for Barzio.*

10 Barzio

Barzio is the best-known resort in Valsàssina, partly because of its splendid position, on a terrace overlooking the valley and facing the Grigne mountains. Well equipped for winter

sports (skiing on the nearby Piani di Bobbio slopes), it has a charming, traditional old centre. The most famous building is the 17th-century home of the family of Alessandro Manzoni, at No 6 on the street of the same name and today housing the civic library; the inner courtyard bears the family coat of arms in stone.

[i] *Piazza Garibaldi 9*

▶ *Follow the signs to Cremeno and then Ballabio.*

11 Ballabio

The village is divided into two parts – Ballabio Inferiore and Ballabio Superiore. The latter is the more historically interesting, with a tower once used to control the Gerenzone and Pioverna valleys below. From here you can climb up a lovely scenic road to Piani Resinelli, a large plateau 1,200m (3,937 feet) above sea level and the starting point for hikes into the Grigne mountains. Popular among winter sports enthusiasts and summer climbers, with houses, hotels and refuge huts, the area also comprises the 120-hectare (296-acre) Valentino Park.

▶ *Follow the signs to Lecco.*

BERGAMO, BRESCIA & LAKE ISÉO

Surrounded by an impressive amphitheatre of mountains, Lake Iseo may not be one of the better known Italian lakes, but it is certainly one of the most fascinating. Rising from its deep waters is the lake-island of Monte Isola, the largest in Europe, and the small isles of Loreto and San Paolo. Also known as Sebino, the lake occupies a hollow dug thousands of years ago by the Val Camònica glacier. The River Oglio, a tributary of the Po, enters the lake from the north between Lóvere and Pisogne, and leaves it to the south, close to Sàrnico. The east shore is in the province of Brescia and the west in the province of Bergamo, and two tours are specifically devoted to the provincial capitals, each with its rich artistic heritage.

The Sebino landscape is extremely varied – ranging from the peat bogs close to Iseo, a protected area unique in Europe and of great interest for its flora and fauna, to the beautiful, sheer rocks of the northern shore. For art- and history-lovers the lake has countless treasures to explore – Romanesque churches and abbeys, fresco cycles (splendid ones by Romanino in the church of the Madonna della Neve at Pisogne and by Lorenzo Lotto at Trescore Balneario), and old towns with perfectly preserved centres. The main tourist attractions are Iseo, Sulzano, Pisogne, Lóvere and Sàrnico. Olive groves, vineyards and orchards bear witness to a mild climate that make a visit in spring particularly enjoyable.

The Franciacorta hills, a land of abbeys, villas and vineyards (with excellent wine cellars), surround the lake to the south, and Val Camònica stretches away to the north. Although heavily industrialised and busy with traffic, the valley has a few surprises for visitors in its nature parks, Adamello and Stelvio, three well-known winter resorts (Ponte di Legno-Tonale, Borno and Montecampione), the Boario spa and a wealth of historical and artistic attractions. Val Camònica is also the site of the greatest concentration of rock drawings ever discovered.

Mooring at Monte Isola, one of the loveliest spots to visit on Lake Iseo

Vineyards in Franciacorta, a land of great wines and refined cuisine

Tour 12

Lying at the mouth of the Seriane and Brembana valleys, Bergamo is divided into two parts – the old upper town on the hill and the modern lower town at its feet. Ringed by approximately 5km (3 miles) of walls constructed by the Venetians in the 16th century, Upper Bergamo is a remarkably preserved citadel, with medieval and Renaissance buildings. The heart of the city is its two squares – Piazza Vecchia, the seat of political power, and Piazza Duomo, the seat of religious power. On these stand the most famous monuments: on the former, Palazzo della Ragione and the Comune tower; on the latter, the Colleoni chapel, Duomo (cathedral) and the basilica of Santa Maria Maggiore. The birthplace of composer Gaetano Donizetti (1797–1848), to whom the theatre is dedicated, Bergamo has an impressive artistic heritage which includes works by the Venetian painter Lorenzo Lotto (1480–1556) and the collections in the picture gallery of the Accademia Carrara, one of the most prestigious in Italy.

Tour 13

The route circles Lake Iseo completely before venturing into Val Camònica to visit the Capo di Ponte rock drawing park, declared a world heritage site by UNESCO. The first section of the journey winds along the east shore and offers two detours – to Monte Isola (by boat) and to the Zone pyramids, tall stone pinnacles formed by thousands of years of erosion of water and wind. Stops include Pisogne, with its precious 16th-century fresco cycle by the Brescian painter Girolamo Romanino. At the tip of the lake you continue up Val Camònica and, after visiting the Capo di Ponte rock drawings, return along the west shore, stopping in the delightful town of Lóvere.

Tour 14

History and art plus food and wine are the attractions of this tour. Franciacorta, the home of the sparkling queen of Italian Spumante wines, is a succession of vine-covered hills and wine cellars open to visitors – a perfect opportunity to purchase excellent wines. Food is of the same high standard, with traditional dishes (such as beef in oil and stuffed tench), as well as interesting new takes on regional cuisines. The hills are dotted with medieval towers, abbeys, old villages and stately villas. Close to the lake is the Torbiere del Sebino nature reserve, where famously, in spring, thousands of water lilies burst into flower.

Tour 15

Brescia is well known for its industries and financial activities, less so for its fine old monuments and art collections. The beautiful old centre has accumulated centuries of fine art and architecture, dating from Roman times to the Middle Ages and the days of the Lombard and Venetian Renaissance. The Tosio Martinengo Picture Gallery and the Luigi Marzoli Armoury Museum are particularly important features.

Brescia's Tempio Capitolino from Roman *Brixia*

Bergamo

Surrounded by more than 5km (3 miles) of mighty walls, Bergamo Alta, the upper town, is an extraordinary citadel perfectly preserved in its original form, incorporating medieval and Renaissance buildings such as the Palazzo della Ragione, the Colleoni Chapel and the basilica of Santa Maria Maggiore. Of particular note in Bergamo Bassa, the lower town, is the picture gallery of the Accademia Carrara, one of the richest in Italy. Begin on foot in the upper town, then return to the car for a tour of the lower town and the Venetian walls.

i *Piazza Marconi (railway station); Via Gombito 13*

▶ *Drive to the upper town along Viale Vittorio Emanuele II. After passing the Sant'Agostino gate, follow Via della Fara and take Via San Lorenzo, at the end of which is Piazza Mercato del Fieno, where you can park your car. Continue on foot to Piazza Vecchia.*

❶ Piazza Vecchia

Piazza Vecchia is reached along Via Gombito, one of the oldest and most characterful streets in the Città Alta, now lined with shops. The very heart of old Bergamo, Piazza Vecchia was built in the second half of the 15th century following the demolition of the medieval quarter. This popular local meeting place has an 18th-century fountain at its centre, and is blocked at one end by the austere stone mass of Palazzo della Ragione. Built in the mid-12th century and altered over the following 400 years, it has a large ground-floor loggia and a first-floor salon with a

The Palazzo della Ragione as seen from the Piazza Vecchia

three-mullioned window surmounted by the Lion of St Mark, the symbol of Venice. On the right is the high 11th-century Comune tower, known as the Campanone. On the left stands Palazzo Podestà, which was decorated with frescoes in 1477 by Bramante; most of the paintings have since been lost, but three surviving portraits of philosophers are now kept in

Left: detail from the façade of the Colleoni Chapel
Below: the Città Alta

RECOMMENDED WALK

A cable-car climbs from Colle Aperto to scenic Colle San Vigilio. From the cable-car station, continue on foot to the top of the hill and the ruins and castle towers, an ancient stronghold set in a strategic position. The upper square, now a public park, has a fine view of Bergamo and the plain.

Palazzo della Ragione. Occupying the fourth side of the square is Palazzo Nuovo, redesigned in 1611 by Vincenzo Scamozzi, and now housing the Angelo Mai Civic Library, which holds precious old manuscripts.

▷ *Pass beneath the loggia of Palazzo della Ragione to emerge in Piazza Duomo.*

❷ Piazza Duomo

This is one of the loveliest religious squares in northern Italy, surrounded by the impressive lines of the Baptistery, the Colleoni Chapel, the basilica of Santa Maria Maggiore and the Duomo (cathedral). Ringed by wrought-iron railings, the Baptistery is a small 14th-century octagonal construction, which originally stood inside the nearby church of Santa Maria Maggiore, but was moved in the 19th century to stand in front of the gardens of the Vescovado. Built between 1472 and 1476 by Gian Antonio Amadeo, the Colleoni Chapel was commissioned as a mausoleum by *condottiere* (district governor)

SCENIC ROUTES

One of Bergamo's most scenic routes winds over 5km (3 miles) along the ring of walls encircling the Città Alta, interrupted by four monumental gates. The Republic of Venice started to build the walls from 1561 to protect its territory on the border with the State of Milan.

Bartolomeo Colleoni of Bergamo, and is a masterpiece of Lombard Renaissance architecture. Inside are the tombs of the *condottiere* (two sarcophagi, one on top of the other, and a gilded equestrian statue), and of his daughter, Medea. The Duomo, begun in 1459 and finally completed in 1886, is rich in works of art, including a canvas by Giambattista Tiepolo (1743) in the apse and an 18th-century carved choir. The 12th-century basilica of Santa Maria Maggiore is a complex building, adorned with doorways, small balconies, statues and bas-reliefs. On the exterior, among other things, is a porch built in the mid-14th century by Giovanni da Campione; inside are precious 16th- and 17th-century tapestries and a splendid wooden choir, most of whose inlay was designed by Lorenzo Lotto (1522–5).

▷ *Return to Piazza Vecchia and take Via Colleoni to Piazza Mascheroni.*

❸ Piazza Mascheroni

Bergamo's market was once held in this square, then called Piazza

Nuova; note the 16th-century merchants' loggia on the left of the square, now incorporated into the 18th-century Palazzo Roncalli. At the centre stands a mighty 14th-century tower, flanked by Palazzo Benaglio, its façade decorated with 16th-century frescoes.

▷ *Pass below the tower and proceed to Piazzale Colle Aperto, where you turn left along Viale delle Mura.*

The cable-car from Bergamo Bassa to Bergamo Alta

FOR HISTORY BUFFS

The oldest part of Bergamo (Città Alta), which sits on the hill, was successively inhabited by Celts, Goths, Romans and Lombards. In 1428 Bergamo, which had been under the rule of the Visconti family of Milan from 1332, was passed to the Venetian Republic and remained in its possession as an outpost in the centre of the Po plain until 1796. During that period, the two cities were united by a close cultural and financial bond.

The monument erected in honour of Gaetano Donizetti in 1897 in Piazza Cavour

SPECIAL TO...

Venetian painter Lorenzo Lotto (c1480–1556) considered Bergamo his spiritual home, where his art was expressed to the highest degree. Many of his works are still found in churches and museums in Bergamo and its province. In Bergamo they can be admired at the Accademia Carrara Picture Gallery and in the churches of Sant'Alessandro della Croce, San Bernardino, San Spirito, San Bartolomeo, Sant'Alessandro in Colonna and San Michele al Pozzo Bianco.

4 Cittadella

The citadel was built in the late 14th century on the orders of Bernabò Visconti who wanted to defend the west section of the city, but by the 16th century it had been abandoned and converted to civilian use. Today it is the seat of the civic natural science and archaeological museums.

▶ *Return along the same road to Piazza Mercato del Fieno, collect your car and drive along the Via Porta Dipinta, passing mansions and old houses to Piazza Sant'Agostino. From the*

square, follow Via Pignolo and Via San Tommaso to Piazza Carrara.

5 Pinacoteca dell'Accademia Carrara

The Accademia Carrara Picture Gallery is one of the richest and most interesting in Italy. It shows about 1,600 paintings by Italian and other artists, mainly dating from the 15th to 18th centuries, with works by Raphael, Titian, Durer and Brueghel the Elder. Of particular note is the collection of Lombard and Venetian art. Masterpieces include a portrait of Lionello d'Este by Pisanello and one of Giuliano de'Medici by Sandro Botticelli, both 15th-century Tuscan masters. There are works by the greats of Venetian Renaissance painting (a *Madonna and Child* by Giovanni Bellini and one by Andrea Mantegna) and Lombard Renaissance painting, starting with portraits by Giambattista Moroni (c1510–1578) and Fra' Galgario (1655–1743), both from Bergamo, as well as still-life paintings of the Italian, Flemish and Dutch schools. Near the Accademia is the Gallery of Modern Art.

▶ *Follow Via C Battisti, Via San Giovanni and Via Verdi to Piazza della Libertà, where you leave your car. Cross Piazza Dante to come out on the Sentierone.*

6 Il Sentierone

Il Sentierone is the heart of the lower town and has for centuries been the place where the people of Bergamo come to meet and stroll. Created by the city's merchants in the early 17th century, this is where the Sant'Alessandro fair was conducted. It's not so much a square as a wide avenue, lined on one side with porticoes, and ending with the imposing façade of the church of San Bartolomeo, housing a *Madonna with Child and Saints* by Lorenzo Lotto (1516), better known as the Martinengo altarpiece. Continuing along Via Torquato Tasso, you come to the church of San Spirito; its façade was never completed, but it houses major works of art, including an *Enthroned Madonna with Saints and Angels* by Lotto (1521). Near the Sentierone is Piazza Cavour and the Bergamo Donizetti Theatre, founded in 1786 and venue for major music festivals.

Lake Iseo
& Val Camònica

1/2 DAYS • 195KM • 121 MILES Iseo, also known as Sebino, is one of the most fascinating Italian lakes, with the green slopes of Monte Isola reflected in its waters and the imposing ring of mountains sloping down to the south towards the Franciacorta foothills.

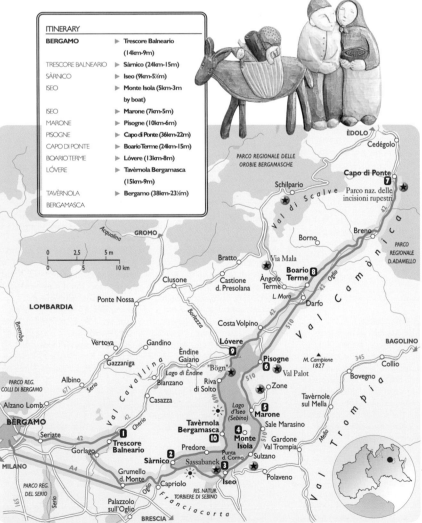

ITINERARY		
BERGAMO	▶	**Trescore Balneario** (14km-9m)
TRESCORE BALNEARIO	▶	Sàrnico (24km-15m)
SÀRNICO	▶	Iseo (9km-5½m)
ISEO	▶	Monte Isola (5km-3m by boat)
ISEO	▶	Marone (7km-5m)
MARONE	▶	Pisogne (10km-6m)
PISOGNE	▶	Capo di Ponte (36km-22m)
CAPO DI PONTE	▶	Boario Terme (24km-15m)
BOARIO TERME	▶	Lóvere (13km-8m)
LÓVERE	▶	Tavèrnola Bergamasca (15km-9m)
TAVÈRNOLA BERGAMASCA	▶	Bergamo (38km-23½m)

i *Piazza Marconi (railway station); Via Gombito 13, Bergamo*

▶ *Leave Bergamo and follow the SS42 to Trescore Balneario.*

1 Trescore Balneario

The most important centre in Val Cavallina, Trescore Balneario has been known since ancient times for its saline-sulphurous springs. Inhabited in the prehistoric era, it became a Roman centre and was fortified during the Middle Ages. The interesting old centre unfolds around Piazza Cavour, lined with 17th- and 18th-century buildings.

Outside town, in the park of Villa Suardi (not open to visitors), is the 15th-century church of Santa Barbara, containing a masterpiece by Lorenzo Lotto (*c*1480–1556). This fresco cycle dates from 1524 and features stories from the life of St Barbara, including rare scenes of peasant life, painted with great attention to detail. Portrayed at the bottom is Battista Suardi, who commissioned the work, with two members of his family.

▶ *A fork in the state road descends towards Gorlago, from where you proceed to Sàrnico.*

2 Sàrnico

Lying on the southwest shore of Lake Iseo, Sàrnico was already inhabited in prehistoric times; the remains of pile-dwellings have been excavated here. In the Middle Ages it developed as a fortified village, and still has the ruins of the castle and walls. The old centre is particularly delightful, with houses featuring porticoes and loggias, narrow streets and small squares; the 15th-century main church is dedicated to San Paolo. Also of interest are buildings designed by the architect Giuseppe Sommaruga, one of the leading representatives of Italian art nouveau style. On the lakeside, just outside town, you can

Fresco of *The Life of St Barbara* by Lotto at Trescore Balneario

admire Villa Faccanoni (1912), among others. This area was once famous for its quarries, where Sàrnico stone was extracted to embellish doorways, columns, fireplaces and public and private buildings all over Lombardy. Today the town has major shipyards and is popular with water skiing and speedboat enthusiasts.

▶ *Skirt the bottom of the lake to Iseo.*

SCENIC ROUTES

A lovely scenic road climbs from Iseo to Polaveno before descending again into Val Trompia. At the highest point there is a splendid view of the lake and Monte Isola. If you're hankering for some exercise, leave the car on the outskirts of the village at Zoadello and take the hour-long walk to the 15th-century church of Santa Maria del Giogo (968m/3,176 feet), which has one of the loveliest views of Sebino.

3 Iseo

This is one of the loveliest and best equipped resorts on the lake, with good hotels, restaurants, sports amenities and beaches. In the well-kept medieval centre, visit the 12th-century parish church of Sant'Andrea, the 11th-century Oldofredi castle (now a cultural centre and exhibition venue), the church of Santa Maria del Mercato (fine 13th- and 14th-century frescoes), the church of San Silvestro and the baptistery of San Giovanni. Along the lakeside and around the harbour are bars and ice-cream parlours. The small central squares are ideal for strolls and shopping. A few minutes from the town centre is Sassabanek; spread over 12 hectares (30 acres), this is one of the largest tourist, leisure and sports centres in the entire Lombard lake area. It's equipped with three swimming pools, two harbours, a bar, a restaurant, gymnasiums, a sauna, and tennis and volleyball courts,

Above: Lake Iseo
Left: the Zone pyramids
Right: traditional cotton-spinning
in Monte Isola

as well as parking for 500 cars, a beach, a large picnic area and an amusement park.

[i] *Lungolago Marconi 2/c*

▶ *Leave your car and take the ferry to Monte Isola.*

4 Monte Isola

At this point a detour must be made to Monte Isola, the largest lake-island in Europe, rising distinctively at the centre of the lake with its green woods and 599m (1,965-foot) peak. Cars are not permitted, making it an ideal spot for walking, sunbathing and swimming. It can be reached from Iseo on a half-hour boat trip (ferries also sail from Sulzano – at 15 minutes the fastest crossing – Sale Marasino, Sàrnico and Lóvere). All its little villages deserve a visit, and the appetising fish dishes and local *salame* served in the trattorias are well worth sampling. Particularly interesting villages are Peschiera Maraglio (where fishing nets are

still woven, once the principal occupation of the local women) and Carzano, with its arched houses on the waterfront. Fishermen dry sardines – the main ingredient in the island's cuisine – along the shores. Monte Isola has two peaks, which command spectacularly scenic views of the lake. On the highest is the Sanctuary of the Madonna della Ceriola and on the other the Renaissance Rocca Oldofredi Martinengo (not open to visitors).

▶ *Return to Iseo by boat and then skirt the Brescian shore of the lake on the SS510.*

5 Marone

Marone marks the beginning of the most rugged and rockiest stretch of the Brescian lakeshore, battered by winds and therefore particularly popular with surfers. From here on, the small pebble beaches give way to rocks that descend sheer into the lake waters. An excellent scenic spot from which to enjoy the spectacle is the church of San Pietro, built on a spur above the hamlet of Vesto. Numerous paths climb more than 1,000m (3,280 feet) from Marone to Monte Guglielmo and the Croce di Marone. In the

TOUR 13

Lake Iseo & Val Camònica

SPECIAL TO...

The church of Santa Maria della Neve at Pisogne houses an important fresco cycle by Girolamo Romanino (1484–c1559) who, along with Vincenzo Foppa, Gerolamo Savoldo and Alessandro Bonvicino ('il Moretto'), was one of the leading representatives of the Renaissance Brescian school. Painted around 1533, the frescoes cover the church walls and ceiling with stories from the Passion of Christ, portrayed in a popular style; the Prophets and Sibyls are depicted on the vaults. The counter-façade bears a large Crucifixion. The church is not always open – for times check at the town hall.

village, visit the beautiful ruins of a Roman villa dating from the 1st century AD.

▶ *Continue along the lake to Pisogne.*

6 Pisogne

Pisogne is the last village on the lake before Val Camònica. The heart of the community – enlivened from spring to autumn by concerts, spectacles, festivals and a multitude of gastronomic events – is the central and elegant Piazza Corna Pellegrini, flanked by porticoes, old mansions, shops and bars. Pisogne's ancient origins are evident in the layout of its old centre and monuments such as the 7th-century parish church of Santa Maria in Silvis, the medieval Vescovo tower and the 15th-century church of Santa Maria della Neve. Nature-lovers can enjoy a lovely excursion from here to Val Palot, with splendid views of the lake.

i *Via Lungolago Tempini 5*

▶ *Continue towards Val Camònica on the SS510. Just before Darfo take the SS42 right for Capo di Ponte.*

7 Capo di Ponte

Capo di Ponte is the home of the Naquane National Park, the largest and most important park in Europe devoted to rock drawings. A hundred or so rocks scattered among meadows and woods across an area of 30 hectares (74 acres) are adorned with around 30,000 drawings; particularly striking is the 'large rock' decorated with more than 1,000 figures drawn between the end of the Neolithic Age (4000 BC) and the Iron Age (after 1000 BC). The park is protected by UNESCO as a world heritage site, but these are not the only drawings found in the area. Two large decorated boulders in the hamlet of Cemmo were the first to prompt research into Camun art, in the early 20th century. One has the oldest representation of a cart ever discovered. It's worth paying a visit to the nearby Romanesque parish

church of San Siro. Along with San Salvatore, the other Cluniac church at Capo di Ponte, which stands in isolation north of the village, this is one of the most interesting early medieval buildings in northern Italy.

▶ *Descend the valley following the provincial road to Boario Terme.*

i *Via Briscioli 42*

8 Boario Terme

This famous spa's waters are renowned principally for the treatment of liver ailments. Exploited systematically since the early 1900s, they now flow from four springs in a modern spa establishment, one of Italy's biggest, that forms the main

Above: Capo di Ponte, the 'roccia grande' (great rock)
Left: detail of a horseman with axe

focus of a large leisure park. This oasis is equipped for sports and activities – the ideal place to get into shape. With about 40 hotels and a modern conference centre, Boario Terme is an excellent point of departure for visits to Val Camònica (access also to the Adamello Nature Park).

Just outside the village, visit the Luine and Lake Moro Rock Drawing Park. Excursions in the immediate vicinity include travelling along Via Mala, a lovely road hewn into the rock and flanked by spectacular gorges. After passing Gorzone, with its medieval Federici castle and small family-run spa of Angolo Terme, another half-hour or so brings you to Val di Scalve, one of the loveliest and wildest valleys in the Bergamo mountain area.

i *Piazza Einaudi 2*

▶ Follow the **SS42** to Lóvere.

The Fonti di Boario Terme park

SPECIAL TO...

The 19th-century Palazzo Tadini, overlooking the lakeside at Lóvere, is the setting for the gallery of the Academy of Fine Arts, founded in 1828 by Luigi Tadini, a benefactor from Crema. It exhibits an important collection of paintings by Venetian and Lombard artists of the 14th to 20th centuries, including a *Madonna and Child* by Jacopo Bellini (c1400–70), one by Lorenzo Veneziano (second half of the 14th century), a portrait of a gentleman by Parmigianino (1503–40) and works by the Venetians Palma the Younger, Paris Bordon and Giambattista Tiepolo. A second section contains archaeological finds, porcelains, bronzes, armour and a collection of minerals.

⑨ Lóvere

Lóvere is the most important town on the Bergamo lakeshore, the terminus of the boat service that links the lake's main centres. With hotels, camping sites, holiday apartments, small beaches and sports amenities, it's ideal for lovers of sailing, wind-surfing and speedboating. Its strategic position, at the tip of

The Iseo lakeside at Tavèrnola Bergamasca

Lake Iseo and at the mouth of Val Camònica, led to its fortification in the Middle Ages. The town grew in importance between the 15th and 16th centuries, when the Republic of Venice made it the capital of a *quadra* (administrative district) and encouraged the development of industry. Lóvere's history is visible in the well-restored town centre, with its medieval nucleus centred around Piazza Vittorio Emanuele. Here you'll find the civic tower, rebuilt in the 19th century on the remains of 14th-century Celeri castle; the church of San Giorgio, built in the 14th century but enlarged several times; and the 13th-century Alghisi and Soca towers. All around is the Renaissance district, with streets laid at right angles along the axis of Via Santa Maria. The basilica of Santa Maria in Valvendra was built between 1473 and 1483; the interior (now in baroque style) houses fine frescoes by Floriano Ferramola (1513), a 16th-century organ and, on the main altar, a large *Annunciation* carved and gilded by Pietro Marone (late 16th century).

☐ *Piazza 13 Martiri 34*

▶ *Skirt the lake along the SS469 to Tavèrnola Bergamasca.*

⑩ Tavèrnola Bergamasca

Surrounded by limestone quarries and processing plants, this village was partially destroyed in 1906 when a section slid into the lake. Still standing in the ancient centre are the tower of the 14th-century Fenaroli castle, now used as the parish bell tower and – high up and close to the cemetery – the church of San Pietro, built between the 13th and 15th centuries. Inside are precious 16th-century frescoes, including an *Enthroned Madonna* by Romanino (c1484–c1559). After leaving the village, it's worth stopping a little further on at Punta del Corno, where water erosion has created a glacial well known as the 'Giant's Pot'.

▶ *Follow the lakeshore to Sàrnico and then the same road to Grumello. Return to Bergamo on the A4.*

SCENIC ROUTES

The SS469 Sebina Occidentale road, particularly along the stretch between Lóvere and Tavèrnola Bergamasca, offers delightfully scenic views of high cliffs descending sheer into the water. The most beautiful spot is the Zorzino Bögn, the wildest and most solitary bay on the lake, edged by white calcareous rocks.

From Sebino
to Franciacorta

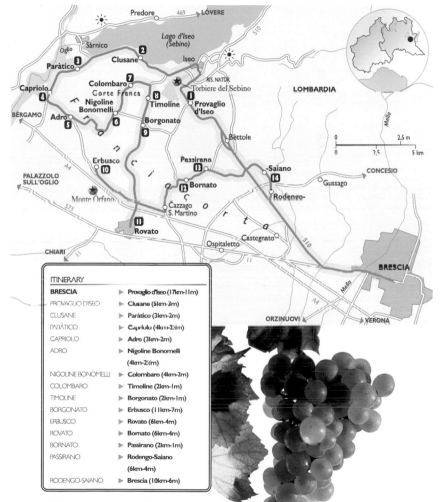

ITINERARY

Hills covered with vineyards, medieval towers, abbeys, old villages, elegant villas and splendid wine cellars can be found along this tour. Vines have been cultivated in Franciacorta since Roman days. The heirs of this ancient tradition produce wines of the highest quality, the most outstanding being Spumante. **1 DAY • 85KM • 53 MILES**

▶ *Leave Brescia on the SS510 and take the provincial road to Provaglio d'Iseo.*

1 Provaglio d'Iseo

This small village between Franciacorta and Lake Iseo has two highlights to explore – the monastery of San Pietro in Lamosa and the Torbiere del Sebino (see Back to Nature). The history not only of Provaglio but of all Franciacorta is bound to this monastery. Founded in the 11th century by French monks from the abbey of Cluny, it soon became the hub of social, economic and agricultural life in the area, which had been all but abandoned after the division of the Roman Empire (AD 395). The monastery is a Romanesque complex of several buildings – one of the most interesting in the province of Brescia. The oldest part is the church of San Pietro, beside which a chapel

The landscape of the Torbiere del Sebino, a precious natural habitat

was constructed in the baroque era. The parvis offers an exceptional view of the peat bogs below.

▶ *Continue towards Iseo and here turn left towards Sàrnico for Clusane.*

2 Clusane

Gourmets are well acquainted with this fishing village on the south shore of Lake Iseo. Its restaurants prepare one of the lake's most appetising dishes – baked tench stuffed with polenta. Every year in mid-July the dish is celebrated with 'Tench Week', a popular gastronomic event. Dominated by the imposing 15th-century Carmagnola castle, the village is centred round the harbour where the *naècc*, the traditional boats used by the local fishermen, are moored. With its beaches and camping sites, this

is an ideal spot for relaxing open-air holidays.

BACK TO NATURE

The Torbiere del Sebino peat bogs, bordering Lake Iseo to the south, form an oasis of a kind found nowhere else in Europe. The bogs, pools of water and marsh vegetation extend over about 360 hectares (889 acres). Late spring is the best time to visit, when thousands of water lilies are in bloom. This unusual habitat developed gradually from the late 18th century, when the basins where the peat was extracted for fuel started to fill with water, forming the marshland of today and providing an ideal habitat for numerous bird species. To visit the peat bogs, follow the route (with birdwatching posts) beneath the monastery of San Pietro in Lamosa, where you can leave the car.

▶ *Leave the lakeshore and follow the signs for Paràtico, towards Franciacorta.*

3 Paràtico

Paràtico lies at the westernmost tip of Franciacorta, where the hills slope down towards Lake Iseo. Probably founded by the Lombards, it is dominated by the ruins of the 13th-century castle of Lantieri, where, tradition has it, the poet Dante Alighieri (1265–1321) stayed. The scenery is said to have inspired one of the cantos of his *Purgatory*. Visit the 15th-century parish church and the 18th-century church of San Pietro, in the square of the same name.

▶ *Continue along the same road to Capriolo.*

4 Capriolo

As you arrive at Capriolo you enter the heart of wine-producing Franciacorta. This medieval

---

village perched on its hill is well known for its wine cellars. The Ricci Curbastro Agricultural and Wine Museum displays thousands of objects tracing the story of peasant life in these parts.

▶ *Leave the village and turn left for Adro.*

5 Adro

So old is the tradition of wine-producing at Adro that even the municipal coat-of-arms includes bunches of grapes. The village lies on the lower slopes of Monte Alto (at 651m/2,136 feet the highest peak in Franciacorta) and is dominated by a Ghibelline stone watchtower, the best known of all the towers built in the Middle Ages to defend the region. Also on the hill is the 16th-century church of Santa Maria Assunta, decorated with a fine fresco cycle by the school of the Brescian painter Ferramola. In the compact little centre, visit the parish church of San Giovanni Battista and Palazzo Bargnani, seat of the town hall.

▶ *Return towards the lake, following the signs for Nigoline Bonomelli.*

6 Nigoline Bonomelli

The journey from Adro to Nigoline is just a few kilometres, passing rows of vines and cultivated fields. Before its end, a detour leads to the 18th-century sanctuary of the Madonna della Neve, which displays several ex-votos. Nigoline, with the nearby

---

villages of Colombaro, Timoline and Borgonato, forms the *comune* of Corte Franca, the heart of wine-producing Franciacorta. This is the home of many of the most prestigious wine-makers in the area, who encourage you to buy wines and visit the cellars. Many old country villas, once the homes of aristocratic Brescian families, are found in this area, some now housing prestigious wine-cellars (and therefore partially open to visitors); others are private, but their spectacular façades can be admired from the road. The most important building in town is Palazzo Monti della Corte,

A classic Franciacorta view

constructed from the 15th century on, which faces the 17th-century parish church. Of note is the church of Santa Eufemia, founded in the 10th century and extended in the 15th, when the frescoes in the apse, attributed to Floriano Ferramola, were created. Castagnola is the home of the 18-hole Franciacorta Golf Club.

▶ *Continue along the same road to Colombaro.*

7 Colombaro

With its old houses and vineyards set within drystone and pebble walls, Colombaro is a medieval town which developed around the monastery of Santa Maria and was later fortified with a castle. There are impressive stately homes here, in particular Palazzo

tallest Cedar of Lebanon in Italy, over 300 years old.

▶ *Turn left for Timoline.*

8 Timoline

Timoline was founded in an area reclaimed by the monks of the nearby monastery of Provaglio. Visit the 15th-century parish church of SS Cosma e Damiano, with its fine frescoes, and the church of Santa Giulia, traditionally considered the early nucleus of the village. Facing the church is one of the loveliest villas in Franciacorta, Villa Pizzini, built between the 17th and 18th centuries with a large park and a spectacular grotto.

10 Erbusco

One of Franciacorta's leading wine-production zones, Erbusco was, as early as the 15th century, a favourite holiday destination of the Brescian nobility. Here stands the villa that has practically become the symbol of Franciacorta, Villa Lechi. Constructed between the 16th and 17th centuries, its distinctive silhouette and large loggias dominate the rows of vines. In the attractive old village, the parish church of Santa Maria Assunta is one of the finest examples of Lombard Romanesque style in the Brescia area and is beautifully decorated with fine 15th-century frescoes.

Barboglio de Gaioncelli (which incorporates the tower of the old castle) and Villa Conti Lana, in whose park you can admire the

The entrance and façade of Villa Lechi at Erbusco

▶ *Return towards inland Franciacorta, following the signs for Borgonato.*

9 Borgonato

A tiny village surrounded by vineyards and home to prestigious wine cellars, Borgonato lies on a low hill with the old church of San Salvatore (long deconsecrated) and the nearby ruins of a castle.

▶ *Continue towards Rovato and turn right for Erbusco.*

▶ *Return along the same road and turn right at the crossroads for Rovato.*

11 Rovato

This is Franciacorta's 'city', an important farming and commercial centre, famous for its old cattle market held on Mondays, and for its trattorias, which serve boiled meats and beef in oil.

On the main square, edged with porticoes designed by architect Vantini around 1840, stand the Palazzo Comunale, the Palazzo Porcellaga and the Venetian walls with their imposing bastions.

RECOMMENDED WALK

From Rovato you can climb quickly to Monte Orfano and the 15th-century Convent of the Annunziata, one of the loveliest in Lombardy and a haven of peace. Inside are several artistic masterpieces, including an *Annunciation* by the 16th-century Brescian painter Girolamo Romanino; outside, there are splendid views of the countryside.

Right: inside Rodengo Abbey
Below: the crenellated walls of Passirano Castle

▶ Back at the crossroads, turn right for Cazzago San Martino and from here proceed to Bornato.

12 Bornato

Here's another village known for first-class viticulture and historic buildings. These include Villa Monte Rossa, on the hill of the same name, reached via a spectacular flight of steps designed by Antonio Marchetti (the 18th-century architect also responsible for the Brescia cathedral); and the castle, with a 16th-century villa built within its medieval walls.

▶ A small road leads past fields to Passirano.

13 Passirano

South of the village stands Passirano Castle, the most striking castle in Franciacorta, built in the 10th century. With its round and square towers and high pebble walls, surmounted by crenellated Ghibelline additions, it is more a fortified enclosure than a castle. Inside are a large courtyard and the modern cellars of a wine-producing firm.

▶ Leave the village and continue to Rodengo.

14 Rodengo-Saiano

The Benedictine abbey of San Nicolá is one of the most impressive monastic complexes in northern Italy. Founded in the 10th century by Cluniac monks and passed in the mid-15th century to the Olivetans, the abbey is distributed around three large cloisters and the church. It is embellished with works by artists of the Brescian school of the 16th and 17th centuries (Foppa, Romanino, Moretto, Gambara and Cossali).

▶ Return to Brescia on the SS510.

FOOD & WINE OF THE LAKES

An itinerary exploring the pre-Alpine lakes will inevitably turn into a gastronomic tour. From Lake Maggiore to Lake Garda you will encounter a variety of dishes based on the various regional cuisines of northern Italy, each one quite different from the other, but all equally inviting. They range from the Piedmontese and Lombard recipes of Verbano to those of Mantua, Veneto and Garda Trentino. Unfailingly these will be combined with a remarkable variety of wines, directly produced in the region of some of the lakes.

Villa cuisine

More than any other, the cuisine of Verbano is influenced by the international tastes brought to its tables by the noble families that, in centuries past, built their villas here – as well as by the foreign travellers produce such as olive oil, vegetables (particularly the asparagus of Rogaro and Drezzo) and, naturally, fish from the lake. These include the tasty *missultit*, dried and salted in the sun, soused fish (fried and marinated in water and

Red endive risotto – an icon of the Veneto's cuisine

who, in the 18th and 19th centuries, elected it as a favourite destination on the Grand Tour. Stresa's pastries, for instance, rich in butter and dusted with icing sugar, are still called *Margheritine* in honour of Queen Margherita of Savoy, whose pastry-makers created them for the royal household's Feast of the Assumption receptions in August.

Dining in Como

Risotto with fish fillets is the highlight of Como's cuisine, which is simple, popular and based on wholesome local

vinegar), smoked trout in oil and Tremezzina fish soup. Among typical dishes are stuffed chicken, usually made for Whit Sunday, and a dessert called *resta* made in Como, with dried fruit, candied peel and a small olive twig inside as a sign of peace.

From tench to wine

Stuffed tench, superbly baked according to an old Clusane recipe, is the most notable dish of the Lake Iseo area, closely followed by char, whitefish, perch and eels. The excellent 'sardines' of Monte Isola are actually *aole* (*Alburnus alburnis alborella*) and other lake fish dried in the sun, preserved in oil and then barbecued. The most traditional Lake Iseo starters are grilled sardines, soused *aole*, perch risotto, pike terrine and salads or soups made with fish from the lake. Fish is often accompanied by polenta, well cooked and sometimes sliced and toasted on the grill. All is combined with fine wines from nearby Franciacorta – red and white Terre di

Great wines carefully conserved in the Franciacorta cellars

Different faces of lake gastronomy – fish laid out to dry at Monte Isola (above) and Taleggio cheese from Valsàssina

Franciacorta and Franciacorta Spumante, a stylish all-round wine (also good as aperitifs).

Discoveries on Lake Garda's shores

Fish, oil, citrus fruits and wine are the ingredients of Lake Garda's cuisine. Local produce is used in a variety of ways in the traditional recipes of Brescia, Trentino, Verona and Mantua, accompanied by seasonal vegetables, preserved meat and cheese. These apparently humble ingredients are rich in flavours, light and wholesome.

The undisputed king of the table is the lake fish, and especially the rare Lake Garda carp,

whitefish (lavaret), lake trout, eel, pike, tench, carp and perch. First courses comprise potato, spinach or pumpkin gnocchi and a thousand different ravioli and soups; second courses are generally mixed grills or game and mushrooms, accompanied by the ever-present polenta. Garda's extra virgin olive oil, with its strong flavour, excellent nutritional properties and low acidity, is one of the finest in Italy.

Equally famous are the DOC wines, from Chiaretto to Bardolino, Lugana and the aromatic wines of the Trentino area, produced from vines that surround the lakeshores. The most valued wine-producing

areas are Valtènesi (in the province of Brescia) and the Bardolino area. Oil and wine can be purchased directly from the producers, who open their presses and cellars to visitors.

Other typical Garda products are truffles and lemons on the Brescian shore, chestnuts and salted meat on the Trentino shore, and white asparagus on the Verona shore, where you can also try exquisite meat tortellini in the Valeggio area. Everywhere you will find a great variety of tasty cheeses. The ancient recipes of Mantua make up the most refined regional cuisine; Garda is a veritable gourmets' paradise. Its roots lie in the culinary arts of the Court of Gonzaga, to which Austrian and Venetian recipes have been added over the centuries. The most typical dishes are pumpkin tortelli, rice *alla pilota*, tagliatelle with game sauce, pike in sauce, other river and lake fish such as trout and tench, and game. To round off your meal, sample the popular local almond cake, *brisolona*.

Brescia

Just half an hour's drive from Lake Iseo, and an equal distance from Lake Garda, Brescia offers museums, exhibitions, entertainment, shopping and good food. But, although it is well known for its industrial and financial sectors, it remains to some extent undiscovered as a tourist destination. The Roman Capitoline Temple, the early medieval convent of Santa Giulia and its hidden treasures, the Venetian Loggia, the castle … a long history is there for all to see in the buildings of Brescia's lovely old centre.

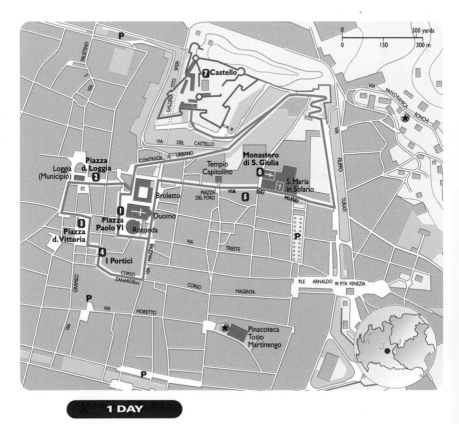

1 DAY

i **Via Musei 32**

▶ *This walking tour starts from
Piazza Duomo.*

❶ Piazza Paolo VI (del Duomo)

The heart of Brescia lies in its
three large squares – Piazza
Duomo, Piazza della Loggia and
Piazza Vittoria. These have
always been the centre of political and religious power, around
which the life of the city flourished. You can reach them using
the shuttle-bus that runs
between the outlying car parks
and the old centre (the price of
the ticket is included in the
parking fee) or on foot, leaving
the car at a parking meter or
multi-storey car park (there are
convenient ones in Via Vittorio
Emanuele II and Piazza
Vittoria).

Much of the centre of
Brescia is pedestrianised. Lined
up, one after the other, in Piazza
Duomo (now named after Paul
VI, the Pope from Brescia), are
the Duomo Vecchio (old cathedral) or Rotonda, a splendid
example of a circular-plan
Romanesque construction, built
in the late 11th century; the
Duomo Nuovo (new cathedral),
with its imposing 18th-century
façade in white Botticino
marble; and the Broletto, seat of
the *comune* in the Middle Ages
and one of the major examples

of secular Lombard architecture
from that period.

▶ *Walk along Vicolo Beccaria.*

❷ Piazza della Loggia

Piazza della Loggia is one of the
most beautiful 'Venetian
squares' on dry land, created in
the first half of the 15th century
by the Venetian Podestà Marco
Foscari. Another 100 years saw
the construction of the Loggia

FOR HISTORY BUFFS

The name Brescia comes from
Brixia, the Celtic root of which,
brig, indicates an elevated
place. In fact the first nucleus
of the city appeared on the
Cidneo hill, where a tribe,
probably the *Liguri*, settled in
about 1200 BC.
During the 4th century BC the
Cenomani from Gallia made the
town their capital. In 89 BC
Brixia became a Latin colony
and in the 1st century AD it
was one of the main towns in
the Cisalpine province. From
568 to 773 it was the seat of
one of Italy's 36 Lombard
duchies. It became a free
comune in the 12th and 13th
centuries, but in 1426 joined
the Venetian Republic, in whose
possession it remained (save
for a few brief intervals) for
four centuries.

Brescia's Loggia; Sansovino and
Palladio contributed to its design

(the symbol of the city and now
the city hall, built between
1492 and 1570 by the leading
architects of the time, from
Sansovino to Palladio), the
Monte Vecchio and Monte
Nuovo di Pietà, and the porticoes with their clock tower. Two
figures have beaten the hours
on the clock's bell since 1581;
they're affectionately known to
Brescians as the *macc de le ure*, or
'time maniacs'.

▶ *Follow Corsetto Sant'Agata.*

❸ Piazza della Vittoria

With its monumental geometry,
Piazza della Vittoria represents
one of the most coherent
projects by Marcello Piacentini
(1881–1960), the leading official
exponent of architecture and
town planning of the Fascist
regime. It was built between
1926 and 1932 on the site of the
city's medieval quarter. Blocking
it at one end is the Palazzo delle
Poste, faced with travertine
stone, and at its side a 60m
(197-foot) tower. Opposite is
the Quadriportico and the
Rivoluzione tower. An antiques
fair is held in the porticoes every
second Sunday of the month.

▶ *At the end of Piazza Vittorio
turn right for Via X Giornate.*

4 I Portici

Around these three squares
wind streets full of shops, cafés
and art galleries. The best place
to shop is the so-called Portici
area, built in the 18th century in
what used to be Via Spaderie
and is now Via X Giornate. Its
imposing buildings house pastry
shops, boutiques, jewellers'
shops and bookshops. The
section on Corso Zanardelli also
frames the entrance to the
Teatro Grande (theatre).

▶ At the end of Corso
Zanardelli turn left into Via
Mazzini, walk past Piazza
Paolo VI, then turn right into
Via dei Musei.

> SPECIAL TO...
>
> The Tosio Martinengo Picture
> Gallery contains one of the
> most important Italian
> collections of old paintings.
> Works exhibited here date
> from the 13th to the 18th
> century, with the main
> collection concentrating on the
> great masters of the
> Renaissance Brescian school
> (Foppa, Ferramola, Romanino,
> Moretto and Savoldo).
> Masterpieces by other great
> names in Italian art include
> works by Raphael, Paolo
> Veneziano and Lorenzo Lotto.

Above: Piazza del Vescovado
Left: the oratory of Santa Maria in
Solario at Santa Giulia

just behind it, the theatre and
private dwellings. Also in Piazza
del Foro is Palazzo Martinengo,
the home of 'Brescia Mostre
Grandi Eventi', which organises
a calendar of excellent exhibitions all year round.

6 Monastero di Santa Giulia

Modern Brescia grew gradually
on the foundations of Roman
Brixia. Continue along Via dei
Musei and, beyond Piazza del
Foro, you will come to the
convent of Santa Giulia, one
of the most imposing early
medieval Lombard complexes.

5 Via dei Musei

The area between Via dei Musei
and Piazza del Foro – the centre
of city life in Roman times –
contains one of the most interesting archaeological sites in
northern Italy. Roman *Brixia*
was uncovered during a number
of excavations started in the
19th century. Around the square
are the remains of the Forum,
the Tempio Capitolino
(Capitoline Temple; closed for
restoration), the Basilica and,

> SPECIAL TO...
>
> The Luigi Marzoli Armoury
> Museum is one of the most
> important in Europe. It exhibits
> more than 500 arms and
> weapons made between the
> late 14th and 18th centuries,
> including a precious collection
> of rare firearms, some of them
> masterpieces of technology.
> Many were made in Brescia
> and illustrate the development
> of the successful local arms
> industry, which still has its main
> centre at Gardone Valtrompia.

in Solario (with 16th-century frescoes by Floriano Ferramola) houses the treasure of San Giulia. Of particular note is the Cross of Desiderius, a precious piece of 9th-century goldwork. From the late 15th century onwards, additions were made to the complex; today, features of interest include the three cloisters and the choir of the nuns of the church of Santa Giulia, decorated with frescoes by Floriano Ferramola and Paolo da Caylina. The complex of San Giulia is the setting for the city museum, which exhibits more than 11,000 pieces ranging from prehistoric times to the 19th century.

1343, erected a mighty keep surrounded by crenellated walls and protected by a deep moat. Around this nucleus (still the heart of the citadel) the Venetians built the ramparts

Mountain biking just a stone's throw from the city

It was founded by King Desiderius, whose daughter Desiderata took refuge here after being jilted by Charlemagne. Until its dissolution in 1798 it was run by Benedictine nuns. The convent is a maze of courtyards, buildings and churches constructed in successive phases. The church of San Salvatore dates from the early Middle Ages; the 13th-century oratory of Santa Maria

▶ *At the end of Via dei Musei climb the steps to Via Brigida Avogadro and the Castello.*

7 Castello

Surrounded by splendid gardens, at the top of the Cidneo hill, the castle is actually a citadel fortified with towers, ramparts and drawbridges constructed between the 13th and 16th centuries. The Mirabella tower dates from the 11th century, but took on its present appearance thanks to the Visconti family, who, in

between the 15th and 16th centuries, along with stores for provisions and the monumental entrance crowned with the Lion of St Mark. The castle now houses the Luigi Marzoli Armoury Museum, Museum of the Risorgimento, the Specola Cidnea (astronomical observatory) and large model railways.

▶ *Descend to the city along Contrada San Urbano, which leads to Piazzetta Tito Speri; from here Vicolo Sant'Agata goes back to Piazza Paolo VI.*

LAKE GARDA

Visiting Juliet's alleged home in Verona, a great local tourist attraction

With a surface area of 368sq km (142 square miles), Garda (the ancient Roman *Bernacus*) is the largest Italian lake, and has always attracted more tourists – from Italy and abroad – than any other. Lying among the mountains in a long valley, which widens towards the plain, it is 52km (32 miles) long and only 2.4km (1½ miles) across at its widest point. Five small islands rise from its waters: Garda, San Biagio, Olivo, Sogno and Trimeleone. The Sarca river, at Tórbole, is the Garda's principal tributary, and the waters find their outlet in the Mincio, which flows to the south at Peschiera. The lake's shores lie in three regions – Lombardy, Trentino-Alto Adige and the Veneto – and four provinces – Brescia, Trento, Verona and Mantua.

Transparent, clean and moderately warm water, sunny beaches, a mild climate, a Mediterranean landscape of vines, olive trees, citrus groves, palm trees and oleanders, fine oil and wine, modern sports and leisure facilities – all help make Lake Garda a marine haven between the last spurs of the Alps and the Po Plain. Dramatic rocks and crags are reflected in its water: Garda is dominated to the east by the Monte Baldo ridge; to the west by the pre-alpine peaks of Tremalzo, Carone and Pizzoccolo; and to the north, its shores are touched by the Trentino Mountains, with the Brenta Dolomites in the background. To the south, the harsh mountains slope down to a gentler amphitheatre of morainic hills and the shallow shoreline has created some excellent beaches.

Poets and writers from Catullus to James Joyce, Goethe and Gabriele d'Annunzio have all sung the lake's praises, extolling the charm of the varied scenery, or of its many fine historical attractions. These include the prehistoric settlements of Valtènesi and the Ledro Valley, the imposing remains of Sirmione and Desenzano, medieval hilltop castles and harbour defences, Romanesque country parish churches, 18th- and 19th-century villas and gardens and elegant art nouveau health resorts. All tell a fascinating story and add to Lake Garda's special appeal.

Tour 16
From the Sirmione peninsula you follow the southwest lakeshore, passing some of Garda's most interesting historic locations, such as the archaeological site of the Grotte di Catullo in Sirmione and Il Vittoriale at Gardone Riviera, home of Gabriele d'Annunzio. Lying on the gentle coastal landscape are famous holiday resorts such as Desenzano, Salò and Toscolano Maderno; inland are unspoiled areas such as the Alto Garda Bresciano park, as well as vineyards and olive groves producing excellent DOC wines and extra virgin olive oil.

Tour 17
Starting from the elegant Riva del Garda, the route explores the northern lakeshore and the high Tignale and Tremòsine plateaux, with their sweeping views of Gargnano, Campione and Limone – sailing and windsurfing hotspots, popular for their constant high winds. The tour then ventures as far as Lake Ledro, known for its prehistoric pile-dwellings, and Lake Idro, on the border between Lombardy and Trentino.

Tour 18
This tour remains in Trentino, visiting the characteristic medieval villages behind Riva del Garda and skirting romantic Lake Toblino to arrive in Trento, austere and beautiful within its ring of mountains.

The return journey visits lakes Lèvico and Caldonazzo, and Tórbole, well known to windsurfers. Along the way you will pass cellars where you can buy excellent wines, and restaurants and trattorias serving typical examples of Trentino cuisine.

Tour 19
Lying between two bends in the Adige River, beautiful Verona is full of extraordinary monuments: the Arena, stage of world opera; the Roman theatre; the basilica of San Zeno, a Romanesque masterpiece; and the Della Scala's Castelvecchio. Enjoy a walk along the riverside, and wander through the old centre's streets and the city's squares.

Above: a view of the observatory on Monte Baldo
Below: Torri del Benaco, halfway up the lake

Tour 20
Behind the Veronese coast, from Peschiera to Bardolino, Lake Garda becomes a gigantic amusement park. Some of Italy's best-known theme parks are found here, starting with Gardaland, the Italian version of Disneyland. The tour also visits towns peppered with ancient ruins, such as Peschiera and Lazise, and Bardolino, famous for its wines and oil.

Tour 21
Winding through the amphitheatre of gentle hills south of Garda, this tour centres on Mantua, one of Italy's richest cities of Renaissance art. Nature-lovers can expect a treat at the Mincio Nature Park and the Sigurtà garden park at Valeggio, and there's a reminder of more turbulent times at the great battlefields of the Risorgimento.

Tour 22
Olives, vines, oleanders and palms cover the land between lakeside and steep mountains on the Riviera degli Olivi, the eastern shore of Garda, where beaches alternate with harbours, traditional villages and old strongholds. From Garda (via the enchanting Punta San Vigilio), you follow the coast to Malcésine and Tórbole, before returning via Monte Baldo, the 'garden of Europe', and its remarkable botanical collection.

The Southern
Brescian Shore

From the rolling scenery extolled by Catullus to elegant Gardone Riviera, the Brescian shore of Lake Garda is a succession of towns teeming with history, art and life. On the shores are beaches and charming little harbours; inland are wine cellars and olive presses.

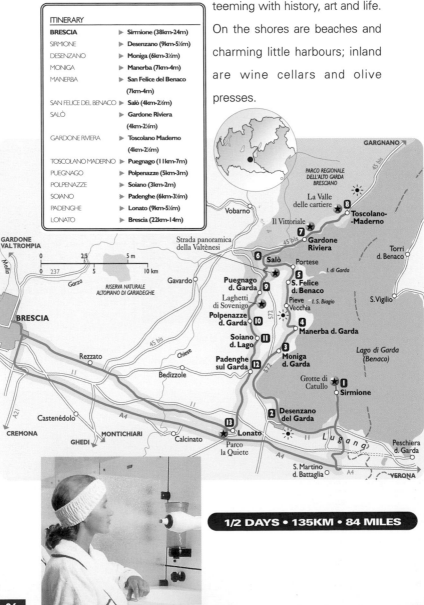

ITINERARY		
BRESCIA	▶	**Sirmione (38km-24m)**
SIRMIONE	▶	**Desenzano (9km-5½m)**
DESENZANO	▶	**Moniga (6km-3½m)**
MONIGA	▶	**Manerba (7km-4m)**
MANERBA	▶	**San Felice del Benaco (7km-4m)**
SAN FELICE DEL BENACO	▶	**Salò (4km-2½m)**
SALÒ	▶	**Gardone Riviera (4km-2½m)**
GARDONE RIVIERA	▶	**Toscolano Maderno (4km-2½m)**
TOSCOLANO MADERNO	▶	**Puegnago (11km-7m)**
PUEGNAGO	▶	**Polpenazze (5km-3m)**
POLPENAZZE	▶	**Soiano (3km-2m)**
SOIANO	▶	**Padenghe (6km-3½m)**
PADENGHE	▶	**Lonato (9km-5½m)**
LONATO	▶	**Brescia (22km-14m)**

GARGNANO

PARCO REGIONALE
DELL'ALTO GARDA
BRESCIANO

La Valle
delle cartiere **8**
Toscolano-
-Maderno

Vobarno

Il Vittoriale

GARDONE
VAL TROMPIA

Strada panoramica
della Valtènesi

7 Gardone
Riviera

Torri
d. Benaco

0   2.5   5 m
0 237   5   10 km

Gavardo

RISERVA NATURALE
ALTOPIANO DI GARIADEGHE

6 Salò

Portese

I. di Garda

Puegnago
d. Garda **9**

S. Felice
d. Benaco

S.Vigilio

Laghetti
di Sovenigo

Pieve — I. S. Biagio
Vecchia I. S. Biagio

BRESCIA

Polpenazze
d. Garda **10**

4 Manerba d. Garda

Rezzato

Chiese

Soiano
d. Lago **11**

Padenghe
sul Garda **12**

3 Moniga
d. Garda

Lago di Garda
(Benaco)

Bedizzole

Grotte di
Catullo **1**
Sirmione

Castenédolo

A4

2 Desenzano
del Garda

CREMONA

MONTICHIARI

13 Lonato

Lugang

Peschiera
d. Garda

GHEDI

Calcinato

Parco
la Quiete

A4

S. Martino
d. Battaglia

VERONA

1/2 DAYS • 135KM • 84 MILES

i *Via Musei 32, Brescia*

▶ *Leave Brescia on the A4*
Milan-Venice motorway, turn-
ing off at the Sirmione exit.

❶ Sirmione

Sirmione is one of Lake
Garda's most famous and
loveliest spots. Long renowned
for its splendid position and
spas, it stands on a narrow
peninsula that extends about
4km (2.5 miles) into the water.
At its tip, where there are
splendid views, is the archaeological site of the Grotte di
Catullo, so called because,
according to tradition, it was
the location of a villa belonging
to Roman poet Catullus (1st
century BC) Lying among
oleanders and olive trees are
the remains of an impressive
residential complex built
during the early period of the
Roman Empire. It extends over
an area of 2 hectares (5 acres),
and is the grandest example of
a Roman villa found in northern Italy (admission fee).

Strictly prohibited to traffic
(the only exceptions being residents at hotels in the zone),
Sirmione's old town centre is a
mass of narrow streets and small
squares overlooked by ice-
cream parlours, boutiques and
craft shops. Entry to the town is
across the drawbridge of the
Rocca Scaligera castle, built in
the 13th century by Mastino I
della Scala, Lord of Verona, as a
garrison and landing-place for
his fleet. Surrounded by water,
the castle now houses a
museum of stone tablets; from
the top of the keep there is a
magnificent view of the lake.
Go on to visit the church of
Santa Anna della Rocca, with its
16th-century frescoes, the 15th-
century parish church of Santa
Maria Maggiore, and San Pietro
in Mavino, dating from the 8th
century and the oldest church in
the town. Sirmione's spas are
famous for the alleged healing

Garda lemons, a touch of the
Mediterranean in the north,
beneath the Rocca Scaligera

Floor mosaic in the Roman villa at Desenzano del Garda

powers of the waters that flow from the bottom of the lake, used for mud baths, massages and inhalations.

i *Viale Marconi 2*

▶ *Follow the SS11 to Desenzano del Garda.*

2 Desenzano del Garda

This is one of the most popular tourist resorts on Lake Garda, a lively seaside town and major sailing centre. The waterfront, Piazza Malvezzi, with its characteristic Porto Vecchio (old harbour) and the porticoed streets of the old centre, lined with restaurants, bars and shops, form the bustling heart of town. The whole area around Porto Vecchio is a pedestrian precinct; this is where you will find the Duomo (cathedral), which has a *Last Supper* by Giambattista Tiepolo (1696–1770). Founded by the Romans, disputed by Brescia and Verona in the Middle Ages and brought under Venetian rule in the 15th century, Desenzano preserves the legacies of its past in its

buildings and monuments; numerous finds on display in the Giovanni Rambotti Civic Archaeological Museum include the remains of a Roman villa, with splendid mosaic floors. The upper part of town, Capo la Terra, is dominated by the castle, probably founded in the early Middle Ages and rebuilt in the 14th and 15th centuries. Around it run the charming narrow streets of old Desenzano.

i *Via Porto Vecchio 34*

▶ *Take the SS572 to Moniga del Garda.*

3 Moniga del Garda

Moniga is guarded by a crenellated stone castle with round towers, built in the 10th century to resist Hungarian invasions. From the centre of the village, you descend through olive groves and vineyards to the lakeshore and the small harbour overlooked by trattorias. There are fine restaurants, sunny beaches facing the Sirmione peninsula, and camping sites shaded by olive trees. Moniga is the home of Chiaretto, a rosé wine which is one of Lake Garda's oldest and best loved.

▶ *Continue along the provincial road to Manerba del Garda.*

4 Manerba del Garda

Divided into five hamlets (Solarolo, Balbiana, Gardoncino, Montinelle and Pieve Vecchia), Manerba stands on a headland still known as the Rocca di Manerba. The name recalls a castle built on its summit in the 8th century and partially revealed by recent archaeological excavations. From the top there is a splendid view of the lake. Beneath the Rocca is the Sasso, a rock of great naturalistic interest and an ideal habitat for rare flowers, Mediterranean shrubs and orchids. Swimmers will find well-equipped beaches at Dusano harbour, Punta San Sivino, Torchio and Romantica, from where they can wade through the shallow water to the islet of San Biagio.

▶ *Pass Pieve Vecchia and follow the road that skirts the edge of the lake to San Felice del Benaco.*

5 San Felice del Benaco

Before you arrive in San Felice, a cypress-lined avenue on the right leads to the Sanctuary of the Madonna del Carmine, built around the middle of the 15th century and containing votive frescoes. San Felice is a peaceful holiday resort, set at the edge of the lake on a headland that circumscribes the gulf of Salò to the south. Standing on the main square is Palazzo Comunale, built around 1570. To the left stands the parish church, which houses a valuable 16th-century altarpiece by Romanino. Opposite San Felice, and contrasting with the blue waters of the lake, are the green gardens of Isola di Garda, occupied by monasteries from the 13th to the 18th centuries but now privately owned. In the early 1900s a white villa was built in Venetian neo-Gothic style on the island – the largest on the lake.

▶ *Drive on to Portese and Salò.*

6 Salò

A stylish holiday resort on the gulf of the same name, Salò was founded in Roman times, when it was called *Salodium*. In the 13th century it became the capital of the Magnifica Patria, a community formed by the towns on Lake Garda's Brescian Riviera (and some in Valsabbia). The old town centre is a maze of small squares and narrow, stone-paved streets, lined with mansions built between the 15th and 17th centuries. Of note is the Duomo (cathedral), built in the 15th century in late-Gothic style. Summer concerts held on its forecourt feature some of Europe's most prestigious orchestras – which is fitting, as Salò was the home of the inventor (or perfecter) of the violin, Gaspare da Salò (1540–1609). Near by, 16th-century Palazzo Fantoni houses documents relating to the Magnifica Patria, and the Nastro Azzurro Museum contains archives from the period between the Risorgimento (Resurgence) of the 19th century and World War II, including from 1943 to 1945, when Salò was the capital of the Italian Social Republic. The lakeside promenade is a great place for an evening stroll.

i *Piazza Sant'Antonio 4*

▶ *Leave Salò and take the SS45 bis to Gardone Riviera.*

7 Gardone Riviera

In the late 19th and early 20th centuries Gardone Riviera was a popular international destination for high society. It still maintains much of the charm that drew its wealthy visitors. Most of the cafés and shops are found along the lake's edge, now a stylish pedestrian area, and on the parallel Corso Zanardelli. Via Roma leads to the Hruska Botanical Gardens, created in the early 20th century by naturalist Arturo Hruska, doctor to the tsars. Extending over a surface area of 10,000sq m (107,642 sq feet) is a collection of more than 2,000 plant and flower species from every continent. Situated on the edge of the town are Villa Alba (a neo-classical building now used as a conference centre) and, on the

d'Annunzio (1863–1938) built his home, Il Vittoriale, which, according to his wishes, was turned into a national museum after his death.

lakeshore, the San Marco tower, once the villa's mooring-place. A road climbs past the gardens to Gardone di Sopra, the oldest part of the town, with its delightful views, 18th-century parish church and art nouveau villas. Here, poet Gabriele

Gabriele d'Annunzio's workshop and study at the Vittoriale in Gardone Riviera

i *Corso Repubblica 8*

▶ *Continue on to Toscolano Maderno.*

8 Toscolano Maderno

The two resorts of Maderno and Toscolano, now a single *comune*, are popular with sailing enthusiasts and sports-lovers; Bogliaco Golf Club, with the oldest green on Lake Garda, lies just inland. Both villages have ancient origins, evident in their buildings and old centres. In Maderno, the 12th-century church of Sant'Andrea is one of the loveliest Romanesque basilicas in the province of Brescia; there's also an 18th-century parish church with a painting by Paolo Veronese. Toscolano has the 16th-century church of SS Pietro e Paolo and the sanctuary of the Madonna del Benaco, housing 16th-century frescoes.

Golfing at Lake Garda

The remains of a large villa dating from the 1st century AD have been found beside the church, a reminder that Toscolano was once the most important centre on the Riviera.

i Via Statale I

▶ Return to Salò via the same route, then climb towards the interior of Valtènesi going via Cisano to Puegnago.

9 Puegnago del Garda

Puegnago marks the beginning of the leg of this tour that winds through Valtènesi, past vineyards and olive groves. Remains of medieval fortifications tower above the village and the main square offers a sweeping view of the lake and surrounding hills.

Stops can be made near by to buy DOC Garda Classico wine straight from the cellars.

▶ Drive on to Polpenazze.

10 Polpenazze del Garda

Every year Polpenazze holds one of the most important wine festivals in the province. This was one of the first settlements in Valtènesi, and major prehistoric finds have been made near by, in the area formerly occupied by Lake Lucone, where a community formed as early as the 4th millennium BC. Objects uncovered include a *pirogue* (narrow canoe), dug out of a tree trunk 4m (13 feet) long; a cast of it is displayed in the Valle Sabbia museum at the nearby village of Gavardo, along with other Bronze Age finds from the area. At Polpenazze visit the 16th-century parish church, built inside the walls of a medieval castle (of which sections

<hr/>

SCENIC ROUTES

The road that crosses Valtènesi between Salò and Padenghe winds through a beautiful hilly landscape of vineyards and olive trees, with delightful views of the lake. Inland are old villages, castles and aristocratic villas; on the coast are small towns, beaches, harbours and rocky coves.

<hr/>

survive), and the church of San Pietro in Lucone, rebuilt in the 15th century over an earlier Romanesque construction, with its fine frescoes and an old organ.

▶ Continue along the same road to Soiano del Lago.

11 Soiano del Lago

Dominated by a 10th-century castle and the 16th-century parish church of San Michele, Soiano is the highest centre in Valtènesi (196m/643 feet), and there is a magnificent view of Lake Garda from the castle's main tower.

▶ Proceed to Padenghe.

12 Padenghe sul Garda

Padenghe was once defended by a castle, built on the hilltop between the 10th and 15th centuries, and this still gives its upper parts the appearance of a medieval village. Further on is the Romanesque church of San Emiliano (12th century). Descend to the centre and the monumental Villa Barbieri (now the town hall), which forms a handsome ensemble with the nearby parish church.

▶ Take the inland provincial road to Lonato.

13 Lonato

Lonato is easily recognised from a distance thanks to the outlines of its medieval *rocca* (fortress), Maestra tower and the dome of the 18th-century Duomo (cathedral). Fortified and fought over from the 10th century AD for its strategic position, Lonato has a well-restored old centre. A pleasant stroll takes you to the castle and a spectacular view of Lake Garda. At its foot is the Casa della Podestà (first built in the 15th century and rebuilt in neo-Gothic style in 1910), containing period objects and furniture. Home to the Ugo da Como Foundation, this museum-residence has a fine picture gallery and a rich library.

▶ Return to Brescia on the SS11.

The Northern
Shore

This is the upper west-
ern shore of the Trentino
part of Lake Garda – windsurfing and sailing territory.
From Lake Ledro, with its prehistoric pile-dwellings,
you move on to Lake Idro, high in the mountains, to
enjoy the unspoiled scenery of the Tignale and
Tremòsine plateaux, balconies overlooking the
lake, and then on to
Limone, known for
its mild climate.

1/2 DAYS • 150KM • 93 MILES

ITINERARY	
RIVA DEL GARDA	▶ Pieve di Ledro (16km-10m)
PIEVE DI LEDRO	▶ Anfo (31km-19m)
ANFO	▶ Idro (11km-7m)
IDRO	▶ Gargnano (39km-24½m)
GARGNANO	▶ Tignale (21km-13m)
TIGNALE	▶ Tremòsine (13km-8m)
TREMÒSINE	▶ Limone (9km-5½m)
LIMONE	▶ Riva del Garda (10km-6m)

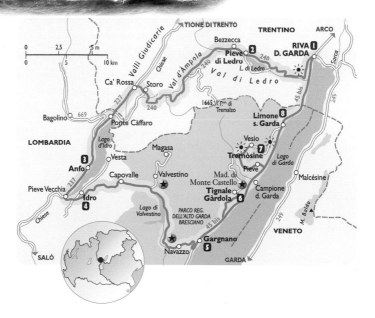

❶ Riva del Garda

The main town on Lake Garda's Trentino shore occupies a splendid position at the point where the lake meets the Brenta Dolomites and the Mediterranean vegetation of olive, lemon and palm trees contrasts with the rocks that descend sheer into the water. It's an elegant resort with ancient origins which, in the 13th century, became a major mercantile port.

Because of its strategic position, Riva del Garda was long

FOR HISTORY BUFFS

Riva is blessed with a mild climate and the *ora*, the wind that blows from the north, giving it an incredibly clear sky. In the mid-19th century, these attributes made it a popular health resort and fashionable holiday destination for the nobility and central European upper classes. It was also loved by poets and intellectuals such as Goethe, Stendhal, Mann and Nietzsche.

octagonal plan, and the 18th-century parish church of the Assunta, with baroque altars and stucco work.

i Largo Medaglie d'Oro al Valor Militare 5

▶ From Riva climb up Val Ledro, turning off to the south on to the **SS45 bis** then right for the **SS240** to Pieve di Ledro.

❷ Pieve di Ledro

Pieve di Ledro is the main tourist resort on the lake of the

Above: Riva del Garda
Opposite: Lake Ledro, the site of a Bronze Age lake-village

fought over by the della Scala family of Verona (1349), the Visconti family of Milan (1380) and the Venetians (1440). Evidence of the past is preserved in the old centre, with Piazza III Novembre at its heart, overlooking the port. Here stand the 15th-century Town Hall, Palazzo Pretorio (1375) and the 13th-century Apponale tower. Not far away, in Piazza Battisti, is the Rocca (stronghold), built in the 12th century and altered many times. It now houses the civic museum (with finds from the Ledro lake-village) and a picture gallery. The characteristic narrow streets that branch off the two

squares are lined with old houses and 18th-century mansions, now a succession of souvenir shops, rôtisseries, boutiques and restaurants. Historic buildings include two churches – the Inviolata, dating from the 17th century, a baroque masterpiece with an

FOR CHILDREN

How did primitive man live? This is the question explored at the Molina di Ledro Lake-dwelling Museum, which contains a reconstructed pile-dwelling and displays of finds made during the archaeological digs (including a canoe). Annexed to the museum are a library and an educational section.

same name, which stands out blue against one of the loveliest backdrops in the Trentino valleys. Just 3km (2 miles) long and 1.5km (1 mile) wide, Lake Ledro has attracted settlers to its shores since prehistoric times. The remains of pile-dwellings were uncovered in 1929, following a considerable fall in the level of the waters during construction work on a hydro-electric station. More than 10,000 wooden poles emerged from the bottom of the lake – the foundations of a large prehistoric village dating from approximately 4,000 years ago.

▶ Continue along the **SS240** to Ca' Rossa, where you take the **SS237** towards Lake Idro to Anfo.

3 Anfo

Situated about halfway up Lake Ledro, Anfo is one of the best-equipped resorts for visitors, partly thanks to its beaches, the largest on the lakeshores. In places the lakeshore descends steeply; in others it slopes gently down to white beaches. In the attractive old centre are the church of Sant'Antonio, with 14th- and 15th-century paintings; just outside Anfo is the Rocca, an imposing fortress built by the Venetians in 1486 and the scene of clashes in both Venetian and Napoleonic periods.

Lying 370m (1,214 feet) above sea level, this is the highest lake in Lombardy. It's well

BACK TO NATURE

As you climb Capovalle, a detour leads to Valvestino, one of the most beautiful and interesting natural settings in the entire Garda hinterland. Along with its greenery, woods, rocks and lake, the valley has two small characteristic villages – Magasa (a starting point for excursions to the Rest and Denai plateaux) and Valvestino.

ciborium, organ and choir by the Boscaì family of woodcarvers, who were active on the lake and in nearby Valsabbia from the

September, this is the starting point of the Centomiglia, the most prestigious regatta raced on Italian lakes. Set in beautiful surroundings of vegetable gardens, olive groves, gardens and old lemon-houses, this was – between 1943 and 1945 – the capital of the Social Republic of Salò; its ministers stayed in the local mansions. Palazzo Feltrinelli, overlooking the lake, was the headquarters of the Republic, and Villa Feltrinelli – a neo-Gothic building set in a park on the edge of the town – was the residence of the Mussolini family. At the centre of Gargnano is a little square that frames the harbour, dominated by the former Palazzo Comunale, an elegant 16th-century construction. At Bogliaco, Palazzo Bettoni is one of the most imposing 18th-century buildings on the Brescian shores of Lake Garda. This grandiose Lombard baroque building was the seat of the Prime Minister of the Social Republic, and is graced with a spectacular Italian garden.

i Piazza Boldini 2

▶ Take the **SS45 bis** (Gardesana occidentale road) north and after approximately 4km (2 miles) climb up a road on the right, between olive trees, towards Gàrdola.

equipped for all kinds of sports, and is ideal for windsurfers and sailors. Along its shores, historic villages alternate with camping sites and holiday villages. The waters are deep (up to 122m/400 feet) and quite cold, but you can happily swim here in summer.

▶ Continue along the lakeshore to Idro.

4 Idro

Set at the end of the lake named after it, Idro is an old village whose narrow streets are lined with stone houses and gardens. In the well-restored centre, the parish church of San Michele contains an elaborate main altar

Villa Bettoni, one of Gargnano's fine aristocratic residences

16th to 18th centuries. You can also visit the 14th-century parish church of Santa Maria ad Undas.

i Via Trento 15

▶ From Idro drive to Garda, climbing Capovalle and then descending towards Navazzo, enjoying sweeping views of the lake as far as Gargnano.

5 Gargnano

Gargnano (which, with nearby Villa and Bogliaco, forms a small *comune*) is well known to sailing enthusiasts. Every

6 Tignale

Sitting at a height of 555m (1,821 feet) on the plateau of the same name, Tignale consists of six small villages surrounded by olive trees, orchards, meadows and woods arranged on terraces high above Lake Garda. This haven of tranquillity commands a spectacular view of the lake. Gàrdola is the seat of the *comune*; from here you climb (1.5km/1 mile) to the sanctuary of the Madonna di Monte Castello, perched with the nearby hermitage on a 700m (2,296 feet) rock overhanging the lake. It was built on the ruins of a castle erected by the della Scala family, and houses the

Casa Santa, a shrine dating from the 9th century.

[i] *Piazza Umberto I 18*

▶ *Descend on the Gardesana road and after approximately 8km (5 miles) take the turning on the left that climbs to the Tremòsine plateau.*

7 Tremòsine
The Tremòsine plateau (north of Tignale) is known as the 'lake terrace' because of its exceptionally scenic position, which dominates the entire lake basin from above. You reach it along a spectacular road that winds through tunnels along the gorge excavated by the Brasa stream. Pieve is the capital of the *comune*, 18 hamlets lying in beautiful surroundings, of which only one sits on the lake – Campione del Garda. These tiny villages feature typical vernacular buildings and minor masterpieces of architecture and art such as the church of San Giovanni Battista at Pieve, with an 11th-century bell tower, San Bartolomeo at Vesio, with an organ by Gaetano Callido (1727–1813), and the sanctuary of San Michele, in the valley of the same name, where there is also a hermitage.

[i] *Piazza Marconi 12; Via Alessandro Voltino*

▶ *Descend along the same road to the Gardesana road and follow towards Riva and Limone sul Garda.*

8 Limone sul Garda
Olive groves and old lemon-houses form a backdrop to Limone sul Garda, the northernmost *comune* on Lake Garda's

Brescian shore. Popular for its mild climate, it's now known also as the 'village of longevity'. In 1979, a protein called Apolipoprotein A-I Milan Gene

A typical northern Garda road running high above the lake, with frequent tunnels

Limone was discovered in the blood of one of the village inhabitants. This protein is capable of eliminating fats from the arteries and therefore effectively combats arteriosclerosis and heart attacks. It's also hereditary, and seems to be exclusive to some of the inhabitants of Limone – attracting the interest of researchers all over the world.
    The town is perched on a small bay, set against high rock walls, and has 17th- and 18th-century Venetian buildings and some old fishermen's houses.

See the parish church of San Benedetto, 17th- to 18th-century Casa Gerardi and the Castèll lemon-house (18th-century). The shoreline, which stretches from the old centre to the Reamòl point, is a succession of some of the largest and most monumental lemon-houses on the lake. They feature characteristic structures of white stacked stone pillars (which once supported a glass and timber roof in winter), surrounded on three sides by high stone walls and open on the fourth side towards the lake. In the 18th century these glasshouses were used to grow lemons, an activity that has practically vanished.

[i] *Via Comboni 15*

▶ *Continue along the Gardesana road to Riva.*

Garda in Trentino
& Other Lakes

Nature and sport are the main pursuits of Lake Garda's Trentino shore. Not far away, elegant Arco and medieval-looking Tenno, Dro and Drena are a prelude to the discovery of Trento, a Renaissance jewel set in the heart of the Alps.

1/2 DAYS • 150KM • 93 MILES

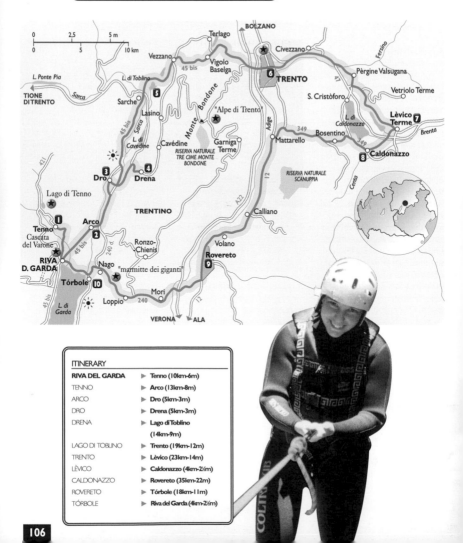

ITINERARY	
RIVA DEL GARDA	► Tenno (10km-6m)
TENNO	► Arco (13km-8m)
ARCO	► Dro (5km-3m)
DRO	► Drena (5km-3m)
DRENA	► Lago di Toblino (14km-9m)
LAGO DI TOBLINO	► Trento (19km-12m)
TRENTO	► Lèvico (23km-14m)
LÈVICO	► Caldonazzo (4km-2½m)
CALDONAZZO	► Rovereto (35km-22m)
ROVERETO	► Tórbole (18km-11m)
TÓRBOLE	► Riva del Garda (4km-2½m)

i Largo Medaglie d'Oro al Valor Militare 5, Riva del Garda

▶ *Leave Riva, following the signs for Tenno.*

❶ Tenno

Dominated by the ruins of a 12th-century castle, Tenno is a medieval-looking town set about 400m (1,312 feet) up in an exceptionally scenic position, with a view of Lake Garda. A little further north is a small lake surrounded by green woods. From Tenno climb to the old fortified village of Frapporta, which overlooks the Garda plain below.

i Via Roma 67

▶ *Return towards Riva and take the SS45 bis northbound to Arco.*

❷ Arco

Arco was a prestigious health resort under the Habsburg Empire, towards the end of the 19th century. Today it's the local capital of climbing. The oldest part of Arco lies at the foot of the castle, built in the early Middle Ages on a rock overlooking the Sarca Valley. In one of its main rooms you can admire a cycle of Gothic frescoes depicting games and ladies and cavaliers. The town's predominant style, however, is art nouveau. The villas standing in extensive grounds, the public gardens, the Casinò, the neo-Gothic evangelical church of Trinitas Kirche

The remains of Arco Castle, surrounded by olive trees and cypresses

---

SPECIAL TO...

Canale is one of the loveliest medieval villages in Trentino, where time seems to have stood still. Not surprisingly, it's much loved by painters. Artists of international renown (including Paloma Picasso) come to spend time at the Giacomo Vittone house of artists, which also organises exhibitions and summer courses.

FOR HISTORY BUFFS

Arco's success as a holiday resort was largely due to Albert of Habsburg, Archduke of Austria. From 1872 onwards he spent long periods in his villa, set in the centre of a large park full of exotic plants, and it was at Arco that he died in 1895. Today the park still features his Arboreto, with plants from the four continents.

---

and the hotels were all built in the second half of the 19th century, when the town was a holiday destination frequented by the Habsburg upper middle classes. Other buildings of note are the 17th-century collegiate of the Assunta, the baroque

---

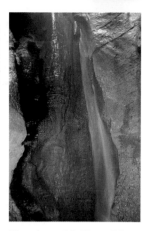

The colours of the Varone falls, at Riva del Garda

SPECIAL TO...

The Varone falls, just above Riva, are a fantastic spectacle that will take your breath away, plunging from a height of about 100m (33 feet) into a gorge excavated by the waters over the millennia. Admission fee.

---

town hall and the Romanesque church of San Apollinare. Arco was the birthplace of Giovanni Segantini (1858–99), the leading Italian Divisionist painter.

i Viale delle Palme 1

▶ *Continue along the SS45 bis to the turning on the left for Dro.*

3 Dro

Dro, with its stone houses, sculpted doorways and high-walled courtyards, is dominated by the ruins of the castle and the chapel of San Abbondio, with its 16th-century frescoes. Its layout is typical of many of the old villages in the upper Garda area. The surroundings are marked by *marocche*, a mass of huge boulders that slid, thousands of years ago, down from the sides of Monte Casale. With a surface area of 14.5sq km (6 square miles), this is the largest landslide in the Alpine range.

▶ *Return to the SS45 bis and follow this to the turning on the right for Drena.*

The medieval Castel Toblino

4 Drena

Drena has a lake climate but mountain habitat and vegetation. This tiny rural village developed at the foot of a medieval castle founded in the 12th century by the counts of Arco and destroyed in 1703 by the French general Vendôme. Inside the restored manor, with its crenellated walls and high tower, an exhibition illustrates local history with finds from various epochs.

▶ *Return to the SS45 bis and continue towards Trento to Lago di Toblino.*

5 Lago di Toblino

Preceded by minute Lake Cavèdine, enchanting Lake Toblino owes its name to the romantic castle built on a small headland in the 12th century and altered several times (it's now a restaurant). All around are ancient woods, vineyards and olive groves.

▶ *Continue along the SS45 bis to Trento.*

6 Trento

The capital of Trentino, and a bridge between Italian and central European culture, Trento is a city rich in art and history. It sits in a beautiful position, surrounded by majestic mountains and crossed by the Adige River. Trento was founded by the Romans, and was for 200 years a Lombard ducal city. Then, for nearly eight centuries (1027–1796), it served as the seat of an episcopal principality. It acquired universal fame in the 16th century as the venue, from 1545 to 1563, of the 19th Ecumenical Council, which promoted the Counter-Reformation. The 16th century was the city's golden age, when it acquired the churches, mansions and squares that still stand in its old centre.

The two most significant sites are Piazza del Duomo and Buonconsiglio castle. The route that links them winds along Via Belenzani, Via Manci and Via San Marco, which spread out into a tangle of narrow side streets and squares. These are lined with Renaissance mansions with painted façades, churches such as San Francesco, the most important 18th-century example, and Gothic, Romanesque and baroque buildings. Piazza Duomo, with the Nettuno fountain, is the focal point of Trento's social and cultural life. Around it stand the austere Romanesque-Gothic duomo (cathedral), Palazzo Pretorio, with the 13th-century civic tower, and old mansions including the Cazuffi houses, whose façades are decorated with 16th-century frescoes. Buonconsiglio Castle, symbol of the city, is in the east. Built in the mid-13th century as the residence of the bishop-princes, it was extended and altered many times to become one of the most significant defensive-residential complexes in Italy. The oldest part, dating from the

Middle Ages, is Castelvecchio, to which the Magno Palazzo was added in the 16th century. Many rooms in both are decorated with extraordinary fresco cycles, notably the 15th-century *The Months*, one of the most famous examples of international Gothic painting. The castle displays a rich art and history collection including paintings, coins, manuscripts, archaeological finds and statues. Other places worth a visit in the centre are the Museum of Modern and Contemporary Art (a new sister museum, MART, with a large part of this museum's former

collection, has opened in Rovereto, see page 110), the Tridentine Museum of Natural Science and the Caproni Museum of Aeronautics.

Across the River Adige is San Apollinare Church, reconstructed by the Benedictines in 1320 with a magnificent high façade.

ℹ️ *Via Manci 2*

▶ *Follow the **SS47** to Pergine Valsugana and from here drive towards Lèvico along*

The jetty at Lake Caldonazzo

Piazza del Duomo, the monumental centre of Trento

the shore of the lake of the same name.

7 Lèvico Terme

Lèvico (506m/1,660 feet) lies in a depression overlooking the lake named after it. The first spa here opened in 1860, although the waters had been in use since the previous century. Today they're exported all over the world. North of the town (12km/7.5 miles), overlooking Valsugana, is Vetriolo Terme, at 1,500m (4,921 feet) the highest spa in Europe.

i *Via Vittorio Emanuele 3*

▶ *Drive towards Lake Caldonazzo on the SS349.*

8 **Caldonazzo**
Caldonazzo gives its name to its lake, the largest in Trentino and, since the 1950s, Trento's 'lido'. In the old part of the village are the Magnifica Corte, a fortress-house rebuilt in the 15th and 16th centuries, and the church of San Sisto, rebuilt in the 18th century.

▶ *Continue along the lakeshore, passing Bosentino, still on the SS349. Approximately 13km (8 miles) before Trento, turn left for Mattarello, and take the SS12 south to Rovereto.*

9 **Rovereto**
Rovereto is known as the 'Athens of Trentino' because of its rich cultural tradition and status as the birthplace of philosophers such as Antonio Rosmini, scholars and musicians. The most interesting part of town is the medieval quarter, which starts from Piazza Cesare Battisti and continues along Via della Terra, passing the Fortunato Depero Museum, dedicated to the futurist artist who designed its furnishings. Visit the MART gallery of contemporary art, with more than 9,000 works. Eventually you arrive at the castle, now housing the Italian War History Museum. Focusing on World War I, this is the most important museum of its kind in the country. On Miravalle Hill, to the southeast, the monumental Bell for the Fallen tolls 100 times every evening in memory of those who died at war.

i *Corso Rosmini 6*

▶ *Leave in the direction of Mori and here take the SS240 for Lake Garda and Tórbole.*

10 **Tórbole**
Tórbole sits at the centre of the so-called 'windsurf triangle', created by the air turbulence of Campione, Riva and Malcésine. Even Goethe spoke with vivid admiration of the strong winds and the resort's position on the

RECOMMENDED WALK

Near Nago, where the Loppio valley converges on that of the Sarca, an undemanding walk leads to the 'giants' kettles', spectacular round cavities produced by the erosion of boulders and detritus carried downstream by the water.

lake. Windsurfers come here from all over Europe and the lake is used for international competitions. Windsurfing schools – annexed to hotels and camping sites – are popular with those seeking to improve their skills. Tórbole forms a single *comune* with Nago, on the hill behind it; here stand the ruins of 13th-century Castel Penede, reached along a scenic route through the woods.

i *Lungolago Verona 19*

▶ *Continue along the lakeshore to Riva del Garda.*

Sailing the waters off Tórbole

Verona

1/2 DAYS

Immortalised by Shakespeare in *Romeo and Juliet*, lovely Verona is known the world over for its Arena, an outstanding opera venue, but visitors will also find many other treasures of art and culture tucked into this bend in the River Adige.

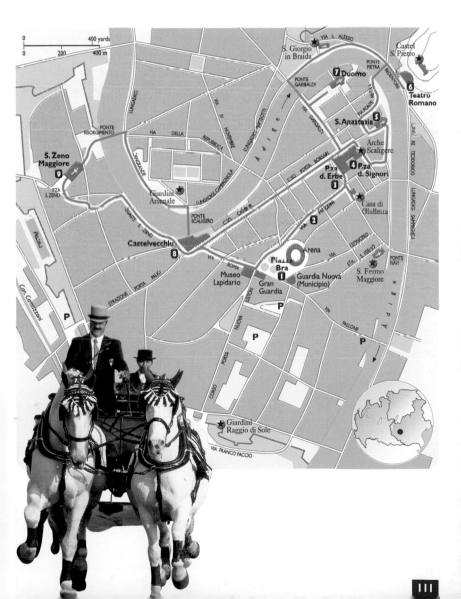

[i] *Aeroporto Valerio Catullo; Via degli Alpini 9; Piazza XXV Aprile*

❶ Piazza Bra

Piazza Bra, at the centre of Verona, is dominated by the massive structure of the Arena. On it stand the neo-classical Gran Guardia Nuova (city hall), Palazzo della Gran Guardia, with the Bra doorways (1480), the philharmonic theatre and the Maffei Stone Tablet Museum. The *listón* – an elegant pavement in pink marble – runs along one side of the square.

The Arena, built in the 1st century AD, is one of the largest surviving Roman amphitheatres, seating 25,000 spectators. Much of its outer ring has collapsed (only the north wing remains), but the second ring of walls, consisting of a double row of 72 arches, is well preserved. Spectators come from all over the world every summer to see the operas that make Verona one of the capitals of music.

▶ *Walk along Via Mazzini.*

❷ Via Mazzini

This is the most elegant and busiest street in the city, full of gift shops and clothes shops. At the end, on the right, a detour to Via Cappello leads to the so-called Casa di Giulietta (House of Juliet), a 13th-century building at No 23. Actually the only feature recalling Shakespeare's heroine is the balcony, added to the inner courtyard during restoration work in 1935.

▶ *Continue along Via Mazzini to Piazza delle Erbe.*

❸ Piazza delle Erbe

This was the forum of Roman Verona and is now the picturesque market square. Fruit and vegetable stalls are set up around the Gothic Colonna del Mercato, the Madonna Verona fountain, built in the 14th century using a Roman statue, and the Venetian column of San Marco, erected in 1523. Overlooking the square at the

end is the Gardello tower (1370); beside it, the baroque Palazzo Maffei. On the right side are the neo-classical minor façade of Palazzo Comune, connected to the Domus Nova (or Palazzo dei Giudici) by the Arco della Costa ('rib arch'), so-called because a whale bone hangs from it. These are followed by the della Scala Mazzanti houses, decorated with 16th-century frescoes. On the opposite side is the 14th-century Casa dei Mercanti, with double windows and crenellation.

▶ *Pass beneath the Arco della Costa into Piazza dei Signori.*

4 Piazza dei Signori
This was Verona's real centre of political and administrative power. It has the harmonious and consistent appearance of a splendid city courtyard. Here is

The Pietra bridge with the Duomo bell tower (below) and a view of Piazza delle Erbe (left)

Performing Verdi's opera *Aida* at Verona's Arena

the main façade of Palazzo del Comune (or della Ragione), with the medieval Lamberti tower (wonderful view of the city from the top). The fine inner courtyard, known as the old market, contains the spectacular Gothic 'della Ragione' steps. Next come the 14th-century Palazzo del Capitano and Palazzo della Prefettura, and the elegant Loggia del Consiglio, built in 1485 as the prestigious seat of the city council. The Volto della Tortura leads to the Arche Scaligere, the monumental tombs erected for the lords of Verona beside Santa Maria Antica Church. Visible above the church doorway is the tomb of Cangrande I, who died in 1329, with his equestrian statue (a copy: the original is in

Castelvecchio). Especially interesting within the enclosure are the tomb of Mastino II (who died in 1351) and, slightly set back, that of Cansignorio.

▶ *Take the picturesque Via Sottoriva to Sant'Anastasia.*

5 Sant'Anastasia
The church of Sant'Anastasia was founded by the Dominicans and is an important example of Venetian Gothic architecture of the 12th and 13th centuries. The façade, which was never completed, has a fine doorway featuring polychrome marble, bas-reliefs and 15th-century frescoes. Inside are major works of art including a fresco of *St George and the Princess*, a 15th-century masterpiece by Pisanello.

▶ *Walk along Via Ponte Pietra and cross the Adige on the Roman Pietra bridge (rebuilt), then turn right into Rigaste Redentore.*

6 Teatro Romano

The Roman theatre was built in the 1st century BC and still has some of its original steps. This area was the site of Verona's first Reto-Euganean settlement and subsequently of the Roman city. The theatre sits at the centre of an archaeological area, which also comprises the Archaeological Museum.

▶ *Return towards Ponte di Pietra and follow the Lungoadige towards the great dome of San Giorgio in Braida (Sanmicheli, 1477–1536), then cross the river on Ponte Garibaldi and turn left into Via Arciduca Pacifico.*

7 Duomo (cathedral)

Begun in the middle of the 12th century and modified many times, the cathedral has an elegant doorway with a porch adorned with sculptures and

reliefs executed in 1139 by Maestro Nicolò. The Romanesque cloister and nearby churches of San Giovanni in Fonte and Santa Elena, dating from the 11th century, are also lovely.

▶ *Return along Via Arciduca Pacifico and turn left into Via Garibaldi and Via Rosa, at the end of which you take Corso Porta Borsari. Beyond the Roman gate, continue along Corso Cavour past 16th-century mansions.*

8 Castelvecchio

This splendid example of 14th-century military architecture was the most imposing della Scala construction, built and occupied by Cangrande II. The interior is

Carnivale in Verona, with the Duomo in the background

arranged around two courtyards and houses the Civic Art Museum, exhibiting major paintings and sculptures, particularly by artists from Veneto (masterpieces include works by Andrea Mantegna, Giovanni Bellini, Vittore Carpaccio, Veronese, Tintoretto and Tiepolo), and a fascinating collection of arms. The Ponte Scaligero across the Adige was blown up by German soldiers during World War II, but rebuilt around 1950.

▶ *Follow the lovely Regaste San Zeno, Via San Giuseppe and Via Porta San Zeno.*

9 San Zeno Maggiore

A Romanesque masterpiece, the basilica of San Zeno was founded at the end of the 9th century and rebuilt in the 12th. Since then it has been central to the city's religious life. Of note are the doorway, made in 1138 by Maestro Nicolò, and the 24 bronze panels on its leaves, which date from the 12th century and constitute a masterpiece of medieval sculpture. The imposing interior has a nave and two aisles, as well as works of art including, on the main altar, a *Madonna and Child with Angels and Saints* painted in 1459 by Andrea Mantegna.

▶ *Return to Piazza Bra either along Regaste San Zeno again or by crossing the Adige on the Ponte del Risorgimento and following Lungoadige Cangrande to Ponte di Castelvecchio (there is a pavement along the riverside). After the bridge take Via Roma.*

Opposite: the basilica of San Zeno

The Lower Lake
near Verona

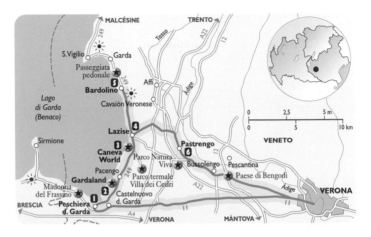

This tour is an ideal way to entertain the children and combines the beautiful towns near Verona with some of Italy's most famous amusement **1/2 DAYS • 70KM • 43 MILES** parks. Nature, history and Garda wines and oil complete the experience.

ITINERARY		
VERONA	▶	**Peschiera del Garda** **(23km-14m)**
PESCHIERA DEL GARDA	▶	**Gardaland (3km-2m)**
GARDALAND	▶	**CanevaWorld (5km-3m)**
CANEVAWORLD	▶	**Lazise (2km-1m)**
LAZISE	▶	**Bardolino (6km-4m)**
BARDOLINO	▶	**Parco Natura Viva di** **Pastrengo (6km-4m)**
PASTRENGO	▶	**Verona (25km-15m)**

i Via degli Alpini 9, Verona

▶ Follow the **SS11** for Lake
    Garda to Peschiera.

1 Peschiera del Garda

Since Roman times, this has
been an important stronghold,
guarding southern Lake Garda
and the roads passing near it.
Gradually fortified with imposing walls built by the della Scala
family, the Venetians and the
Austrians, Peschiera still has the
appearance of a walled town,
surrounded by mighty bastions
guarding the water. The Mincio
River forms here; this main
outlet of Lake Garda crosses the
town in three arms. Most of the
old centre is a pedestrian zone,

FOR HISTORY BUFFS

Peschiera, together with
Verona, Legnago and Mantua,
constituted one of the corners
of the famous Quadrilateral,
conceived in 1859 by the
Austrians to protect communi-
cations with Austria through
the Adige Valley and defend
a vast mustering zone
for troops.

i Piazzale Betteloni 15

▶ Continue along the **SS249**
    (Gardesana Orientale road),
    following the signs for
    Gardaland

the Wizard's Castle, the
Medieval Tournament, Ikarus,
Blue Tornado, Jungle Rapids,
Space Vertigo, Canyons, Rio
Bravo, the Elves village, the
Arab Souk, the Pirates, Colorado
Boat, the Valley of the Kings,
Flying Island (a fantastic
panoramic orbiting platform),
Prezzemolo Baby Fun (devoted
to tiny tots) and the Buccaneers'
Cove.

Gardaland also has more
relaxing areas – particularly a
huge green park where you can
stroll and discover flowers,
bizarre topiary sculptures and
rare trees such as the *Metasequoia
glyptostroboides*, a giant sequoia
that can grow to a height of
100m (330 feet).

Descending a giant water chute
on a 'pirogue' – just one of the
thrills of Gardaland

enclosed within a 16th-century
fortress with five bastions. The
buildings, churches and gardens
are a delight. Visit the Museum
of the History of the
Risorgimento or Palazzina
Storica and the Rocca (stronghold). This is a major railway
junction, along with nearby
Castelnuovo del Garda, and
provides the ideal point of
departure for visits to the local
amusement parks.

2 Gardaland

Gardaland, at Ronchi di
Castelnuovo del Garda, is the
largest and most famous amusement park in Italy. It was also
one of the first – in 2000 it celebrated its 25th birthday.
Essentially it's a small town
devoted to fun, animated all day
long by shows and dozens of
attractions, including four theme
villages, as well as restaurants,
bars, snack bars, ice-cream
parlours, shops and the PalaBlu
(a large dolphin pool). New
features are introduced every
year: favourites include Merlin

SPECIAL TO...

About 3km (2 miles) from
Peschiera is the sanctuary of
the Madonna del Frassino,
attached to a 16th-century
convent. This pilgrimage site
dates in its present form from
the early 17th century, with
some early 20th-century
changes, and stands on the
spot where, according to
legend, the Madonna appeared
in 1510 to a peasant. Inside are
works of art and ex-votos.

Venice to control trade on this section of the lake.

i *Via F Fontana 14*

▶ *Continue along the SS249 to Bardolino.*

5 Bardolino

Bardolino, one of the liveliest spots on the lake, is extremely popular with young people. With an old traditional centre, a well-equipped harbour offering a sweeping view of Lake Garda, camping sites, holiday villages, discos and pubs, it is also known

The towers of Lazise, restored by the della Scala family in the 14th century

▶ *Proceed along the SS249 towards Lazise, following the signs for CanevaWorld, just before the town.*

3 CanevaWorld

Established more than 20 years ago as a water park, CanevaWorld is the other main fun haven on Lake Garda. According to its publicity it's not just an amusement park – it's a world of amusement. Three theme attractions – Acqua Paradise, Medieval Times and the Rockstar Café – exist side by side and are expanded every year. Acqua Paradise is a large water park covering an area of 30,000sq m (322,920 square feet) with oases, sea-beds, waterfalls and tropical villages. Slides include the highest in Europe – more

than 30m (98 feet), and attractions and beaches are specially designed to create a Caribbean atmosphere. During the day there are games for the children and plenty of cafés, spaghetti houses, ice-cream parlours and fast food outlets. In Medieval Times you travel back in time to a tournament between knights on horseback in an unpaved arena. Spectators are divided into teams and side with one or the other. The entertainment includes dinner with a themed menu. The Rockstar Café is a temple of Italian pop music, filled with curios, gadgets and lots of memorabilia.

▶ *Enter Lazise on the state road.*

4 Lazise

Surrounded by olive trees and stretches of lake-water, Lazise is dominated by its powerful castle, one of the best examples of its kind on Lake Garda, with high crenellated walls, built as a strategic outpost of the della Scala family, lords of Verona. Enter the old centre, passing through the old walls and the narrow medieval streets, which date from the time when Lazise was one of Italy's first communes, formed in 983. These lead you to the delightful harbour, overlooked by the Romanesque church of San Nicolò and the Dogana (customs house), built by the Republic of

SCENIC ROUTES

Bardolino is the starting point of the Strada del Vino wine route, which leads through hills, farms and old villages to Cavaion Veronese, Affi and the Garda Rocca, giving you the chance to taste and buy the best local products. A useful complimentary map provided by the Consorzio Tutela Vino Bardolino will help you find your way to the wine cellars and vineyards.

for its excellent wines and extra virgin olive oil, which can be tasted and bought directly from the producers. On the hills between Bardolino and Garda, there are about 30 oil presses and more than 60 wine cellars selling oil and wine, plus two museums – the Cantine Fratelli

BACK TO NATURE

Villa dei Cedri Park, at Colà di Lazise, has ancient trees, a lake extending over about 5,000sq m (53,821 square feet), with hot water at a temperature of 37°C (99°F) and an impressive neo-classical villa (with an excellent restaurant). It's the ideal place to spend a relaxing day surrounded by nature, having hydromassage and swimming in the lake.

FOR CHILDREN

At Ferlina di Bussolengo, on the road back to Verona, the Paese di Bengodi (Land of Plenty), located entirely underground, looks at first glance like a Renaissance village. There are games rooms, a mechanical rodeo and a Laser Dome here, as well as shops and restaurants. On Sundays it's reserved for children, with games organised by the resident mascot 'mouse'.

FOR CHILDREN

Particularly suited to tiny tots, the Rio Valli Cavaion Veronese Water Park is one of the largest in Italy. Spread over approximately 50,000sq m (538,000 square feet), with a vast area of swimming pools, it's equipped with water games, slides and other amenities for a day of fun and sport.

RECOMMENDED WALK

A footpath winds from Bardolino along the lake to Garda. This beautiful and relaxing walk takes about an hour.

Zeni Wine Museum and the Cisano Olive Oil Museum.

i Piazzale Aldo Moro 5

▶ Return along the SS249 to Lazise and here turn inland, following the signs for Pastrengo.

6 Parco Natura Viva di Pastrengo

Pastrengo's Natura Viva Park is a tranquil spot where you can observe hundreds of wild animals. It's divided into two sectors – the fauna park and the

Exhibit in the Cisano Olive Oil Museum in Bardolino

safari park. The fauna park is home to about a thousand animals from all continents and belonging to 200 different species. The safari park can only be visited by car or bus and offers the chance to observe jungle animals close up. It also has a community of chimpanzees, the only ones in Italy to have reproduced. One section of the park contains life-sized reproductions of the most famous dinosaur species, such as the tyrannosaur, triceratops and pteranodon.

▶ Return to Verona on the provincial road via Bussolengo.

Top: boats moored in the water at Bardolino
Above: one of the dinosaurs in Pastrengo's Parco Natura Viva

THE FLORA OF THE LAKES

One of the great delights of the pre-Alpine lakes is the exceptional variety of plants and flowers and the lush vegetation, partly indigenous and partly introduced, which make each lake a unique environment.

Botanical mountain

Monte Baldo, on the east shore of Garda, is known as the 'botanical garden of Europe' for the extraordinary wealth of its flora. En route from lakeside to peak (2,218m/7,277 feet), it passes from olive trees to alpines. Gradually, as you go higher, the Mediterranean vegetation of vines, olive trees, cypresses, oleanders and ilex gives way to woods of chestnuts, rovella and ash, as well as beech and pine woods above 1,000m

Water lilies and cypresses in the Sigurtà Park at Valeggio sul Mincio

(3,280 feet) and then meadows and high pastures. Even edelweiss flower at high altitude. In spring primroses, anemones, violets, daffodils and soldanella stretch as far as the eye can see, and orchids flower in autumn.

Novezzina is the home of Monte Baldo Botanical Garden. Inaugurated in 1989, it collects only indigenous species – approximately 500 so far, though more will be planted in future years. Its numerous rare and protected flowers include specimens of Baldo anemone, columbine, asphodel, snowdrop, summer snowflake, daphne, gentian, yellow gentian, orange lily, martagon lily, lily of the valley, nigritelle, daffodil, auricula, peony, pasque-flower, rhododendron, Christmas rose, lady's slipper and edelweiss. Guided tours are organised.

Lake Garda's parks

Another zone of particular naturalistic interest is Alto Garda Bresciano Park, which extends over an area of more than 38,000 hectares (93,896 acres), rising from lake level, at 65m (213 feet), to almost 2,000m (6,560 feet) on the highest mountains, between Salò and Campione. Marked by greatly contrasting scenery that typifies this area, it combines the coastal strip with palm trees, oleanders, bougainvillaea and mimosa, and the mountainous inland area with almost Alpine traits.

The predominant vegetation of Lake Garda is typically Mediterranean, with palm, agave and laurel trees. In spring mimosa, broom, jasmine, bougainvillaea and oleanders all bloom to produce a rainbow of colours. Olive trees, vines and citrus fruits flourish in the Limone area, growing on the shores and inland hills of the Brescian shore.

The mild climate has also allowed many plant and flower species from other continents to acclimatise perfectly, and these now constitute a major attraction in some famous botanical gardens such as Villa Hruska at Gardone Riviera, the Sigurtà Park at Valeggio sul Mincio and the Arboreto in the Arciducale park at Arco.

Villa flowers

The most spectacular parks are on lakes Maggiore and Como, annexed to some of their most famous villas. The vegetation of Lake Maggiore is quite unusual as, from the 18th century on, exotic and rare species from all over the world have been added to the typical flora of the pre-Alpine lake areas. Flowering

shrubs, in particular, remain a distinguishing feature of the splendid parks for which Lake Maggiore is well known. The abundance of parks has given rise to the increased production of flowers and vegetables, especially greenhouse specimens. In fact, the nursery business has acquired considerable economic importance.

Lake Maggiore's most famous park is that of Villa Taranto, at Pallanza; and other very popular areas, particularly in spring when the rhododendrons and azaleas flower, are the gardens of Isola Bella, Isola Madre and Villa Pallavicino in Stresa. Inland, in the Vergante area, is an interesting alpine botanical garden.

Lake Como's gardens

Lake Como is also known for its parks, visited by plant enthusiasts from all over the world. Among the most spectacular are those of Bellagio (starting with Villa Melzi and Villa Serbelloni) and that of Villa Carlotta at Tremezzo. The gardens of Villa Balbaniello, near Lenno, are famous for their climbing plants, trained to cover the buildings; Villa Pizzo's gardens at Cernobbio are celebrated for their ancient rose garden.

On the Riviera del Brenta

Some of the gardens belonging to the Venetian villas are also spectacular, particularly on the Riviera del Brenta. Perhaps the star of them all, though, is the park of Villa Pisani at Strà, with its box tree maze.

Above: gathering olives
Below: camellia and citrus fruit in the gardens of Villa Carlotta in Tremezzo

Around
Mantua

1/2 DAYS • 150KM • 93 MILES

Although centred on Mantua, a splendid Renaissance city, and the masterpieces found there by Mantegna, Giulio Romano and Leon Battista Alberti, this tour also visits places of historical and natural interest – from Mincio Nature Park to the villages in Garda's amphitheatre of hills, and the hills of the Risorgimento.

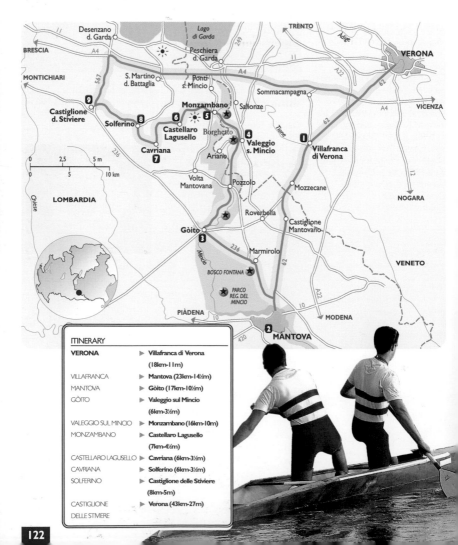

ITINERARY

VERONA	▶	**Villafranca di Verona** (18km-11m)
VILLAFRANCA	▶	Mantova (23km-14½m)
MANTOVA	▶	Gòito (17km-10½m)
GÒITO	▶	Valeggio sul Mincio (6km-3½m)
VALEGGIO SUL MINCIO	▶	Monzambano (16km-10m)
MONZAMBANO	▶	Castellaro Lagusello (7km-4½m)
CASTELLARO LAGUSELLO	▶	Cavriana (6km-3½m)
CAVRIANA	▶	Solferino (6km-3½m)
SOLFERINO	▶	Castiglione delle Stiviere (8km-5m)
CASTIGLIONE DELLE STIVIERE	▶	Verona (43km-27m)

▶ *Leave Verona through Porta Nuova and follow the SS62 to Villafranca di Verona.*

❶ Villafranca di Verona

Founded in 1185, Villafranca di Verona now has a 19th-century appearance, but still has evidence of its earlier past in the mighty 13th- to 14th-century castle, surrounded by a moat now almost entirely filled in. Inside, a museum displays mementoes, arms and documents from the time of the Risorgimento, when Villafranca was at the centre of major historic events – most notably the signing of the armistice between Napoleon III and Francis Joseph, an event that brought an end to the Second War of Independence (8 July 1859). In the old centre, which spreads around three parallel medieval streets, you can visit the parish church of SS Pietro e Paolo, built at the end of the 18th century as a copy of the Palladian church of the Redentore in Venice; and the Church of the Disciplina, with its late-baroque façade.

▶ *Proceed along the SS62 to Mantova (Mantua).*

❷ Mantova (Mantua)

Mantua is one of the most charming and artistically interesting cities in northern Italy. Surrounded by the waters of the Mincio River, which form three lakes (used by boats which travel as far as Venice), it was developed over the centuries by the Gonzaga family, who made it a city-court of the utmost splendour. At the heart of the city is Piazza Sordello, on which stand Palazzo Vescovile, the Duomo (cathedral) of San Pietro, with an impressive neo-classical façade and 16th-century interior designed by Giulio Romano, and Palazzo Ducale, and the Gonzaga palace complex, constructed between the mid-13th and the 17th centuries. With more than 500 rooms,

hanging gardens and courtyards, the palace extends over a vast area. The oldest section is made up of Palazzo del Capitano and the Magna Domus, which overlook Piazza Sordello. The Gonzaga family made this their residence after gaining power in 1328; gradually, more buildings were added, linked with covered passageways and tunnels. The sectors of greatest historical and artistic interest include the Sala dei Principi, with the sinopites (preparatory drawings) found beneath frescoes painted by Pisanello as part of a major cycle before 1444 (now kept in the

nearby Sala Pisanello); the Appartamento degli Arazzi, with copies of Flemish tapestries designed by Raphael; the Appartamento Ducale; the Appartamento Estivale, designed by Giulio Romano, the great 16th-century painter and architect responsible for many parts of the palace; and the Galleria della Mostra, built to house the art collection of Vincenzo I Gonzaga (died 1627). From the Galleria dei Mesi you walk through rooms decorated

The Camera Picta fresco in Mantua's Palazzo Ducale

greatest masterpieces of the Italian Renaissance.

From Palazzo Ducale you come to Piazza Broletto, with Palazzo Podestà and the communal tower, and Piazza delle Erbe, with Palazzo della Ragione, the clock tower (1473), the Rotonda di San Lorenzo (late 11th century, the oldest religious building in the city), and the basilica of San Andrea, a masterpiece of Renaissance architecture inspired by classical models, designed by Leon Battista Alberti in 1470 and completed in 1765 with the baroque dome.

In the east of the city is Palazzo Te, a grandiose suburban villa designed for Federico II Gonzaga in 1525 by Giulio Romano, also responsible for the

▶ *Leave Mantua on the SS236 for Gòito.*

🔒 Gòito

Gòito was an important fortress, scene of memorable battles during the Risorgimento (8 April and 29 May, 1848); it still has legacies of its long past in the medieval tower and in the criss-cross structure of the old village. Most importantly, however, it is a point of departure for visits to the Mincio Nature Park. Near Gòito is the Bertone park centre, with many trees over 100 years old. This was once the hunting ground of the Gonzaga family; you can explore it on a guided tour. Divided into two main areas – one to the north towards Lake Garda, and a marshy area near the Mantua lakes – the

Mantua at sunset as seen from one of its lakes

with frescoes and stucco work by Giulio Romano and his pupils (Sala di Troia, Sala di Giove, Sala dei Cavalli). After passing the Sala del Manto, with its rich coffered ceiling, climb to San Giorgio Castle, a massive construction dating from the late 14th century, which houses the most famous room in the entire palace – the Camera degli Sposi (or Picta), decorated between 1465 and 1474 with frescoes by Andrea Mantegna – one of the

richly decorated interiors. The rooms are named after their frescoes – the most famous being Sala Psiche, considered a masterpiece of Mannerism.

A host of other mansions and churches worthy of a visit include the church of San Sebastiano, designed by Alberti in 1460, Mantegna's home, conceived perhaps by the painter himself, the 17th-century Palazzo di Giustizia, the house of Giulio Romano and the 14th-century church of San Francesco.

🛈 *Piazza Andrea Mantegna 6*

park was established in 1984, and is now one of the most important wetlands in Italy.

bushes and water-chestnuts. The lotus flowers in bloom in July and August provide a splendid spectacle.

▶ *Take the road to Pozzolo and continue to Valeggio.*

4 Valeggio sul Mincio

Once a military stronghold and a major trading centre, this small town set in a strategic position on the border between Veneto and Lombardy is well known for its exquisite tortellini. Every year, on the second Tuesday in June, a table is laid to seat 4,000 people for the Nodo d'Amore festival, celebrating the delicious 'queen' tortellino. Valeggio's other claim to fame is its massive medieval fortifications. The town is dominated by

library and civic hall) date from the 18th century; Villa Maffei is 17th century, and, behind it, in the old orchard, is splendid Sigurtà Park. With 600,000 irises, 25,000 roses, 30,000 tulips, water lilies, aquatic gardens and thousands of other plants and flowers, this green haven, created in the early 1800s by Giuseppe Carlo Sigurtà, is spread over an area of 50 hectares (123 acres) near the town centre. Entry is only by car, motorcycle or bicycle; there are 13 car-parks, from which you can set off past lawns, woods and small lakes on a 7km (4-mile) trail.

ℹ *Piazza Carlo Alberto*

▶ *Follow signs to Monzambano.*

Japanese maple trees in the Sigurtà Park at Valeggio sul Mincio

Several zones of considerable natural and environmental interest protect the Mincio River, including the Valli del Mincio Nature Reserve and the Bosco della Fontana, at Marmirolo. This area is a mini-ornithological paradise, where herons, mallards, coots, teal and various birds of prey can gather undisturbed. The flora is typical of marshy areas, and includes cane-brakes and aquatic plants, water lilies, buttercups, hibiscus

an imposing medieval castle with towers and crenellated walls, built by the della Scala family, lords of Verona; the Rocca can be visited. There's a splendid view from the top of the plain and Garda's morainic amphitheatre. Another impressive military work, the Visconti dam-bridge (1393), approximately 650m (2,132 feet) long, also forms a distinctive part of the landscape.

The oldest, central part of Valeggio is medieval; the parish church of San Pietro and Palazzo Guarienti (now the

5 Monzambano

This medieval centre overlooking the Mincio Valley is dominated by the walls and towers of its castle, built in the 12th century by the della Scala family to protect access routes to their estates and to garrison the river fords, with a defence line that included nearby Ponti Castle. The old centre, at the foot of the hill, dates mainly from the 15th and 16th centuries. An antiques fair is held on the third Sunday in the month in the handsome Piazzetta delle Arti; the 18th-century parish church of San Michele is impressive. Monzambano and its environs are renowned for excellent cuisine and typical Mantuan dishes.

▶ *Follow the signs to Castellaro Lagusello.*

6 Castellaro Lagusello
A 13th-century castle is reflected in the waters of a small, heart-shaped lake in this charming medieval village. Within its ring of walls are the stronghold, old mansions, low houses and an 18th-century

The Mincio shore within sight of Monzambano

SCENIC ROUTES

The Strada del Vino wine route starts from Ponti sul Mincio and visits Volta Mantovano, Cavriana, Solferino, Monzambano, Castellaro Lagusello and Castiglione delle Stiviere (about 50km/31 miles), winding through the green hills of Mantua and stopping at vineyards that produce DOC Colli Mantovane wines, which can be bought directly from the cellars.

church dedicated to San Nicola. Castellaro Lagusello sits in the centre of a nature reserve named after it and providing a protected habitat for marsh flora and numerous migratory birds.

The lake must have been much larger in the past: the remains of a Bronze Age lake village and relics from the Roman period came to light when the waters receded.

▶ *Follow the signs for Cavriana.*

7 Cavriana
Cavriana Hill was inhabited in neolithic times, and given its castle during the Middle Ages. From the 15th century onwards the Gonzaga court met here, but the settlement was destroyed by Austrians in the mid-18th century (only the tower of the stronghold remains). Villa Silliprandi was built on its foundations and numbered among its guests the Austrian Emperor Franz Josef and King Vittorio Emanuel II. Nineteenth-century Villa Mirra houses the Alto Mantovano Archaeological Museum, one of the most important in Lombardy, which displays finds from Cavriana and the morainic hills of Mantua. Eight rooms tell the history of the entire area, from prehistoric settlements to the Roman period and the Middle Ages, and through to the Renaissance. Of particular interest are finds from the lake villages of Bande di Cavriana and Castellaro Lagusello, which demonstrate that the local populations engaged in trade

and were in contact with the Mediterranean and transalpine areas as early as the 2nd millennium BC. The museum ends with a room where Napoleon III stayed during the battle of San Martino and Solferino.

Just outside Cavriana is the parish church of Santa Maria, a Romanesque building with an attractive brick façade and frescoes.

▶ Continue to Solferino.

8 Solferino

In 1859 Solferino and nearby San Martino witnessed some of the most decisive and bloodiest battles of the century: 40,000 were killed in two clashes – between the Austrians and the Piedmontese army, and between the Austrians and the French. The Austrians were in retreat when a violent storm turned the whole scene into a quagmire. The Rocca, built in the 11th century, now houses a history museum and ossuary, beside which is a memorial to the International Red Cross, built in 1959 with marble from all over the world to celebrate the organisation's centenary.

i Piazza Torelli I

▶ Continue west to Castiglione delle Stiviere.

9 Castiglione delle Stiviere

Castiglione delle Stiviere is the birthplace of Luigi Gonzaga (1568–91), whose remains lie in the baroque basilica; his relics are in the Aloisiano Museum of Holy Art. This is also the home

Little bitterns hidden in the reeds in the Mincio Nature Park

of the International Red Cross Museum, set up to commemorate the historic events that led to the birth of the humanitarian institution. Henri Dunant was a businessman from Geneva, on holiday in the area immediately after the terrible battles of Solferino and San Martino. More than 6,000 wounded were brought to the town and the entire population then numbering about 5,300 – rallied to assist them, providing aid, food, money and clothes. Dunant played his part, too, and was profoundly affected by the experience. Back in Geneva, he organised an international conference with the aim of creating groups of volunteers who could intervene and treat the wounded during battles. The museum has unusual and eloquent historical notes, as well as several displays about the assistance given to, and transportation of, the wounded, including stretchers and field surgical instruments.

i Via Marta Tana I

▶ Return to Verona on the **SS567** towards Desenzano and from here the **A4** motorway towards Venice.

The Upper Lake
near Verona

From the Riviera degli Olivi, with the holiday atmosphere of Garda and Malcésine and the enchantment of Punta San Vigilio, you climb the great mountain of the Veronese and Trentino Riviera: Monte Baldo.

2 DAYS • 180KM • 112 MILES

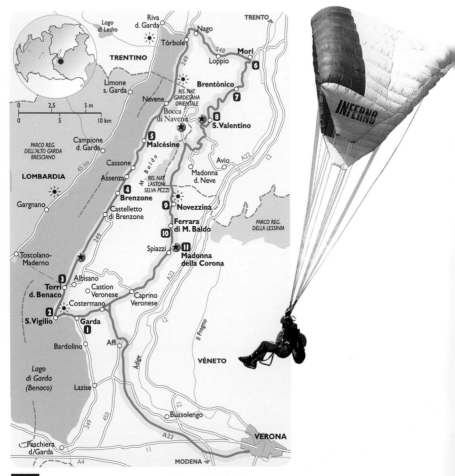

i Via degli Alpini 9, Verona

▶ Follow the signs for the **A22** Brenner motorway and take this northbound to Affi. Here follow the signs for Garda.

❶ Garda

Garda is a traditional holiday resort and the main town on the Riviera degli Olivi – the Veronese shore of Lake Garda – sitting at the centre of a large gulf in Lake Garda. The lakeside and Piazza Catullo form the bustling heart of the town, where people meet and stroll. During the Venetian Republic, Garda was one of the leading lake centres, as is evident in the grand buildings of the old centre. Palazzo dei Capitani, built in the 14th and 15th centuries, was the residence of the Captain of the Lake, who represented the authority of Venice on this shore; the Portico della Losa, built in the 16th century as a landing stage for Palazzo Carlotti, is behind it; Palazzo Fregoso was the residence of the *condottiere* (mercenary leader) Cesare Fregoso, a Genoese exile who served Venice. The parish church of Santa Maria Maggiore dates from the 18th century. Outside town, on the road to San Vigilio, are Villa Albertini, reworked in the 19th century as a castle. During the first War of Independence King Carlo Alberto stayed here, and it was here that, on 10 June, 1848, he ratified the act annexing Lombardy to Piedmont. Villa Carlotti-Canossa was the home of Marchesa Alessandra di Rudini, who had a stormy

relationship with poet Gabriele d'Annunzio.

i Piazza Donatori di Sangue

▶ Continue along the **SS249** (Gardesana Orientale road) to Punta San Vigilio.

❷ Punta San Vigilio

This is one of the most fascinating locations on Lake Garda, extending into the lake, green with olive trees and cypresses. It's been inhabited since Roman times and is probably named after the monk and saint, Vigilio, who lived here in the 13th century. Alternatively, according to a romantic legend in keeping with the spirit of the place, Vigilio was a satyr who loved the nymph Stella; his love

Relaxing at the café tables on a summer's day in Garda

was unrequited, and in a rage he turned her into the rock that emerges from the water beyond the peninsula. Punta San Vigilio is reached along a long avenue lined with centuries-old trees (it leaves the coast road just outside Garda). At the end is the spectacular Villa Guarienti, built in the mid-16th century to a design by Michele Sanmicheli, a famous Venetian architect. Privately owned, and only visible from the outside, it stands austere and imposing in a geometric Renaissance garden. Descending along a cobbled street, you come to a small harbour overlooked by the Locanda San Vigilio, one of the

FOR HISTORY BUFFS

The name 'Garda' probably derives from the German *Warte* – guard, or fortress. This referred to the rampart, now destroyed, that stood on the Rocca hill. It must have been a castle of great strategic importance, giving its name to the lake in place of its original Latin name, *Benacus*.

Winston Churchill and Prince Charles). Further on is the small medieval church of San Vigilio.

▶ *Continue along the lake to Torri del Benaco.*

8 Torri del Benaco

Torri del Benaco was an important Roman fortress, built in a strategic position between Peschiera and Riva. A later stronghold with crenellated towers was built in 1383 for Antonio della Scala, and this still survives. Inside is an art and folk museum, which looks at local industries such as lake fishing, olive oil and quarrying. On the south side of the stronghold, visit the Serra dei Limoni lemon-house, dating from 1760. At the centre of the village is Piazzetta Calderini, lined with

a castle and old Venetian mansions, shaded by olive and plane trees and overlooking a harbour. A car ferry service links Torri del Benaco and Maderno, on the opposite lakeshore.

i *Via Fratelli Lavanda 5*

most exclusive hotels on Lake Garda (past guests include

Above: San Michele's fair at Prada di Brenzone
Left: Punta San Vigilio

▶ *Continue along the shore, called Riviera degli Olivi (Olive Tree Riviera), to Brenzone.*

4 Brenzone

Castelletto di Brenzone is one of the 16 hamlets that form the *comune* of Brenzone; some (such as Magugnano, Porto di Brenzone, Assenza and Cassone) sit on the lakeshore; others (Marniga, Biazza, Fasor, Crero) lie on the slopes of Monte Baldo. Brenzone has a traditional harbour and narrow cobbled

---

RECOMMENDED WALK

On the hillsides behind Torri, surrounded by olive groves and woods of hornbeam, ilex and ash, are the lovely old hamlets of Pai di Sopra and Albisano. (They can also be reached on foot along paths.) The whole area is perfect for mountain biking. Another enjoyable walk, about 10km (6 miles) long, is the Strada dei Castelli, along the old route from Torri to Garda and offering exceptional views.

TOUR

22 **The Upper Lake** near Verona

Upper Lake Garda from the slopes of Monte Baldo

streets that climb from the lake to the oldest quarter, clustered around a small square with an ancient olive tree at the centre.

ⓘ *Frazione Porto, Brenzone*

▶ *Continue for Malcésine.*

5 Malcésine

Malcésine is one of the principal holiday resorts on Lake Garda and is extremely busy in summer. The charm of the old centre, with picturesque old-fashioned narrow streets, is combined with beaches for swimming and sunbathing, and winds that make it a paradise for sailing and windsurfing enthusiasts. Behind it is the high ridge

of Monte Baldo, reached by cableway (Tratto Sino, 15 minutes). In the old centre are the 15th-century Palazzo dei Capitani (containing, among other things, a library named after Goethe, who visited Malcésine in 1786); the 16th-century parish church, and the church of the Madonna del Rosario. Dominating everything is a castle with a massive crenellated tower, which commands a spectacular view of the lake and village.

ⓘ *Via Capitanato 6/8*

▶ *After reaching Tarbole, at the tip of the lake, take the* ***SS240*** *for Nago to Mori.*

6 Mori

This farming town is actually made up of four villages lining the main road. It has an interesting 12th-century parish church with a grand Romanesque bell tower, and some grand 18th-century villas.

▶ *Take the turning that climbs in large bends to the Brentònico plateau.*

7 Brentònico

At an altitude of about 700m (2,296 feet), the green Brentònico plateau was formerly known for its carpenters' and stone-cutters' workshops. Brentònico is the main centre; its oldest houses date from the 17th and 18th centuries. The crypt of the 16th-century church of SS Pietro e Paolo is decorated with 14th-century frescoes.

▶ *Proceed along the road that climbs Monte Baldo towards San Valentino.*

8 San Valentino

This little mountain village, at a height of 1,315m (4,314 feet), is an expanding tourist resort with ski runs, and provides a base for excursions to the nearby winter sports area of Polsa. It's also the starting point for a route that winds up Monte Baldo (2,218m/7,277 feet) through unspoiled scenery and with exceptional views. This area has been described as 'the botanical garden of Europe' and can be explored along numerous routes of varying difficulty and lengths, on foot or mountain bike. A short distance outside the village is the Bes-Cornapiana Nature Reserve, extending over 150 hectares (371 acres) and rich in endemic and rare species.

▶ *Continue along the same road to Novezzina.*

9 Novezzina

Novezzina, at a height of 1,232m (4,042 feet), is the home of the Monte Baldo Botanical Garden, which numbers approximately 500 species of plants and flowers indigenous to Monte Baldo. In spring there are panoramic expanses of primroses, anemones, violets and daffodils; in autumn, there are buttercups and orchids.

▶ *Descend the hairpin bends towards Ferrara di Monte Baldo.*

10 Ferrara di Monte Baldo

Iron mines were worked here in the Roman era, but today Ferrara di Monte Baldo is a small holiday resort (856m/2,808 feet) in the heart of the Monte Baldo area, equipped for winter sports. The hamlet of Novezza has cross-country ski runs, ski lifts and a snowboard run.

▶ *Continue towards Spiazzi.*

11 Madonna della Corona

Shortly before Spiazzi, the sanctuary of the Madonna della Corona (774m/2,539 feet) sits in a spectacular position on a sheer rock face above the Adige Valley.

Hermits once lived here, and a church was built on the site in the 16th century. This sanctuary was erected in 1625 and worshippers venerate a statue of the Virgin Mary which, according to popular belief, was miraculously transported here from Rhodes. You can also reach the sanctuary from Brentino by climbing a long flight of steps.

▶ *Descend to Caprino Veronese and drive to Affi, where you take the **A22** to Verona.*

The sanctuary of the Madonna della Corona above Val d'Adige

THE VENETO

In its heyday, Venice was a mighty city-state that based its power on dominion of the seas. Over several hundred years this power extended beyond the confines of the lagoon and left its mark on part of northern Italy – the two Adriatic shores and the Mediterranean. From the 14th to the 16th century Venice was one of the world's leading centres of political and economic power, and the most independent city in Europe: the only great state to govern itself, without deferring to monarch or bishop. Built on 118 islets in the lagoon, with 411 bridges and 150 canal, including the 3,800m (12,464-foot) Grand Canal, hundreds of mansions and 190 churches, Venice is a remarkable city – unique in its 'streets' of water, its urban design and its extraordinary historical and artistic wealth. On its maze of *calli* (streets), canals, *campi* and *campielli* (squares) stand mansions, churches and museums housing thousands of works of art, including a number of exquisite masterpieces.

Access to Venice is via a long bridge that connects it to the mainland; within the city people get around on foot or by boat (the romantic gondolas or modern vaporetti, the city's water buses). These also run to the main islands in the lagoon, Italy's largest wetland and a delicate ecosystem that extends north of the Po delta to the Lido, Venice's beach and also the venue for the famous Film Festival, and to the more secluded islands of Murano, Burano and Torcello.

The hinterland of Venice is also rich in works of art, featuring the Riviera del Brenta (the water link between the lagoon and Padua), an extraordinary open-air museum dotted with sumptuous residences where the Venetian aristocrats used to spend their holidays and displayed their wealth. Treviso, Padua, Vicenza and their environs are an extraordinary complex of art, history and nature, renowned for their excellent food and wines, as well as for their traditional hospitality.

Santa Maria della Salute on the Grand Canal, an impressive Venetian landmark

Tour 23

Venice is a city that you never finish exploring. Each visit brings fresh discoveries. Stay at least two days (three with an excursion to the islands) to grasp the basics and enjoy a relaxing visit. One day will be enough only to form first impressions. The best plan is to wander round the city on foot and use the water bus service that links the city's various *sestieri* (districts) and the islands that surround it. Seeing Venice from the water (perhaps taking a romantic trip on a gondola) is a must: the city was designed for it. The tour starts from Piazzale Roma (or the nearby Santa Lucia railway station), where you catch a water bus to San Marco along the Grand Canal. The ideal service is Linea 1, which zigzags from one side of the canal to the other, stopping at all the jetties, where you can disembark to visit monuments, museums or parts of the city. Those in a hurry should take Linea 82, which makes just a few stops before reaching Piazza San Marco. From here the tour continues on foot, although if you wish you can take a water bus to the two islands of San Giorgio and Giudecca, which lie opposite the San Marco basin. The water bus is also used to visit the other islands in the lagoon – the Lido to the east, a narrow strip of sand that separates the lagoon from the open sea; and Murano, Burano and Torcello to the north. The fastest crossing to the latter islands leaves from the Fondamenta Nuove at

From the mansions of Venice to the Venetian villas along the Riviera del Brenta

Cannaregio. If you embark in the San Marco area, at Riva degli Schiavoni, you'll sail round Punta di Sant'Elena proof that Venice really is an island. To find your way through the *calli* and *campielli* follow the visitor arrows indicating main sights and routes. Getting lost is not a problem: there will always be someone along the way who'll be glad to give directions.

Tour 24

This tour explores the hinterland of Venice (with the villas of the Riviera del Brenta) and the gentle lands of the Marca Trevigiana (Castelfranco Veneto, Àsolo, Possagno, Conegliano and Treviso), dotted with buildings and works of art by the leading architects and artists of the Veneto area – from Palladio to Giorgione, Paolo Veronese, Cima da Conegliano and Canova.

Tour 25

Another route that winds through areas of great historical and artistic interest visits Padua and Vicenza (two of the leading artistic and cultural centres in the Veneto and in Italy), and some of the most significant towns in their provinces, including the walled towns of Monsélice, Este, Montagnana, Maròstica, Cittadella and Bassano, the Italian capital of grappa and ceramics.

Venice, loved by visitors from all over the world

Venice

1/2 DAYS

Venice is not the world's only city on water – but no other has preserved the urban layout and most of the buildings that enriched it at the height of its splendour. In its golden age, Venice ruled the Mediterranean and today its charm endures.

i *Piazza San Marco 71; Santa Lucia railway station*

▶ *Leave the car in one of the car parks at Piazzale Roma or Isola del Tronchetto (to the right at the end of the bridge across the lagoon) or before the bridge at San Giuliano in Marghera (from here take a bus to Piazzale Roma). Catch the water bus in Piazzale Roma: Linea 1 zigzags along the Grand Canal to San Marco and the Lido, stopping at all the jetties.*

featuring about 200 mansions, most built between the 12th and the 18th century. The Grand Canal is crossed by four bridges (Calatrava, Scalzi, Rialto, Accademia) and winds in an S-shape, linking, as it did centuries ago, the three cornerstones of the city: the point of arrival from the mainland (now Piazzale Roma and the railway); the mercantile centre (Rialto); and the religious and civic centre (San Marco). On the right along the first section, to the Rialto bridge, you can admire the Fondaco dei Turchi (home of the

and Ca' d'Oro (a masterpiece of Venetian Gothic design, called the 'house of gold' for its poly-chrome marble and the gilding that once adorned its façade; it now houses the Giorgio Franchetti Gallery, which exhibits paintings, marbles, bronzes and ceramics).

On the left beyond the Rialto bridge are Ca' Farsetti, the city hall and Palazzo Grassi, the setting for a major modern art collection. On the right are Ca' Foscari, seat of the university, and the 17th-century Ca' Rezzonico, a masterpiece of

The historic Regatta takes place on the Grand Canal

❶ Grand Canal to the Ponte dell'Accademia

After leaving Santa Lucia railway station on the left, you catch your first spectacular view of the Grand Canal, 'the loveliest street in the world'. Lining it are the entrances, landing stages, stores and loggias of the most prestigious mansions in the city, and some splendid churches. It is a virtually uninterrupted stage-set,

Civic Natural History Museum); Ca' Pesaro (one of Venice's most typical mansions, begun in 1628 to a design by Baldassarre Longhena and now housing the museums of modern and oriental art), and Campo della Pescaria (where the fish market is held), with the Fabbriche Nuove, designed by Sansovino in 1554–6 and seat of the mercantile judiciary. On the left are Palazzo Vendramin Calergi (winter home of the municipal casino, which in summer moves to the mainland),

Venetian baroque-style, housing the museum of 18th-century Venetian art (with period furnishings and works by Tiepolo, Pietro Longhi and Guardi).

▶ *Stop to visit the Accademia galleries.*

❷ Gallerie dell'Accademia

These house Venice's main art collection – a catalogue of outstanding Venetian master-pieces. On display are paintings by Paolo Veneziano and Antonio Vivarini (14th to 15th centuries), Giovanni Bellini, Cima da Conegliano, Mantegna, Carpaccio, Giorgione, Lotto (leading Renaissance painters), Tintoretto, Titian and Veronese (great names of 16th-century Venetian painting), Canaletto, Bellotto and Guardi (famous 18th-century landscape painters).

▶ Take the water bus for San Marco again. On the right you will see Palazzo Venier dei Leoni, seat of the Peggy Guggenheim Collection of Contemporary Art, and further on the church of Santa Maria della Salute, a masterpiece of baroque architecture; then Punta della Dogana, the watershed between the Grand Canal and the Giudecca Canal.

FOR HISTORY BUFFS

Venice developed in the shadow of Byzantium in the 6th to 8th centuries, protected by the waters of the lagoon, and was projected on to the world scene by its merchants and mighty institutions. Until 1797 it was known as the Serenissima Repubblica. Mark the Evangelist was the city's patron saint, and his symbol – a winged lion with a book – was in evidence throughout the city's territories. If the book was open it meant that Venice was at peace; if it was closed, the city was at war.

---

3 Piazza San Marco

This is one of the most famous and loveliest squares in the world, the hub of Venetian life. It's closed on three sides by the Procuratie (with famous cafés and shops beneath the porticoes) and on the fourth by the Basilica di San Marco, with nearby Palazzo Ducale; the Campanile (bell tower) di San Marco dominates the scene, rebuilt to its original design after collapsing in 1902. At its base is

---

RECOMMENDED WALK

A beautiful walk along the San Marco Canal leads via Riva degli Schiavoni to the Arsenale (home of the naval museum), the gardens of the Biennale (with the pavilions that house the international exhibition of modern art, one of Venice's most prestigious art events) and the island of Sant'Elena, at the extreme tip of the city. This whole area is the Castello, the working-class district of Venice.

---

the elegant Loggetta by Sansovino (1537–49). The clock tower also stands on the square, erected in 1496–9 and featuring an astronomic clock, the lion of San Marco and a bell on which two bronze Moors strike the hours. The basilica of San Marco, the greatest expression of the Byzantine-Romanesque style that marks Venetian architecture, was founded in the 9th century and subjected over the centuries to many additions and redesigns. Surmounted by five domes, the façade is topped by copies of the four bronze horses brought from Constantinople in 1204; the originals (possibly of Greek origin) are inside the basilica. The interior is decorated with splendid mosaics (11th to 15th centuries) and coloured marble floors, and

---

SPECIAL TO...

Facing Palazzo Ducale, on the opposite side of the San Marco basin, stands the island of San Giorgio Maggiore, reached by water bus, and the church of the same name, designed in 1566 by Palladio. Inside are canvases by Carpaccio, Tintoretto and Bassano, and the monastery, now the home of the Giorgio Cini foundation. The bell tower offers a wonderful view of the city. Giudecca island has another masterpiece by Palladio, the Redentore.

---

houses exquisite works of art, including the treasure of San Marco and the Pala d'Oro (10th to 14th centuries), one of the world's most impressive works of goldsmithery. On the opposite side of the square, the Correr Museum, with its wonderful picture gallery, is housed in the Napoleonic wing that links the old and new Procuratie.

▶ Return towards the canal in Piazzetta San Marco.

Right: the Basilica
Below: The Piazzetta, bell tower, Libreria Sansoviniana and Palazzo Ducale seen from St Mark's Basin

4 Palazzo Ducale

Piazzetta San Marco is the part of Piazza San Marco that opens on to the lagoon, flanked by 16th-century Libreria Sansoviniana (seat of the Marciana library and the archaeological museum) and

Palazzo Ducale, the residence of the doges, lords of the Venetian Republic, and seat of the main city judiciary. The portico, loggia and polychrome marble facing give the building an extraordinarily light appearance, making it the city's foremost work of Gothic architecture. Inside is a succession of chambers and apartments decorated by the leading Venetian artists (of particular note is a *Paradise* by Tintoretto, on the ceiling of the Sala del Maggior Consiglio, perhaps the largest canvas ever painted). It also has a splendid courtyard. To the rear of Palazzo Ducale is the Bridge of Sighs, one of the best-known postcard images in Venice. This covered bridge was built in the early 17th century to connect the old palace prisons with the new prisons, and owes its name to the lamentations of the prisoners crossing it.

▶ *From Piazzetta dei Leoni, pass behind Palazzo Ducale, cross Rio Palazzo and turn left into Calle della Chiesa and Calle dei Mercanti; turn left along Ruga Giuffa to Campo Santa Maria Formosa. Follow Calle Lunga Santa Maria Formosa, on the right, before turning left into Calle Trevisana and Fondamenta Bressana, leading to Campo SS Giovanni e Paolo.*

5 Basilica di SS Giovanni e Paolo (San Zanipòlo)

With its imposing brick façade, the Gothic church of SS Giovanni e Paolo is, together with that of the Frari, one of the great Venetian churches of the preaching orders. Founded by the Dominicans in the 14th century, it contains the funeral monuments of several illustrious figures. Beside it is the white Renaissance façade of the former Scuola Grande di San Marco, now annexed to the city hospital. Also in the square is the 15th-century monument to Colleoni by Verocchio, a masterpiece of Renaissance sculpture.

The Rialto bridge on the Grand Canal, until the 19th century the only link between the two parts of the city

▶ *Follow Calle Larga Gallina and Fondamenta Piovan.*

6 Santa Maria dei Miracoli

Faced with polychrome marble, Santa Maria dei Miracoli was built in 1489 by Pietro Lombardo to house a *Madonna and Child* created in 1408 and believed to have miraculous properties. The church is one of the most elegant Renaissance buildings in Venice.

▶ *Go into Campo Santa Maria Nuova and follow Salizzada San Canciano before turning right into Salizzada San Giovanni Crisostomo. This leads to Campo San Bartolomeo; go along Salizzada Pio X to the Rialto bridge.*

7 Rialto

The Rialto is the oldest bridge on the Grand Canal. Built in wood, probably as early as the 12th century, it was reconstructed in its present form in the late 16th century. Lined with shops, it links the area around Piazza San Marco (reached from the Mercerie, the busiest street in Venice, with dozens of shops) to the bustling and picturesque market quarter.

▶ *Continue along Ruga degli Orefici and turn left into Ruga Vecchia San Giovanni. Then go straight on in the same direction, following the signs for Campo San Polo.*

8 Campo San Polo

This is the largest *campo* in the city (the only square in Venice known as a *piazza* is that of San Marco) – the hub of everyday life and a splendid arena for summer entertainment. On it stands the Byzantine church of San Polo, rebuilt in the 19th century and containing paintings by Tintoretto, Palma the Younger and Giambattista Tiepolo.

▶ *Take Salizzada San Polo and turn left into Calle 2a Saoneri, then right into Rio Terà, leading to Campo dei Frari.*

9 Santa Maria dei Frari

Built from the 14th century on in Gothic style by the Franciscans, the vast church of Santa Maria dei Frari guards many historic and artistic legacies of the Venetian

Republic, as well as masterpieces such as the *Assunta* by Titian (1516–18), on the main altar, an *Enthroned Madonna* by Giovanni Bellini (1488), in the sacristy, and *Madonna of Cà' Pesaro*, by Titian (1526), at the second altar in the left aisle. Funerary monuments include those to Titian and Canova.

▶ *Proceed to nearby Campo San Rocco.*

10 Scuola Grande di San Rocco

Begun in 1489 and completed in 1560, the Scuola Grande is named after St Roch, the patron saint of plague victims, and houses the largest cycle of works by Tintoretto. There are mirrors to allow viewing of the paintings on the ceilings, and you can admire a marvellous cycle of large canvases painted between 1564 and 1587 (upper floor), as well as eight canvases painted between 1583 and 1587 (ground floor).

▶ *Take Calle Scalater and then turn right into Calle dei Preti. Continue in the same direction following the signs for Piazzale Roma and passing through Fondamenta Minotto, Campo dei Tolentini and the former Papadopoli garden.*

Torah scrolls in a synagogue in the city's old Ghetto

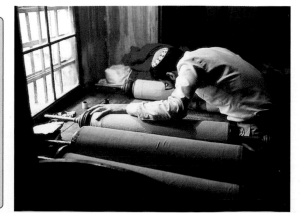

EXCURSION 1

▶ *Linea DM from Piazzale Roma takes you straight to Murano.*

Murano

Murano is the island of glass. In the 13th century the glassworks were confined to the island to avoid the possibility of their furnace flames setting fire to the centre of Venice. Master glassmakers still work on the island, and can be seen creating masterpieces big and small in their workshops. The Museum of Glass Art tells the history of the industry, for which Venice has been world-famous since the Roman era. The island's church, SS Maria e Donato, is a significant example of Venetian Byzantine architecture, built in the 12th century and incorporating part of an earlier building. It has a magnificent apse with two rows of arches and, inside, mosaics dating from the 12th and 13th centuries.

EXCURSION 2

▶ *Burano and Torcello are a 40-minute water bus ride on Linea LN from Murano.*

Murano's artistic glassware

Burano

This is the island of lace-making, the craft traditionally practised by Venetian women. Today you can visit the lace-making school housed in Palazzo del Podestà. Bustling and lively, Burano – with its distinctive, multi-coloured fishermen's houses – is one of the still genuinely working class islands in the lagoon, although the fishing industry that once flourished here is now in decline. The 16th-century church of San Martino stands on the main square.

Torcello

Lying in the northernmost part of the lagoon, Torcello is one of its most fascinating islands, a favourite of writer Ernest Hemingway and of countless other travellers seeking peace, tranquillity and unusual charm.

Visit the beautiful cathedral of Santa Maria dell'Assunta (erected in the 7th century and rebuilt in the 11th), linked by a portico to the baptistery and the Romanesque church of Santa Fosca. Inside are precious and beautiful mosaics dating from the 12th and 13th centuries and created by the Venetian Byzantine school. The 11th-century bell tower is one of the tallest in the lagoon. The Estuary Museum contains finds and works of art that trace the history of the lagoon.

Left: colourful houses on Burano
Opposite: a gondola – *the* way to travel in Venice

Delights of
the Veneto

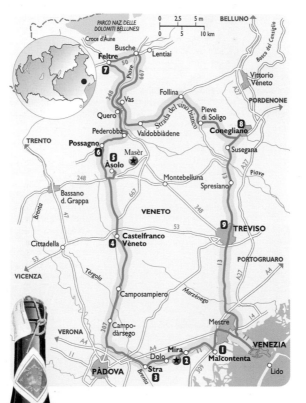

A journey from the spectacular villas of the Riviera del Brenta to the timeless charm of Àsolo, featuring magnificent work by artists from Palladio to Paolo Veronese, and Giorgione to Cima da Conegliano and Canova. At the heart of this tour is the enchanting borderland of Treviso.

ITINERARY		
VENEZIA	▶	**Malcontenta (9km-5½m)**
MALCONTENTA	▶	**Mira (12km-7½m)**
MIRA	▶	**Stra (8km-5m)**
STRA	▶	**Castelfranco Veneto (45km-28m)**
CASTELFRANCO VENETO	▶	**Àsolo (20km-12½m)**
ÀSOLO	▶	**Possagno (9km-5½m)**
POSSAGNO	▶	**Feltre (34km-21m)**
FELTRE	▶	**Conegliano (88km-55m)**
CONEGLIANO	▶	**Treviso (25km-15½m)**
TREVISO	▶	**Venezia (30km-18½m)**

3 DAYS • 280KM • 174 MILES

i *Piazza San Marco 71; Santa Lucia railway station, Venice*

▶ *From Mestre take the SS11 towards Padua and after approximately 5km (3 miles) follow the signs for Malcontenta.*

❶ Malcontenta

Villa Foscari, better known as Malcontenta, in the village of the same name, is a fitting introduction to a visit to the Riviera del Brenta, along the old course of the river that links Venice with Padua. One of the loveliest and best-loved spots in Veneto, the Riviera is virtually an open-air museum, filled with an astonishing number of architectural and artistic masterpieces. Venetian noblemen built their imposing country residences on the banks of the Brenta between the late 15th and 18th centuries, entrusting their construction to the most celebrated architects and artists, starting with Andrea Palladio and Veronese. These villas were more than places to live: they were symbols of vast landed wealth, rivalling each other for pomp and luxury. In

A tourist boat on the waters of the Riviera del Brenta, near Mira

summer they became palaces of pleasure, as the rich took their holidays here.

Malcontenta is the work of Andrea Palladio (1508–80), the greatest 16th-century architect in Veneto, who designed it around 1555. Housing 16th-century frescoes depicting mythological scenes, the villa earned its name ('discontented') from a legend about a noblewoman from Ca' Foscari, who was imprisoned here under suspicion of adultery.

▶ *Back on the SS11, proceed to Mira.*

❷ Mira

Mira has one of the highest concentrations of villas, some of which are open to visitors. Just

before you arrive in Mira, on the left bank of the Brenta, you will see the 18th-century Villa Seriman (Widmann-Foscari) and, on the opposite bank, the 17th-century outbuildings of Villa Valmarana, containing frescoes by Tiepolo dating from the late 18th century. These are followed, slightly set back from the river, by Villa Contarini dei Leoni, Villa Levi-Moreno, Villa Alessandri, Palazzo Bonlini Pisani, Villa Mocenigo-Boldù, Villa Venier-Contarini and Villa Swift-Barozzi on the left; and Villa Querini-Stampalia, Villa Bonfadini, Villa Corner, Villa

Bon, Villa Moro-Lin, Palazzo Persico, Villa Selvatico and Villa Brusoni on the right. Overlooking the Brenta River are Villa Rocca-Ciceri, Palazzo Molin and Villa Fini, facing which are Villa Velluti and Villa Tito.

▶ *Continue along the **SS11** to Stra.*

₃ Stra

Stra is the setting for the well-known and now nationally owned Villa Pisani, the greatest villa in the Veneto, complete with box tree maze, and one of the last to be built. It was built for the Pisani family between 1736 and 1756 to celebrate the appointment of Alvise Pisani as doge. In 1807 it was sold to Napoleon I and is now a national monument. The front, facing the canal, has the look of a palace; the park railings open at its sides. Inside are courtyards, porticoes and a majestic double-height ballroom with a grandiose fresco depicting the glories of the Pisani family, painted in 1760 by Giambattista Tiepolo. Equally impressive is the park, with pools flanked by statues, a semicircular building with the stables in the background and the 1721 box tree maze. While at Stra, pay a visit to Villa

Above: Villa Pisani at Stra
Left: the central block of Villa Barbaro at Màser, resembling a temple with porticoed wings

SPECIAL TO...

Villa Barbaro, perhaps the loveliest of the Venetian villas, stands at Màser, at the foot of the Àsolo hill. It was built for Cardinal Daniele Barbaro around 1557 by Palladio, and was decorated by another great artist, Paolo Veronese, who created one of his best fresco cycles here. Standing in the garden is the Templet, one of Palladio's last works, completed in the year of his death (1580).

Lazara-Pisani, known as the
Barbariga, Villa Badoer-Draghi
(late 15th century), the 16th-
century Villa Gritti and Villa
Foscarini-Negrelli-Rossi.

▶ *Continue along the **SS11**
to the junction with the
SS307, which leads to
Castelfranco.*

4 Castelfranco Veneto
Developed at the end of the
12th century as Treviso's military
and administrative outpost on
the Brenta plain, Castelfranco
Veneto occupied a strategic position, where the Via Postumia
and the Padua-Àsolo road
crossed. In a bid to attract
residents after the town's
foundation, anyone who moved
here was exempt (*franchi*) from
taxes. The castle still forms the
town's centre – a fortified square
with walls 930m (3,050 feet) long
and 17m (56 feet) high, which
encircled the original settlement.
Eight towers and four gates
complete the complex. Within
the walls is the Duomo (cathedral, 18th century), which houses
an *Enthroned Madonna with
Saints Liberalis and Francis*, a
famous work by young
Giorgione (1477–1510), the

Below: the walls of Castelfranco
Veneto

master of Venetian painting, who was born in Castelfranco. Not far away is a Gothic building commonly called 'Giorgione's house': a fresco in one of its rooms portraying *The Symbols of the Liberal and Mechanical Arts* is attributed to him.

i Via Francesco Maria Preti 66

▶ Follow signs north for Àsolo.

Right: this poster is a reminder of the connection between Àsolo and the actress Eleonora Duse, who is buried there
Below: old fountain in Àsolo

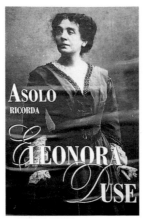

5 Àsolo
Àsolo is one of the most fascinating places in Italy, a splendid garden city with picturesque views, impressive architecture, a mild climate and a sophisticated air. In its time it's been the capital of a non-existent kingdom, a centre of poetry and literature and, more recently, a bolt-hole for poets and artists, English aristocrats, American magnates, dandies and adventurous noblewomen. It all began in 1473, when Caterina Cornaro, a cultured Venetian noblewoman, and recent widow of Jacques II of Lusignano, Lord of Cyprus, decided to give her territories to

Venice. In exchange the Venetian Republic granted her the lordship of Àsolo, where she settled in 1489 and opened her court to poets, scholars, painters and sculptors – a 'kingdom' based not on arms but on culture and devotion to beauty. Cornaro left her mark on the city for centuries to come. Set in splendid isolation at the top of a hill, the town has retained the extraordinary atmosphere that once attracted guests such as Henry James, Ernest Hemingway, Gabriele d'Annunzio and Eleonora Duse, who made this her last refuge and is buried here. At the heart of the old centre is Piazza Maggiore, with the Loggia del Capitano (15th century) housing the Civic Museum. A little further on is Palazzo Beltramini, the town hall, and the medieval Porta del Colmarion. A stepped path leads to the Rocca, built in the 12th century by the Ezzelini family, and giving exceptional views.

i Piazza Garibaldi 73

▶ Follow the signs for Possagno.

6 Possagno
This is the birthplace of Antonio Canova (1757–1822), famous Venetian neo-classical sculptor. You can visit his home and a gallery of plaster casts, with its collection of nearly all his plaster models and original studies, along with bronze preparations

made before the final copies were created in marble. Climb to the Canova Temple, the mausoleum designed and financed by the sculptor from 1819 and now containing his tomb.

▶ Drive towards Pederobba and here take the SS667 towards Belluno. At Quero turn off for Feltre following the SS348.

7 Feltre
Perched on a hill at the westernmost tip of Val Belluno, Feltre was, in its 15th-century heyday, one of the leading suppliers of iron, copper, silver and timber for the Venetian Republic. The link with Venice, which had been so profitable, brought trouble when the town was razed to the ground in the early 16th century by armies of the League of Cambrai. It was promptly rebuilt, from the foundations up. This explains its homogeneous Venetian-style old centre, featuring buildings of the 16th and 17th centuries, with many façades decorated with frescoes and graffiti. The main street, Via Mezzaterra, climbs through the old town past painted mansions with projecting roofs to Piazza Maggiore. Standing on the square are Palazzo della Ragione (mid-16th century; its portico is attributed to Palladio), the neo-Gothic Palazzo Guarnieri and, higher up, the church of San Rocco and the castle. The Civic Museum is of interest and has a picture gallery devoted mainly to Venetian painters (from Gentile Bellino to Marco Ricci), a collection of period furnishings and historic mementoes. On the

> **RECOMMENDED WALK**
>
> Not far from Feltre is the Dolomiti Bellunesi National Park, 32,000 hectares (79,070 acres) of untamed nature with interesting excursions. Its nearest point of access to Feltre is the Croce Daune Pass, approximately 10km (6 miles) to the northwest.

edge of the centre are the 16th-century cathedral and an archaeological site with remains of Roman and early Christian buildings.

i *Piazzetta Trento Trieste 9*

▶ *Follow the SS50 towards Belluno to Busche and here take the SS667 to just past Vas. Follow the road left that leads via Valdobbiàdene, Follina and Pieve di Soligo to Conegliano.*

8 Conegliano
One of the main financial centres in Treviso province, Conegliano has ancient origins, still evident in the scenic Rocca di Castelvecchio that dominates the town; inside, the Civic Museum exhibits archaeological finds and paintings. The old quarter of the town developed around Via XX Settembre, lined with mansions dating from the 15th and 16th centuries and entered by two gates, Porta Ruio and Porta Monticano. On the central Piazza Cima are 18th-century Palazzo del Comune and the Accademia theatre (1846–68).

Near by is the Scuola dei Battuti, entirely adorned with early 16th-century frescoes, and the Duomo (cathedral), with a valuable altar piece, *Enthroned Madonna with Saints*, executed in 1493 by Cima da Conegliano. Rising behind the Duomo is the 15th-century house where the artist was born.

The Calieròn caves at Fregona on the Cansiglio plateau

i *Via XX Settembre 61*

▶ *Follow the SS13 to Treviso.*

9 Treviso
A lively and stylish city, packed with art and culture, Treviso is the capital of one of the most industrious and wealthiest provinces in northern Italy. Elegant, dynamic, full of charm and zest, it's also known for its excellent cuisine, based on the re-interpretation of old traditional recipes, the best of which is the famous Treviso red

endive. The medieval and intricate centre is clustered within a ring of 16th-century walls, punctured with gates, alongside which runs a moat fed from the Sile River. Narrow, often winding streets, small squares and houses with frescoed façades crowd around the two main squares – Piazza del Duomo and Piazza dei Signori, linked by Calmaggiore. Piazza del Duomo is dominated by the grand medieval Duomo (cathedral), whose apse was reconstructed

The colours and atmosphere of Treviso

Palazzo dei Trecento (where the communal assemblies met), whose 16th-century arcade is a popular meeting place. Not far away are the 13th-century Loggia dei Cavalieri (where Treviso's nobility used to assemble) and Monte di Pietà, where the Rettori chapel is richly decorated with 17th-century leather panels and large canvases showing stories from the Bible.

There are many more old churches in the areas near the

Dominicans. The church of San Francesco, which served as the town's pantheon in the Middle Ages, houses the tombs of Francesca, Petrarch's daughter and Piero, Dante's son. Innocenti Chapel, in the 14th-century church of Santa Caterina dei Servi di Maria, has an important cycle of frescoes depicting *The Life of St Ursula*, painted by Tommaso da Modena and taken in 1883 from the church of Santa Margherita. Santa Maria

Maggiore, or the sanctuary of the Madonna Granda, was founded between the 8th and 9th centuries and has been altered many times.

The old civic museum is closing and its collection is gradually being transferred to the former church of Santa Caterina. It has an archaeological collection, a picture gallery with works mainly by Venetian painters (Giovanni Bellini, Cima da Conegliano, Jacopo Bassano) and a modern art collection. Housed in the museum is the Salce collection, a large assortment of advertising posters that records changes in habits and consumption between 1944 and 1962.

in the 15th and 16th centuries; the rest dates back to the 18th century. The cathedral interior is rich in works of art, including frescoes by Pordenone and an *Annunciation* by Titian (1520). Around Piazza dei Signori stand the various buildings of the communal judiciary – Palazzo del Podestà, surmounted by the civic tower, Palazzo Pretorio and

town walls. Gothic San Nicolò was built from 1231 by the Dominicans, and is notable for the tall windows in the apse, the huge pillars and the late 14th-century frescoes by Tommaso da Modena. The same artist created the frescoes for the chapter house of the adjacent convent in 1352, depicting a series of portraits of celebrated

i *Piazza Monte di Pietà 8*

▶ *Return to Venice on the SS13.*

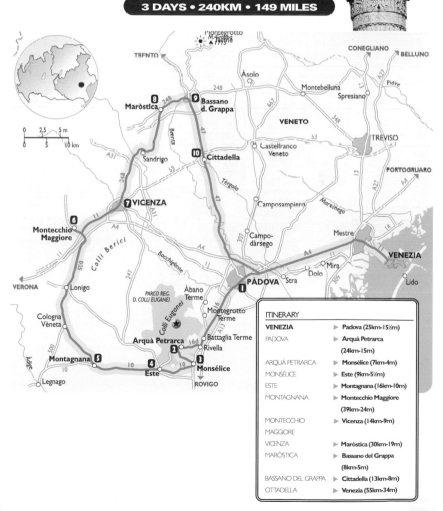

From Padua
to Vicenza

This tour visits Padua – with splendid squares,
the Basilica del Santo and Giotto's frescoes in
the Arena Chapel – and the walled towns of
Monselice, Este, Montagnana and Cittadella,
before arriving in Vicenza, the city of Palladio
and Tiepolo.

3 DAYS • 240KM • 149 MILES

ITINERARY		
VENEZIA	▶	Padova (25km-15½m)
PADOVA	▶	Arquà Petrarca (24km-15m)
ARQUÀ PETRARCA	▶	Monsélice (7km-4m)
MONSÉLICE	▶	Este (9km-5½m)
ESTE	▶	Montagnana (16km-10m)
MONTAGNANA	▶	Montecchio Maggiore (39km-24m)
MONTECCHIO MAGGIORE	▶	Vicenza (14km-9m)
VICENZA	▶	Maròstica (30km-19m)
MARÒSTICA	▶	Bassano del Grappa (8km-5m)
BASSANO DEL GRAPPA	▶	Cittadella (13km-8m)
CITTADELLA	▶	Venezia (55km-34m)

▶ *Take the **A4** motorway to
Padova (Padua).*

❶ Padova (Padua)

The city of St Anthony and
Giotto is full of art treasures. Its
fascinating old centre has
retained much of the medieval
layout on which the Renaissance
and 18th-century city grew. 'The
Saint' is how the locals affectionately refer to St Anthony, whose
Basilica del Santo (raised just
after his death in 1232) has for
centuries been a place of
pilgrimage. Padua boasts what is

perhaps the finest masterpiece
by Giotto, the greatest Italian
painter of the Middle Ages, in
the Arena (or Scrovegni) Chapel,
decorated with frescoes (1303–5)
depicting *The Lives of the Virgin
and Christ*. Right in the heart of
the old centre are Piazza delle
Erbe, Piazza della Frutta and
Piazza dei Signori. Bustling
Piazza delle Erbe, with its fruit
and vegetable stalls, is dominated by the 13th-century
Palazzo della Ragione, beneath
which are tempting food shops.
Erected in the 13th century as
the seat of the law courts, its
large chamber was once decorated with frescoes by Giotto;

Giusto de'Menabuoi. Also in the
centre is Palazzo Bo', seat of the
prestigious university founded
in 1222 (Galileo Galilei taught
here, among others). It also has
the oldest anatomical theatre in
the world (1594).

Of note among the churches
are the Romanesque-Gothic
Eremitani Church, with the
Ovetari Chapel, on which
Mantegna worked (the Civic
Museum is housed in an
annexe), and the 12th-century
Santa Sofia. Set slightly apart
from the centre are Piazza del
Santo and Prato della Valle. The
former is the setting for the
Oratory of San Giorgio, with

Prato della Valle in Padua – one of
the largest squares in Europe

FOR CHILDREN

The Padua Amusement Park is
a multi-purpose centre
comprising leisure and
refreshment areas. In the
Palachildren, kids can dive,
climb and roll about with Soft
Play, and there are mini jeeps
and inflatable games as well as
countless other amusements.
Adults can while away the time
bowling or playing one of the
100-plus video games.

they were destroyed by a fire in
1420 and today it contains one of
the largest cycles of Italian frescoes on an astrological theme
(*c*1430). On the edge of Piazza
dei Signori (dedicated to the da
Carrara family) are the Loggia
del Consiglio or Gran Guardia
(1496–1553) and Palazzo del
Capitanio (1605), with the Arco
dell'Orologio on its façade. Not
far away, in the square of the
same name, are the Duomo
(cathedral, rebuilt in the mid-
16th century to a design by
Michelangelo) and the
Baptistery, decorated with
14th-century frescoes by

frescoes by Altichiero (1379–84),
and the 15th-century Scuola
del Santo, with frescoes by
16th-century Venetian artists,
including Titian. It's dominated,
though, by the basilica of
Sant'Antonio, built between
the 13th and 14th centuries and
rich in works of art. In front of
it is the splendid monument
to Gattamelata created by
Donatello in 1453. The Prato
della Valle is extremely large,
and has the Isola Memmia at
its centre, surrounded by the
canal and adorned with statues
of local dignitaries. The
grandiose 16th-century basilica

of Santa Giustina stands at one end. The nearby botanical garden was the first in Europe, established in 1545.

i *Piazza del Santo; Vicolo Pedrocchi*

▶ *Leave Padua southwards on the SS16. At Rivella turn right towards Arquà Petrarca, following the SS16d.*

2 Arquà Petrarca

Arquà is a medieval village in the heart of the Colli Euganesi Nature Park. Its name is bound to that of Francesco Petrarca (Petrarch, 1304–74), who spent the last years of his life in this secluded spot in the hills. The poet's tomb has stood in the village square since 1389; slightly higher up, you can visit his house.

▶ *From Arquà follow the signs to Monsélice.*

3 Monsélice

Monsélice – the ancient Roman *Mons Silicis* – is, together with Este and Montagnana, one of

the walled towns that guarded the territory south of Padua in the Middle Ages. On its hilltop, the Rocca dominates the old medieval centre; the climb there passes the spectacular sanctuary of the Sette Chiese (designed in 1605 by Vincenzo Scamozzi and decorated with frescoes by Venetian Palma the Younger). The medieval castle was restored in the 1930s by Count Vittorio Cini, who also collected old furnishings to add to the evocation of another age. The halls, library and large kitchen are open to visitors, and house, among other things, a rich collection of weapons

Villa dei Vescovi at Luvigliano, surrounded by the rolling Euganean hills

The Palio parades beneath the famous walls of Montagnana

(halberds, armour, swords) made between the 14th and 18th centuries.

ⓘ *Via del Santuario 6*

▶ *Take the SS10 towards Este.*

4 Este
Surrounded by medieval walls, ancient Este has been inhabited since the 9th century BC, when it was occupied by the *Veneti*, an Indo-European people who may have come from Asia Minor (and who gave their name to the region). It was a major centre during the Roman era, and in

about AD 1000 saw the rise of the powerful Este family, who were destined to become one of the leading Italian dynasties. One branch of the Este family became dukes of Ferrara, Modena and Reggio Emilia. A 14th-century castle and its mighty keep dominate the town; its ring of walls, approximately 1km (half a mile) long, topped with Guelph crenellation and punctuated by 12 towers, surrounds a slope now planted up as public gardens.

Beside the entrance to the gardens is the National Atestine Museum, housed in the only room to have escaped a fire in the 16th-century Palazzo Mocenigo. On display is one of

the most important archaeological collections in northern Italy, giving an overview of this ancient Venetian civilisation. Nowadays the heart of town is Piazza Maggiore, where you'll find the town hall and the Gothic Palazzetto degli Scaligeri. Interesting churches include the 17th-century Duomo and Santa Maria delle Consolazioni, which has a rare Roman mosaic floor.

ⓘ *Via Negri 9*

▶ *Continue along the SS10 to Montagnana.*

5 Montagnana
The crenellated walls enclosing Montagnana, more than 2km (1 mile) long, are one of the most famous and complete examples of medieval military architecture in Europe. Built between 1360 and 1362, they feature 24 towers, four gates and various fortifications including the Rocca degli Alberi and the castle of San Zeno, which today houses the Civic Museum. Within the walls is the well restored medieval village. On its central square, Piazza Vittorio Emanuele II, stands the 15th-century Duomo (cathedral). The cathedral doorway was designed by Jacopo Sansovino around 1530; inside is a *Transfiguration* by Veronese (1555). The town hall was built in 1538 to a design by Michele Sanmicheli of Verona. All around are characteristic old streets, many lined with porticoes (such as Via Carrarese and Via Matteotti), shops, workshops, inns and restaurants. Make sure you taste Montagnana's delicious cured ham. Outside the walls stands Palazzo Pisani, by Palladio.

▶ *Follow the signs for Cologna Veneta and here take the SS500 past Lonigo to Montecchio Maggiore, 39km (24 miles).*

6 Montecchio Maggiore
According to tradition Montecchio was the home of the

Montecchi family, models for the Montagues, the family of Shakespeare's hero Romeo. Approximately 2km (1 mile) up on the hills near Montecchio are two castles said to be those of the Montagues and Capulets; actually they belonged to the della Scala family. The most interesting building, on the edge of the village, is the 18th-century Villa Cordellina Lombardi, designed by Venetian architect Giorgio Massari and of Italy's leading art centres. The 16th century was a period of particular local splendour, and its greatest representative was Andrea Palladio, talented interpreter of classical canons and creator of a new architectural language. Thanks to Palladio's monuments, Vicenza has become one of UNESCO's world heritage sites.

The city's past is visible in its perfectly preserved old centre and in the dozens of villas Vincenzo Scamozzi, begun in the late 16th century and completed in the mid-17th century) and the Duomo (cathedral), rebuilt several times between the 14th and 16th centuries; its large dome was another of Palladio's projects.

On the hills surrounding the city is the Basilica di Monte Berico, now in baroque form, built on the site where the Madonna is said to have appeared in the early 15th

embellished with frescoes by Giambattista Tiepolo in 1743.

▶ *Return to the junction with the SS11 and follow this left to Vicenza.*

7 Vicenza
This is the home of Palladio and Tiepolo, but also of gold – in a thousand goldsmiths' firms – and excellent cuisine, the most typical local dish being *baccalà mantecato* (minced dried cod cooked with milk). But art comes first. Vicenza has the most amazing artistic heritage, dating from the Middle Ages (when it was enclosed within a ring of walls) to the 'Venetian' centuries, when it became one

dotted all around it. Standing on the old streets and squares in the centre are some of Palladio's most important monuments – the basilica (symbol of the city and one of Palladio's masterpieces, started in 1549) and the Loggia del Capitaniato on Piazza dei Signori, the monumental heart of the city; the fascinating Teatro Olimpico (conceived by Palladio and completed by Vincenzo Scamozzi of Vicenza), and Palazzo Chiericati (also by Palladio, 1550), housing the City Picture Gallery, of particular importance for its Venetian paintings. Also of considerable artistic importance in the centre are Palazzo del Comune (one of the most significant works by

The Rotonda, by Palladio, in the environs of Vicenza

century, after being invoked to ward off a plague. The refectory has a large canvas by Paolo Veronese portraying *The Supper of St Gregory the Great* (1572).

About 3km (2 miles) from the centre is Villa Valmarana ai Nani, splendidly decorated by the artists Giambattista and Giandomenico Tiepolo with a cycle of frescoes. Continuing along the Valmarana road you come to Villa Almerico-Capra, a famous masterpiece by Palladio known as the Rotonda.

ℹ *Piazza dei Signori 8; Piazza Matteotti 12*

A chess game is played in costume on the square in Maròstica

i *Piazza Castello 1*

▶ *Leave Vicenza to the north on the SS248 for Maròstica.*

8 Maròstica

Lying at the foot of the Vicenza foothills (Sette Comuni plateau), Maròstica overlooks the plain as far as Vicenza. Protected by walls, this was an important stronghold of the della Scala family, who built Castello Inferiore and Castello Superiore here in the 14th century. The former served as a defence against enemy attacks and the latter to control the territory from its high vantage point. Every two years a famous chess game is held in the main square (marked with a chess-board), between players dressed in period costume. The Castello Inferiore, on the square, houses a small museum containing the costumes. The nearby church of Sant'Antonio Abate houses an important altarpiece by Jacopo and Francesco Bassano (1574). Climbing the steps that lead to the 17th-century church of the Carmine, you pass the path leading to the Castello Superiore, now a romantic ruin.

▶ *Continue along the SS248 to Bassano del Grappa.*

9 Bassano del Grappa

This small town has great charm, and is known for its fine ceramics and its grappa, produced in some of Italy's most famous distilleries. Immortalised in a traditional song, the ancient covered bridge (rebuilt in 1948) that crosses the river has become the town's symbol. At one end of it is a traditional tavern, which leads to the Museum of the Alpine Soldiers, housing relics

---

SCENIC ROUTES

From Bassano the Strada Cadorna climbs in steep hairpin bends to Monte Grappa. Along with the surrounding mountains this was the scene of bloody World War I battles, of which many signs remain. At the top of Monte Grappa, in a splendidly scenic position between the Brenta valleys and the Piave River, is a memorial chapel containing the remains of more than 22,000 casualties.

FOR HISTORY BUFFS

In the Middle Ages Cittadella was, together with nearby Castelfranco, the main administrative and military centre on the Brenta plain. The towns were founded between the late 12th and the early 13th centuries, Cittadella by its Paduan rulers, Castelfranco by Treviso.

---

and war records; at the other is a small Grappa Museum. Extending around squares and irregular streets lined with porticoes, the centre is a succession of old mansions, many with decorated façades.

The history of this area is traced in the local museum, with an archaeological section and a picture gallery containing works by the leading Venetian artists (the da Ponte family, Francesco, Jacopo, Girolamo and Leandro, known as the da Bassano family, Giandomenico Tiepolo, Marco Ricci and Antonio Canova – many of whose sketches and casts are kept here). On the Piazza della Libertà, next to Piazza Garibaldi, are the Loggia del Comune, with a clock dating

The covered wooden bridge that crosses the Brenta at Bassano

from the late 16th century, coats-of-arms and frescoes, and the church of San Giovanni Battista. Palazzo Sturm, built in the 18th century sheer above the Brenta river, houses an interesting Ceramic Museum. Bassano was (and still is) one of Italy's leading ceramic-producing centres. On the edge of the town are the medieval Castello Superiore and the Duomo (cathedral), built over the earlier parish church of Santa Maria and repeatedly extended until the end of the 17th century.

i Largo Corona d'Italia 35

▶ *Return southwards on the straight SS47 to Cittadella.*

⑩ Cittadella
Cittadella was founded around 1220 on a strategic site which the Romans had previously occupied, at the point where the roads from Padua to Bassano and from Vicenza to Treviso met. Its plan combines function with symbolism, making it one of the most interesting examples of the town-fortress: circular, with two main streets intersecting at right angles to divide the town into four symmetrical quarters. The ring of walls, 1,461m (4,793 feet) long, is interrupted by 12 towers, 16 smaller towers and four gates,

placed at the head of each main street. The main streets converge on the central square, where the Loggia (town hall) and neo-classical parish church of SS Prosdocimo e Donato stand. Other interesting monuments are Palazzo Pretorio and the Malta Tower, constructed in 1251 as a prison where Ezzelino da Romano could incarcerate his political enemies, and mentioned by Dante in the Ninth Canto of his *Purgatory*.

i Porta Bassanesi 2

▶ *Continue along the SS47 and join the A4 motorway towards Venice at the Padova est entrance.*

NAVIGATION

To enjoy the beautiful scenery in peace and stay away from the traffic, consider using one of the many ferry, boat and hydroplane services that plough the waters of Italy's main lakes daily. Navigation companies provide daily links between the main lake towns, with stopping points en route. They also organise mini-cruises and dinner dances, as well as regular excursions to the islands (book ahead in high season).

For general information on the services contact: Ministry of Transport and Navigation, Gestione Governativa Navigazione sui Laghi Maggiore, di Garda, di Como, Via Ludovico Ariosto 21, Milan, tel: (02) 467 6101, fax: (02) 4676 1059, www.navigazionelaghi.it.

A useful reference when planning personalised tours is the Regione Lombardia website www.regione.lombardia.it

Lake Maggiore

Navigazione Lago Maggiore has 28 ferries, motorships, hydroplanes and catamarans, which provide the Arona-Angera, Stresa-Intra-Laveno, Cànnero-Luino-Cannobio and Locarno-Magadino services. There are numerous services, approximately every half hour, from Stresa to the Borromean islands. For information and bookings call free phone 800 551801.

Daily services and cruises organised by tourist promotion boards are increased in summer and at weekends between late July and late August. There are also hourly evening services to and from the Borromean islands (Stresa, Isola Bella, Isola Superiore, Baveno and return).

For all information on routes and timetables, which change from season to season, contact: Navigazione Lago Maggiore, Operational Management, Piazzale Francesco Baracca 1,

Arona tel: (0322) 46651, fax: (0322) 249530, email: navimaggiore@navigazionelaghi. it; Central Operations, Piazzale M Flaim 1, Intra, tel: (0323) 407112, fax: (0323) 407133, email: infomaggiore@ navigazionelaghi.it; Locarno office, Viale G Motta 1, Locarno, tel: (0041) 9175 16140, email: infomaggiorech@navigazione laghi.it. Free phone 800 551801.

Lake Orta

Lake Orta's public navigation service uses two motorships, *Ortensia* and *Azalea*, linking the towns on the lake and the isle of San Giulio with daily services from 10 April to 14 October (rest of the year Sundays and holidays only). For information: Navigazione Lago d'Orta, Via Simonotti 35, Borgomanero, tel: (0322) 844 862.

Links with the isle of San Giulio are also provided by motorboats that leave Orta every 10 to 15 minutes. For information on the motorboat service: tel: (0333) 6050288, fax: (0322) 911967, www.moto-scafisti.com.

Lake Lugano

Lake Lugano's boat services link all the main landing places on both Swiss and Italian territory; the routes are Ponte Tresa-Campione d'Italia-Lugano, Lugano-Morcote-Ponte Tresa, Lugano-Porlezza, Lugano-Campione d'Italia-Gandria, Lugano-Capolago connecting with the Mount Generoso railway timetable.

Navigazione Lugano also offers day cruises, concessions (up to 50 per cent) and discounts on all its services for those under 16 years and holders of the Swiss Boat Pass.

For information on routes, tariffs and timetables contact: Navigazione Lugano, cp 566906 Lugano, tel: (0041) 91971 5223, fax: (0041) 91971 2793, email: info@lakelugano.ch.

Lake Como

Navigazione del Lago di Como boasts more than 100 years' experience and currently has a fleet of 20 boats used to connect more than 30 locations on the lake. Five ferries provide services between the shores of Lecco, Como and Bellagio and on the Varenna-Menaggio, Varenna-Bellagio-Cadenabbia and return route. Starting early in the morning, fast hydroplanes cross the lake from Como to Còlico making several stops along the way. The first service usually leaves Còlico at around 6am and Como at approximately 6.30am; the last one generally leaves at 7pm. It takes approximately 1 hour 20 minutes to make the crossing. Also operating on the same route are numerous slower boats, which make the crossing in 3½ hours. On Sundays and holiday afternoons and in the summer months mini-cruises, lasting approximately 1 hour, depart from the landing stages at Lecco and Como. Daily boat excursions run from Como to Piona and back, from Como to Bellagio, from Como to Tremezzo and Piona with a visit to Villa Carlotta at Tremezzo and the Cistercian Piona Abbey. Every Saturday between mid-June and late September the navigation company organises nocturnal cruises, with dinner and dancing on board. For all information on cruises and timetables, which change according to the season and day of the week, contact: Navigazione Lago di Como, Via per Cernobbio 18, Como, tel: (031) 579211, fax: (031) 570080, email infocomo@navigazionelaghi.it Free phone 800 551801.

Lake Iseo

On Lake Iseo the seven vessels belonging to Navigazione Lago d'Iseo link the lake's main towns on the Pisogne-Lòvere-Monte

Isola-Iseo, Peschiera Maraglio-Sulzano and Canzano-Sale Marasino routes. Two cruise ships, *Città di Bergamo* and *Città di Brescia*, have restaurants on board and can carry up to 400 passengers each; the *Iris*, *Gardenia*, *Ninfea* and *Cigno* motorboats carry up to 110 passengers. In summer months the navigation company offers a tour of the lake, stopping at Sàrnico, Iseo, Lòvere and Monte Isola.

For information on routes and timetables contact: Navigazione Lago d'Iseo, Via Nazionale 16, Costa Volpino, tel: (0359) 71483, email: info@navigazionelagoiseo.it.

Lake Garda

Transport on Lake Garda is provided by Navigarda, which has 25 boats and operates on two main navigation routes; the first links Riva del Garda with Desenzano; the second, halfway up the lake, links Toscolano Maderno with Torri del Benaco. Crossing times vary according to the transport used. Powerful hydroplanes cover the first route in just over two hours, whereas the boats take at least four. Crossing the lake on the second route takes approximately half an hour.

In summer, day cruises visit Peschiera, Lazise, Bardolino, Garda and Salò, or depart from Riva del Garda for Tórbole, Limone and Malcésine. Every stop includes a visit. There are also afternoon and evening cruises on speedy hydroplanes or old steamboats, with on-board dining and sometimes dancing. For information on routes, timetables and tourist proposals contact: Navigarda, Navigazione Lago di Garda, Piazza Matteotti 1, Desenzano, tel: (030) 9149511, fax: (030) 9149520, email: infogarda@ navigazionelaghi.it.

Transport in Venice

Public navigation services are run by ACTV (Azienda Consorzio Trasporti Veneziano, information office Piazzale Roma, open every day 7.30am–8pm, tel: (041) 528 7686); www.actv.it. Water buses, motorboats and motorships provide a fairly extensive service all over the city and to the coastal areas (and the main islands in the lagoon). Tickets can be purchased at jetties, from tobacconists or on board (with a surcharge); some tickets, valid for one or more days, are specifically intended for tourists.

Urban lagoon services are displayed at the jetties. The Linea 1 water bus zigzags along the Grand Canal from Piazzale Roma or the railway station to San Marco and the Lido, stopping at all the jetties; this line is used for part of Tour 23. Faster motorship services circumnavigate the city from the railway station to the Lido via Giudecca. ACTV public transport also runs the bus services to the Lido and those between Venice and the mainland.

Gondolas can be booked at various points around the city (Bacino Orseolo; Calle Vallaresso; Danieli; Riva degli Schiavoni; Ferrovia San Simeon Piccolo; Isola del Tronchetto; Piazzale Roma; Rialto; Riva del Carbon; Santa Maria del Giglio; San Marco, jetty; Santa Sofia, Cannaregio; San Tomà; Trinità, Campo San Moisè). It is advisable to agree on a price before starting the trip.

A practical and economic version of the gondola is much used by the Venetians to cross the Grand Canal from one side to the other. The 'gondola ferry' runs between Santa Maria del Giglio and San Gregorio; San Samuele and Cà' Rezzonico (weekdays only); Sant'Angelo and San Tomà; San Silvestro and Riva del Carbon (weekdays only); Santa Sofia and Pescaria di Rialto; San Simeon Piccolo and the railway station (weekdays only).

Taxis are motorboats marked with a yellow band, bearing the communal emblem in black and the vehicle number. Their rates are quite high. Beware of unauthorised taxis, especially at Tronchetto.

MOTORING

Driving is one of the best ways to explore this part of Italy – once you get used to the rather aggressive way of driving most Italian motorists adopt. Avoid the cities if possible as one-way systems, congestion and lack of parking pose problems.

Rules of the Road

Drivers must be at least 18 and hold a full licence.

Seat belts must be worn in the front of a vehicle and (where fitted) in the back.

Drive on the right and give way to traffic approaching from the left, unless signs indicate otherwise.

Speed limits are as follows: 50kph (31mph) in built-up areas; 110kph (68mph) outside built-up areas; 130kph (81mph) on motorways (for cars over 1100cc).

Penalties for drinking and driving are severe. The level of alcohol in the bloodstream must be below 0.05 per cent.

Carry documents with you at all times. Both UK and US driver's licences are valid in Italy, but you should also carry a translation if your licence does not include one.

Motorways and Toll Roads

Motorways *(autostrade)* cover the entire country. As you approach the motorway, take a ticket from the machine on the left-hand side of the car; the barrier will rise. Payment is made when you leave the motorway, either by cash (usually to the official in the booth) or by a pass or credit card (follow signs to the Viacard booth).

Breakdowns

In the event of a vehicle breakdown, turn on your hazard warning lights and place the warning triangle 50m (164ft) behind the car. If you are in your own car, assistance (note this is not free) can be obtained from the Automobile Club d'Italia (ACI) by calling 116. In a rental car, contact the emergency breakdown number given by the rental company.

ACCOMMODATION AND RESTAURANTS

Following is a selection of hotels (◇), farm holiday centres (☺) and camping sites (▲) that can be found along the routes of each tour, with suggestions for restaurants (🍴) to take a break.

Accommodation prices
Accommodation is divided into three price categories based on the cost of a double room per night:
€ – up to €60
€€ – €60–€120
€€€ – over €120

Restaurant prices
Restaurants are divided into three price categories based on the cost of a three-course meal, excluding drink:
€ – up to €20
€€ – €20–€40
€€€ – over €40

TOUR I
STRESA
◇ **Du Parc €€€**
Via Gignous 1. Tel: 0323 30335; www.duparc.it.
21 rooms.
Open Easter to mid-Oct.

◇ **Royal €€–€€€**
Viale Lido 1. Tel: 0323 32777; www.hotelroyalstresa.com.
70 rooms.
Open Apr–Oct.

◇ **Speranza au Lac €€–€€€**
Piazza Marconi.
Tel: 0323 31178;
www.hotelmilansperanza.it.
86 rooms, 3 suites.

🍴 **Piemontese €€€**
Via Mazzini 25. Tel: 0323 30235.
Experimental Piedmontese cuisine. Closed Mon & Dec–Jan, plus Sun dinner Oct–Mar.

BAVENO
◇ **Simplon €€€**
Corso Garibaldi 52. Tel: 0323 924112;
www.zaccherahotels.com.
120 rooms.
Open mid-Apr to Oct.

◇ **Villa Azalea €€**
Via Domo 6. Tel: 0323 924300; www.villaazalea.com.
32 rooms.

▲ **Parisi**
Via Piave 50. Tel: 0323 923156; www.campingparisi.it.
Open mid-Mar to end Sep.

🍴 **Il Gabbiano €€**
Via I Maggio 19. Tel: 0323 924496.
Piedmontese fish and meat specialities. Closed Mon, also lunch on Tue.

FERIOLO
▲ **Orchidea**
Via Repubblica dell'Ossola 11, Tel: 0323 28257;
www.campingorchidea.it.
Open Mar–Oct.

MERGOZZO
🍴 **La Quartina €€–€€€**
Via Pallanza 20. Tel: 0323 80118.
Piemontese cooking; specialising in lake fish. Closed Mon (except Jun–Aug) & Jan to mid-Feb.

INTRA
◇ **Intra €**
Corso Mameli 133. Tel: 0323 581393; www.verbaniahotel.it.
37 rooms.

🍴 **La Tavernetta €€**
Via San Vittore 22, a Intra. Tel: 0323 402635.
Classic Italian cuisine. Closed Tue & Nov.

PALLANZA
☺ **Monterosso €**
Near Cima Monterosso 30. Tel: 0323 556510, fax: 0323 519706.
Closed mid-Jan to mid-Feb, Mon–Tue.

🍴 **La Cave €€**
Viale delle Magnolie 16.
Tel: 0323 503346.
Traditional cuisine. Hotel.

TOUR 2
ARONA
◇ **Giardino €€**
Corso della Repubblica 1.
Tel: 0322 45994;
www.giardinoarona.com.
56 rooms.

🍴 **Il Grappolo**
Via Pertossi 7. Tel: 0322 47735.
Family-run; home-cooking with local ingredients. Excellent tasting menu. Closed Tue, 1 week in Jan, 1 week in Jun.

🍴 **Taverna del Pittore**
Piazza del Popolo 39.
Tel: 0322 243366.
Sophisticated regional and seasonal cooking using local ingredients. Closed Mon, mid-Dec to mid-Jan.

BELGIRATE
◇ **Villa Carlotta €€€**
Via Mazzini 121/125. Tel: 0322 76461; www. bestwestern.it/villacarlotta.
128 rooms.

🍴 **La Terrazza €€**
Via Mazzini 83. Tel: 0322 7493.
Fish dishes. Closed Wed.

TOUR 3
VERBANIA
◇ **Il Chiostro €€**
Via Fratelli Cervi 14. Tel: 0323 404077; www.chiostrovb.it.
100 rooms.

🍴 **Il Torchio €€**
Via Manzoni 20, Pallanza.
Tel: 0323 503352.
Classic Piedmontese cuisine. Closed Wed, also Thu dinner.

CÀNNERO RIVIERA
◇ **La Rondinella €**
Via Sacchetti 50.
Tel: 0323 788098;
www.hotel-la-rondinella.it.
16 rooms.
Closed Jan.

⚐Lido
Viale del Lido 5.
Tel: & fax: 0323 88800.
Open Apr–Sep.

CANNÓBIO
◇**Antica Stallera** €€
Via P Zaccheo 7. Tel: 0323
71595; www.anticastallera.com.
18 rooms.
Closed period in Jan.

SANTA MARIA MAGGIORE
◇ **Miramonti** €€
Piazzale Diaz 3. Tel: 0324
95013; www.almiramonti.com.
11 rooms.
Closed Nov & Dec.

LOCARNO
◇ **Hotel dell'Angelo** €€
Piazza Grande (Switzerland).
Tel: 0041 91 7518175;
www.hotel-dell-angelo.ch.
55 rooms.

TOUR 4
MOTTARONE
◇ ⒪ **Eden** €
Tel: 0323 924873;
www.edenmottarone.it.
9 rooms.
Closed Tue & Nov.

ORTA SAN GIULIO
◇ **La Contrada dei Monti**
€€€
Via Dei Monti 10. Tel: 0322
905114, fax: 0322 905863.
17 rooms.
Closed Jan.

⚐Orta
Via Domodossola 28. Tel: 0322
90267; www.campingorta.it.

⒪ **Leon d'Oro** €€
Piazza Motta 43. Tel: 0322
911991.
*Lake fish, salumeria and local
cheese, and local funghi in season.
Closed 2 weeks in Jan.*

◇ ⒪ **Villa Crespi** €€
Via Fava 18. Tel: 0322 911902;
www.hotelvillacrespi.it.
14 rooms.
Mediterranean cuisine. Closed Mon.

OMEGNA
⒪ **Trattoria Toscana** €€
Via Mazzini 153. Tel: 0323
62460.
Country cuisine. Closed Wed.

TOUR 5
VARESE
⒪ **Al Vecchio Convento** €€€
Viale Borri 348. Tel: 0332 261005.
*Tuscan & classic Italian cuisine.
Closed Sun evening, Mon, 3 weeks
in Aug & period during Dec & Jan.*

⒪ **Da Vittorio** €€€
Piazza Beccaria 1. Tel: 0332
234312.
*Classic Italian cuisine. Closed Fri,
period in Aug.*

SACRO MONTE
⒪ **Sacro Monte** €€
Tel: 0322 90220.
*Classic Piedmontese cuisine. Closed
Tue, period in Jan.*

LAVENO
◇ ⒪ **Il Porticciolo** €€–€€€
Via Fortino 40.
Tel: 0332 667257.
10 rooms.
*Closed Tue (except Tue lunch
Jul–Aug), Wed & period in
Jan–Feb.*

ANGERA
◇ **Lido** €€
Viale Libertà 11. Tel: 0331
930232; www.hotellido.it.
18 rooms.

⚐Città di Angera
Via Bruschera 99. Tel: 0331
930736, fax: 0331 960367;
www.campingcittadiangera.it.
Closed Jan & Feb.

TOUR 6
AZZATE
◇ **Locanda dei Mai
Intees** €€€
Via Monte Grappa 22. Tel: 0332
454603, fax: 0332 459339;
www.mai-intees.it.
12 rooms.

COMABBIO
⒪ **Cesarino** €€–€€€
Via Labiena 1861.
Tel: 0331 968472.
*Lake fish dishes. Closed Wed & 3
weeks in Aug.*

MONATE
⚐Lago di Monate
Biandronno, Via Lago di
Monate 459. Tel: & fax: 0331
968566.
Open Jun–Sep except Jan.

BIANDRONNO
◇ **Continental** €€
Via Nino Bixio 3, Cassinetta di
Biandronno. Tel: 0332 766655;
www.continentalhotelva.it.
71 rooms.

TOUR 7
LUGANO
◇ **Walter au Lac** €€
Piazza Rezzonico 7
(Switzerland). Tel: 0041 91
9227425; www.walteraulac.ch.
42 rooms.

⒪ **Al Portone** €€
Viale Casserate 3. Tel: 0041 91
9235511.
*Innovative Italian cuisine. Closed
Sun & Mon.*

PORLEZZA
◇ **Europa** €€
Lungolago Matteotti 19.
Tel: 0344 61142;
www.hoteleuropaitaly.com.
35 rooms.
Open mid-Mar to Nov.

LANZO D'INTELVI
◇ **Belvedere** €€
Viale Poletti 27, Belvedere.
Tel: 0318 40122;
www.albergobelvedere.it.
36 rooms.

CAMPIONE D'ITALIA
⒪ **Da Candida** €€€
Via Marco da Campione 4.
Tel: 0041 91 6497541.
*Classic Italian cuisine. Closed Mon,
Tue dinner & late Jun–late Jul.*

TOUR 8
COMO
◇ **Barchetta Excelsior** €€€
Piazza Cavour 1. Tel: 0031 3221;
www.hotelbarchetta.it.
84 rooms.

◇ **Park** €€
Viale Fratelli Rossetti 20.
Tel: 031 572615.
41 rooms.
Open Mar–Nov.

◇ **Metropole & Suisse €€€**
Piazza Cavour 19. Tel: 031
269444; www.hotelmetropole
suisse.com.
71 rooms.

◇ **Posta €€**
Via Garibaldi 2. Tel: 031
364011; www.hotelposta.net.
18 rooms.

◇ **Tre Re €€**
Via Boldoni 20. Tel: 031 265374;
www.hoteltrerei.com.
41 rooms.
Closed mid-Dec to mid-Jan.

◇ ▣ **Villa Flori €€€**
Via per Cernobbio 12. Tel: 031
33820; www.hotelvillaflori.it.
45 rooms.
*Open Mar–Oct. Closed Sat lunch,
& Sun.*

▣ **Lo Storico €€€**
Via F Juvara 14. Tel: 0312
260193.
*Welcoming restaurant specialising
in fresh fish. Closed Sun, 1 week in
Jan, 1 week in Aug.*

▣ **Osteria l'Angelo del
Silenzio €€**
Viale Lecco 25. Tel: 0313
372157.
*Local cuisine featuring meat and
fish; tables outside in summer.
Closed Mon & Tue lunch, 1 week in
Jan, 1 week in Aug.*

▣ **Il Solito Posto €**
Via Lambertenghi 9. Tel: 0312
71352.
*Traditional and innovative local
fish and meat dishes.*

▣ **Osteria Rusticana €**
Via Carso 69. Tel: 0313 06590.
*Classic local cooking, home-made
bread, pasta and desserts. Closed
Sun, 2 weeks in Jan, 1 week in Aug.*

**TOUR 9
CERNOBBIO**
◇ ▣ **Regina Olga €€€**
Via Regina 18. Tel: 031 510171,
fax: 031 340604;
www.hotelreginaolga,it.
83 rooms.
Closed mid-Nov to mid-Feb.

MOLTRASIO
◇ **Best Western G.H.
Imperiale €€€**
Via Durini. Tel: 031 346111.
102 rooms.
Closed Jan.

ARGEGNO
◇ **Argegno €€**
Via Milano 14. Tel: 031 821455;
www.hotelaregno.it.
14 rooms.
Closed period in Dec.

TREMEZZO
◇ ▣ **Rusall €€**
Via San Martino 2, near Rogaro.
Tel: 0344 40408,
fax: 0344 40447.
23 rooms.
*Closed Jan to mid-Mar & 2 weeks
in Nov. Restaurant closed Wed
lunch.*

⏃ **Degli Ulivi**
Via Sala 18, loc. Bolvedro.
Tel: 0344 40161, fax: 0344 4015.
Open Apr–Oct.

▣ **Al Veluu €€**
Via Rogaro 11, loc. Rogaro.
Tel: 0344 40510.
*Local lake cuisine. Closed Tue &
Nov–Mar.*

CADENABBIA
▣ **La Cucina della Marianna
€€€**
Via Regina 57. Tel: 0344 43111.
*Local cuisine. Closed Mon, period
during Jan & Mar. Open evenings
only (Sun from midday).*

VARENNA
◇ **Du Lac €€€**
Via del Prestino 11. Tel: 0341
830238, fax: 0341 831081.
17 rooms.

◇ **Villa Cipressi €€–€€€**
Via IV Novembre 22. Tel: 0341
830113; www.villacipressi.it.
32 rooms.
*Usually closed Oct–Mar, but some
years open all year round.*

▣ **Vecchia Varenna €€**
Contrada Scoscesa 10.
Tel: 0341 830793.
*Local lake cuisine. Closed Mon
& Dec to mid-Feb.*

**TOUR 10
LECCO**
◇ **Alberi €€**
Via Lungolago Isonzo 4.
Tel: 0341 350992;
www.hotelalberi.lecco.it.
20 rooms.

▣ **Antica Osteria Casa di
Lucia €€**
Via Lucia 27. Tel: 0341 494594.
*Lombard regional cooking with lake
fish and local meat and cheese.
Closed Sat lunch & Sun, 1 month
in Aug.*

BELLAGIO
◇ **Belvedere €€**
Via Valassina 31. Tel: 031
950410, fax: 031 950102.
62 rooms.
Open Apr–Oct.

◇ **Il Perlo Panorama €€**
Mulini di Perlo (3km/2 miles
from Bellagio). Tel: 0319 50229;
www.ilperlo.com.
17 rooms.
Closed mid-Nov to mid-Mar.

◇ **Grand Hotel Villa
Serbelloni €€€**
Via Roma 1. Tel: 031 950216;
www.villaserbelloni.com.
81 rooms.
Open Apr–Nov.

▣ **Far Out €€**
Salita Mella 4. Tel: 031 951743.
*Classic Italian cuisine. Closed Wed
(Mon–Thu in winter), Jan.*

▣ **Mistral €€€**
Via Roma 1. Tel: 031 950216,
fax: 031 951529.
*Local cuisine. Closed Wed. Open
Jun–Sep, evening only.*

▣ **Silvio €–€€**
Via Carcano 12.
Tel: 031 950322.
*Local fish cuisine. Closed
Epiphany–Feb.*

MERATE
▣ **Villa Ottocento €€**
Via Statale 5. Tel: 0395 981711.
*Elegant surroundings and classic
Italian cooking. Closed Mon,
2 weeks in Aug.*

MONZA
⟡ **Della Regione €€**
Via Elvezia 4. Tel: 039 387205;
www.hoteldellaregione.it.
90 rooms.

🍴 **Alle Grazie €€–€€€**
Via Lecco 84. Tel: 039 387903.
*Experimental cuisine. Closed Wed
& period in Aug.*

🍴 **Derby Grill €€€**
Viale Regina Margherita 15.
Tel: 039 39421.
*Local cuisine. Closed Sat & Sun
lunch & period at Christmas and in
Aug.*

TOUR 11
MANDELLO DEL LAIRO
🍴 **Osteria Sali e Tabacchi €**
Piazza S. Rocco 3, Maggiana.
Tel: 0341 733715.
*Local cuisine. Closed Mon evening
& Tue, also various holidays.*

🍴 **Ricciolo €€**
Via Statale 165, near Olcio.
Tel: 0341 732546.
*Larian cuisine. Closed Sun evening
& Mon (except Jul–Aug),
Christmas–Jan.*

MENÁGGIO
⟡ **Du Lac €€**
Via Mazzini 27. Tel: 0344 35281;
www.hoteldulacmenaggio.it.
10 rooms.

⟡ **Grand Hotel Victoria €€€**
Lungolago Castelli 9. Tel: 0344
32003; www.centrohotelslake
como.com/victoria_mennagio.
55 rooms.
Closed Nov–Feb.

⟡ **Royal €€**
Largo Vittorio Veneto 1, Loveno
(1km/0.5 miles from Menaggio).
Tel: 0344 31444; www.royal-
colombo.com.
18 rooms.

BELLANO
⟡ **Meridiana €**
Via Carlo Alberto 19. Tel: 0341
821126; www.meridianahotel.it.
30 rooms.
Closed Christmas.

BARZIO
⟡ **Grand'Hotel
Ballestrin €€**
Via Coldogna 1. Tel: 0341
996111; www.hotelballestrin.it.
46 rooms.
*Open Christmas–Mar, end Jun
to mid-Sep.*

TOUR 12
BERGAMO
⟡ **Piazza Vecchia €€**
Via Colleoni 3. Tel: 0352 53179;
www.hotelpiazzavecchia.it.
13 rooms.

⟡ **Piemontese €€**
Piazza Marconi 11. Tel: 0352
30400;
www.hotelpiemontese.com.
54 rooms.

⟡ **Best Western Premier
Hotel Cappello d'Oro €€€**
Viale Papa Giovanni XXIII 12.
Tel: 035 2289011;
www.hotelcappellodoro.it.
89 rooms.

🍴 **Baretto di San Vigilio
€€–€€€**
Via al Castello 1 (Bergamo Alta).
Tel: 0352 53191.
*Modern and creative interpretations
of classic local and Italian dishes.
Closed Mon in winter.*

🍴 **Colleoni e dell'Angelo €€€**
Piazza Vecchia 7 (Bergamo Alta).
Tel: 0352 32596.
*Upmarket locale serving classic
Bergamo dishes. Closed Mon.*

🍴 **Lio Pellegrini €€€**
Via San Tomaso 47. Tel: 035
247813.
*Tuscan & classic Italian cuisine.
Closed Mon & Tue lunch, period in
Jan & Aug.*

🍴 **L'Osteria di via Solata €€€**
Via Solata 8, in Città Alta. Tel:
035 271993, fax: 035 4227208.
*Classic & local cuisine. Closed Sun
evening, Tue, Feb & period in Aug.*

TOUR 13
TRESCORE BALNEARIO
⟡ **Della Torre €€€**
Piazza Cavour 26. Tel: 035
941365; www.albergotorre.it.
34 rooms.

ISEO
⟡ **Iseo Lago €€€**
Via Colombera 2. Tel: 0309
889299; www.iseolagohotel.it.
66 rooms.

⟡ **Relais Mirabella Iseo €€€**
Via Mirabella 34, Località
Clusane, 5km (3 miles) from
Iseo. Tel: 030 9898051;
www.relaismirabella.it.
29 rooms.
Closed Jan–Feb.

🍴 **Osteria Il Volto €€–€€€**
Via Mirolte 33. Tel: 030 981462.
*Brescian & lake cuisine. Closed
Wed & Thu lunchtime, 2 weeks
in Jul.*

TOUR 14
PARÁTICO
⟡ **Franciacorta Golf Hotel
€€€**
Via XXIV Maggio 48.
Tel: 035 913333;
www.franciacortagolfhotel.it.
43 rooms.
Closed Christmas.

CAPRIOLO
🍷 **Ricci Curbastro e
Figli €€**
Via Adro 37. Tel: 030 736094;
www.riccicurbastro.it.

COLOMBARO
⟡🍴 **Relais Franciacorta
€€€**
Via Manzoni 29. Tel: 030
9884234;
www.relaisfranciacorta.it.
50 rooms.
*Restaurant closed Mon dinner &
Tue.*

🍴 **Trattoria la Colombara
€€–€€€**
Via Manzoni 29. Tel: 030
9826461.
*Lombard cuisine. Closed Mon
evening & Tue.*

ERBUSCO
⟡🍴 **Relais & Chateaux
L'Albereta €€€**
Via Vittorio Emanuele 11. Tel:
030 7760550; www.albereta.it.
57 rooms.
*Restaurant closed Jun to mid-Feb,
Sun dinner & Mon.*

ROVATO
Due Colombe €€–€€€
Via Roma 1. Tel: 030 7721534.
Speciality beef in oil. Closed Sun evening & Mon, New Year–Epiphany & two weeks in Aug.

TOUR 15
BRESCIA
Ambasciatori €€€
Via Santa Crocefissa di Rosa 92.
Tel: 030 399114;
www.ambasciatori.net.
66 rooms.

Orologio €€
Via Beccaria 17. Tel: 0303 755 4111; www.albergoorologio.it.
16 rooms.

Il Labirinto €€€
Via Corsica 224. Tel: 0303 541607.
Classic Brescian cuisine with a modern twist. Closed Sun.

La Sosta €€
Via San Martino della Battaglia 20. Tel: 0302 95603.
Traditional local cooking combining fish and meat. Closed Sun pm and Mon, 1 week in Jan & Aug.

Trattoria da Ciospa €
Via San Zeno 22. Tel: 0302 21049.
Simple and flavoursome local dishes at keen prices. Closed Sun.

TOUR 16
SIRMIONE
Olivi €€–€€€
Via San Pietro 3. Tel: 0309 05365; www.hotelolivi.com.
64 rooms.
Closed Dec–Jan.

Smeraldo €–€€
Via XXV Aprile 11. Tel: 0309 16077; www.hotellapaul.it.
22 rooms.

Sirmione
Via Sirmioncino 9, near Colombare. Tel: 030 919045.
Open May–Sep.

La Rucola €€€
Vicolo Strentelle 7. Tel: 030 916326.
Elegant setting and creative cuisine. Closed Fri at lunch, Thu & period in Jan & Feb.

DESENZANO
Aquila d'Oro €€€
Via F. Agello 47–49, Località Rivoltella. Tel: 030 9901222, fax: 030 9902350.
21 rooms.

Enrichetta €€€
Via F. Agello 12, Località Rivoltella. Tel: 030 9119231; www.hotelenrichetta.com.
24 rooms.

Vò
Via Vò 9. Tel: 030 9121325; www.voit.it.
Open mid-Apr to Oct.

Cavallino €€€
Via Gherla 30. Tel: 030 9120217.
Fish and seafood restaurant. Closed Sun pm & Mon, 2 weeks in Nov.

Esplanade €€€
Via Lario 10. Tel: 030 9143361, fax: 030 9143361.
Local cuisine. Closed Wed.

MONIGA DEL GARDA
Al Porto €€€
Via Porto 29. Tel: 0365 502069.
Innovative local cuisine. Closed Wed. Open Feb–Oct.

MANERBA DEL GARDA
Villa Schindler €€
Via Bresciani 68. Tel: 0365 651046; www.villaschindler.it.
10 rooms.
Open Easter–Oct.

Capriccio €€€
Piazza San Bernardo 6, near Montinelle. Tel: 0365 551124, fax: 0365 550296.
Classic regional and seasonal cuisine with style. Closed Tue, Jan–Feb. Open evenings only.

SALÒ
Laurin €€€
Viale Landi 9. Tel: 0365 22022, fax: 0365 22382.
33 rooms.
Closed mid-Dec to Jan.

Gallo Rosso €€€
Vicolo Tomacelli 4.
Tel: 0365 520757.
Classic Italian cuisine. Closed Tue evening, Wed lunch Jun–Sep & various holidays.

Lepanto €€€
Lungolago Zanardelli 67.
Tel: 0365 20428.
Local & classic Italian cuisine. Closed Thu, mid-Jan–Feb.

GARDONE RIVIERA
Monte Baldo €€
Corso Zanardelli 110.
Tel: 0365 20951;
www.hotelmontebaldo.it.
40 rooms.
Open mid-Apr to mid-Oct.

Locanda agli Angeli €€€
Piazza Garibaldi 2, near Vittoriale. Tel: 0365 20832; www.agliangeli.com.
16 rooms.
Creative local dishes. Closed Tue. Open mid-Feb to mid-Nov.

La Stalla €€
Via dei Colli 14.
Tel: 0365 21038.
Local cuisine. Closed Tue in winter & period in Jan.

PADENGHE SUL GARDA
West Garda €€€
Via Prais 32. Tel: 030 9907161; www.westgardahotel.com.
71 rooms.

TOUR 17
RIVA DEL GARDA
Bellavista €€–€€€
Piazza Cesare Battista 4.
Tel: 0464 554271;
www.bellavistariva.it
31 rooms.

Du Lac et Du Parc €€€
Viale Rovereto 44.
Tel: 0464 566600;
www.dulacetduparc.com.
164 rooms.
Open Apr–Oct.

Feeling Hotel Luise €€€
Viale Rovereto 9. Tel: 0464 550858; www.hotelluise.com.
67 rooms.

◇ **Sole €€€**
Piazza III Novembre 35. Tel:
0464 552686; www.hotelsole.net.
78 rooms.
*Closed mid-Jan to mid-Mar &
mid-Nov to mid-Dec.*

◯ **Al Volt €€**
Via Fiume 73. Tel: 0464 552570.
*Trentino cuisine with lake fish.
Closed Mon & mid-Feb to mid-
Mar, lunch in Jul.*

GARGNANO
◇ **Du Lac €€€**
Via Colletta 21. Località Villa.
Tel: 0365 71107; www.hotel-
dulac.it.
11 rooms.
Open mid-Mar to Oct.

LIMONE SUL GARDA
◇ **Lido €**
Via IV Novembre 34. Tel: 0365
954574; www.lidohotel.com.
26 rooms.
Open Apr to mid-Oct.

TOUR 18
ARCO
◇ **Palace Hotel Città €€€**
Viale Roma 10. Tel: 0464
531100; www.welcome
togardalake.com.
81 rooms.
*Closed Nov to mid-Dec & mid-Jan
to mid-Mar.*

◯ **Alla Lega €**
Via Vergolano 8. Tel: 0464
516205.
*Local cuisine with accent on Alpine
specialities. Closed Wed, mid-Jan to
mid-Mar.*

TRENTO
◇ **Buonconsiglio €€**
Via Romagnosi 16/18.
Tel: 0461 272888;
www.hotelbuonconsiglio.it.
46 rooms.

◇ ◯ **Villa Madruzzo €€**
Near Ponte Alto 26, Cognola.
Tel: 0461 986220;
www.villamadruzzo.it
51 rooms.
Restaurant closed Sun.

◯ **Antica Trattoria al Vòlt €€**
Via S Croce 16. Tel: 0461
983776.

*Family-run restaurant with local
produce and cooking. Closed Thu
and Sun pm.*

◯ **Chiesa €€**
Parco San Marco.
Tel: 0461 238766.
*Traditional Trentino cuisine.
Closed Sun.*

◯ **Osteria a le Due Spade
€€€**
Via Don Rizzi 11. Tel: 0461
234343, fax: 0461 220201.
*Trentino cuisine. Closed Sun, Mon
lunch, period in Jun.*

LÉVICO
◇ **Eden €€€**
Viale Vittorio Emanuele 14.
Tel: 0461 706103;
www.eden-hotel.com.
39 rooms.

◇ **Parc Hotel du Lac €**
Localitá Lago 3. Tel: 0461
706590, fax. 0461 707252.
47 rooms
Open mid-Apr to mid-Oct.

Λ2 Laghi
Near Costa. Tel: 0461 706290,
fax: 0461 707381.
Open mid-Jun to mid-Sep.

CALDONAZZO
◇ **Due Spade €€**
Piazza Municipio 2.
Tel: 0461 723113;
www.albergoduespade.it.
24 rooms.
Closed Nov.

ROVERETO
◇ **Leon d'Oro €€€**
Via Tacchi 2. Tel: 0464 437333,
fax: 0464 423777;
www.hotelleondoro.it.
56 rooms.

◇ ◯ **Rovereto €€**
Corso Rosmini 82/D. Tel: 0464
435222, fax: 0464 439644;
www.hotelrovereto.it.
49 rooms.

◯ **Novecento €€**
Corso Rosmini 82/D.
Tel: 0464 435454.
*Trentino & Mantuan cuisine. Closed
Sun, period in Jan & Jul.*

TORBOLE
◇ ◯ **Piccolo Mondo €€€**
Via Matteotti 7. Tel: 0464
505271, fax: 0464 505295.
56 rooms.
*Closed 2 weeks in Feb. Restaurant
closed Tue, except in summer.*

TOUR 19
VERONA
◇ **Accademia €€–€€€**
Via Scala 12. Tel: 045 596222;
www.accademiavr.it.
94 rooms.

◇ **Bologna €€€**
Piazzetta Scalette Rubiani 3.
Tel: 045 8006830.
32 rooms.

◇ **Giulietta e Romeo €€**
Vicolo Tre Marchetti 3.
Tel: 045 8003554;
www.giuliettaeromeo.com.
34 rooms.

◇ **Grand Hotel €€€**
Corso Porta Nuova 105. Tel: 045
595600, fax: 045 596385;
www.grandhotel.vr.it.
62 rooms.

ΛCastel San Pietro
Via Castel San Pietro 2.
Tel: & fax: 045 592037.
Open mid-May to Oct

◯ **Al Pompiere €€–€€€**
Vicolo Regina d'Ungheria 5.
Tel: 045 8030537.
*Venetian cuisine. Closed Sun & at
lunch Mon, period in Jan & Jun.*

◯ **Locanda di Castelvecchio
€€–€€€**
Corso Castelvecchio 21/A.
Tel: 045 8030097.
*Classic Veneto cooking specialising in
roast and boiled meat. Closed Tue &
Wed lunch, 1 week in Jan & Aug.*

◯ **Trattoria I Masenini €–€€**
Via Roma 34. Tel: 045 8065169.
*Classic Italian cooking with some
Veneto specialities. Closed Sun &
Mon lunch, 3 weeks in Jan–Feb.*

◯ **Tre Marchetti €€€**
Vicolo 3 Marchetti 19/B. Tel: 045
8030463.
*Veronese cuisine. Closed Sun (Mon
in Jun & Aug), period in Sep.*

TOUR 20
PESCHIERA DEL GARDA
◇ **Residence Hotel Puccini** €€€
Via Puccini 2. Tel: 045 6401428;
www.hotelpuccini.it.
32 rooms.

LAZISE
◇ **Casa Mia** €€€
S.S. 249, Località Risare 1.
Tel: 045 6470244;
www.hotelcasamia.com.
43 rooms.
Closed mid-Dec to Jan.

◇ **Lazise** €€
Via Esperia 38/A. Tel: 045
6470466; www.hotellazise.it.
73 rooms.

BARDOLINO
◇ **Caesius Thermae** €–€€
Via Pescheria 3, Loc Cisano.
Tel: 045 719100;
www.hotelcaesiusterme.com.
185 rooms.

Å **Serenella**
Near Mezzariva.
Tel: 045 7211333;
www.camping-serenella.it.
Open late Mar to mid-Oct.

🍽 **Il Giardino delle Esperidi**
€€
Via Mameli 1. Tel: 045 6210477.
*Local cuisine. Closed at lunch Tue
& Wed.*

TOUR 21
MANTUA
◇ **Bianchi Stazione** €€€
Piazza Don Leoni 24. Tel: 0376
326465; www.hotelbianchi.com.
55 rooms.
Closed Christmas.

◇ **Broletto** €€–€€€
Via Accademia 1. Tel: 0376
223678; www.hotelbroletto.com.
16 rooms.
Closed 22 Dec–4 Jan.

◇ **Italia** €€
Piazza Cavallotti 8. Tel: 0376
322609; www.hotelitalia
mantova.com.
31 rooms.

◇ **Mantegna** €€
Via Filzi 10. Tel: 0376 328019;
www.hotelmantegna.it
42 rooms.

🦞 **Corte Bersaglio** €
Via Learco Guerra 15.
Tel: 0376 320345.
Closed Aug & Jan.

🍽 **Alla Nuova Marasca** €–€€
Piazza Leon Battista Alberti
19/20. Tel: 0376 322620.
*Classic regional cuisine with a
modern twist. Closed Sun pm &
Mon, 2 weeks in Jan–Feb & 1 week
in Aug.*

🍽 **Aquila Nigra** €€€
Vicolo Bonacolsi 4. Tel: 0376
327180, fax: 0376 226490.
*Lombard & local cuisine. Closed
Sun (Sun evenings Apr–May,
Sep–Oct), Mon, period in Aug.*

GÓITO
🍽 **Al Bersagliere** €€€
Via Statale Goitese 260.
Tel: 0376 60007, fax: 0376
689589.
*Mantuan cuisine. Close Mon & Tue,
period at Christmas and Aug.*

CASTIGLIONE DELLE
STIVIERE
🍽 **Osteria da Pietro** €€€
Via Giovanni Chiassi 19.
Tel: 0376 673718.
*Lombard cuisine. Closed Wed (Tue
also Jun–Aug), period in Jan &
Aug.*

TOUR 22
GARDA
◇ 🍽 **Conca d'Oro** €€
Lungolago Europa 2.
Tel: 045 7255275;
www.hotelconcadorogarda.it.
26 rooms.
Closed mid-Mar to mid-Nov.

◇ **Locanda San Vigilio** €€€
Località San Vigilio.
Tel: 045 7256688;
www.punta-sanvigilio.it.
14 rooms.
Open Mar–Oct.

🍽 **Tobago** €€–€€€
Via Bellini 1. Tel: 045 7256340.
*Veronese & fish cuisine. Closed Tue
in winter, Epiphany to mid-Feb.*

TORRI DEL BENACO
◇ **Gardesana** €€€
Piazza Calderini 20.
Tel: 045 7225411;
www.hotel-gardesana.com.
34 rooms.
Closed Nov-Jan.

🍽 **Al Caval** €€–€€€
Via Gardesana 186.
Tel: 045 7225083.
*Local cuisine. Closed Wed, period in
Jan & Feb. Open evenings only
(except during festivals).*

MALCÉSINE
◇ **Alpi** €€
Localita Campogrande. Tel: 045
7400717; www.alpihotel.info.
45 rooms.

Å **Tonini**
Via Polpere 1. Tel: 045 7401324.
Open Apr–Oct.

TOUR 23
VENEZIA (VENICE)
◇ **Ateneo** €€€
San Marco 1876, Calle Minelli.
Tel: 041 5200777; www.ateneo.it.
20 rooms.

◇ **Ca' Pisani** €€€
Dorsoduro 979A, Rio Terrà
Antonio Foscarini. Tel: 041
2401411; www.capisanihotel.it.
29 rooms.

◇ **Flora** €€€
San Marco 2283A, Calle dei
Bergameschi. Tel: 041 5205844;
www.hotelflora.it
44 rooms.

◇ **Locanda Fiorita** €€€
San Marco 3457/A, Campiello
Nuovo. Tel: 041 5234754;
www.locandafiorita.com.
10 rooms.

◇ **Locanda San Barnaba**
€€–€€€
Dorsoduro 2785. Tel: 041
2411233; www.locanda-
sanbarnaba,com.
13 rooms.

◇ **Santo Stefano €€€**
San Marco 2957, Campo San
Stefano. Tel: 041 5200166; www.
hotelsantostefanovenezia.com.
11 rooms.
Closed period in Jan & Feb.

◇ **Villa Rosa €€**
Cannaregio 389, Calle della
Misericordia. Tel: 041 716569;
www.villarosahotel.com.
34 rooms.

⛺ **Europa Camping Village €**
Via Fausta 332, Cavallino
Treporti. Tel. 041 968069;
www.campingeuropa.com.
Open Apr–Sep.

🍽 **Dal Pampo €€**
Castello 24, Calle Generale
Chinotto. Tel: 041 5208419.
*Family-run restaurat serving hearty
Venetian classics. Closed Wed, 2
weeks in May, 7 Aug.*

🍽 **Da Flore €€€**
San Polo 2202/A, Calle del
Scaleter. Tel: 041 721308.
*Venetian cuisine. Closed Sun &
Mon, Christmas–mid-Jan, & period
in Aug.*

🍽 **Trattoria alla Madonna
€€**
San Polo 594, Calle della
Madonna. Tel: 041 5223842.
*Venetian fish cuisine. Closed Wed,
Christmas & 2 weeks in Aug.*

🍽 **Vina da Gigio €€€**
Cannaregio 3628A, Fondamenta
San Felice. Tel: 041 5285140.
*Superlative Venetian cooking featur-
ing both fish and meat. Closed Mon,
3 weeks in Jan–Feb & Aug–Sep.*

TOUR 24
MIRA
◇ **Villa Margherita €€€**
Via Nazionale 416. Tel: 0414
265800, fax: 0414 265838;
www.villa.margherita.com.
19 rooms.

CASTELFRANCO VENETO
◇ **Alla Torre €€€**
Piazzetta Trente e Trieste 7.
Tel: 0423 98707;
www.hotelallatorre.it.
54 rooms.

ÁSOLO
◇ **Hotel Duse €€–€€€**
Via R Browning 190. Tel: 0423
55241; www.hotelduse.com.
14 rooms.

🍽 **Ca Derton €€€**
Piazza D'Annunzio 11. Tel: 0423
529648.
*Traditional Veneto cuisine in elegant
surroundings. Closed Sun & Mon
lunch.*

CONEGLIANO
◇ **Canon d'Oro €€€**
Via XX Settembre 131. Tel: 0438
34246; www.hotelcanondoro.it.
48 rooms.

TREVISO
◇ **Al Foghèr €€€**
Viale della Repubblica 10.
Tel: 0422 432950;
www.hotelalfogher.it.
55 rooms.

◇ **Hotel Continental €€€**
Via Roma 16, Tel: 0422 411216,
fax: 0422 55054,
www.hcontinental.it.
80 rooms.

⛺🍽 **Il Cascinale €**
Via Torre d'Orlando 6/B.
Tel: 0422 402203;
www.agriturismoilcascinale.it.
*Closed period in Aug. Restaurant
open Sat & Sun.*

🍽 **Antica Torre €€€**
Via Inferiore 55. Tel: 0422
583694.
*Sophisticated take on classic Veneto
dishes. Closed Sun & Thu pm,
2 weeks in Jan, 7 Aug.*

TOUR 25
PADUA
◇ **Al Cason €€€**
Via Frà Paolo Sarpi 40. Tel: 0498
62636; www.hotelcason.com.
48 rooms.

◇ **Al Fagiano €€**
Via Locatelli 45. Tel: 0498
753396; www.hotelalfagiano.com.
40 rooms.

◇ **Europa €€–€€€**
Largo Europa 9. Tel: 0496
61200; www.hoteleuropapd.it.
80 rooms.

◇ **Methis €€€**
Riviera Paleocapa 70. Tel: 0498
725555; www.methishotel.com.
59 rooms.

🍽 **Bion €–€€**
Via Vigonovese 427, near
Camin, 4km (2.5 miles) east of
Padua. Tel: 049 8790064.
*Venetian home cooking. Closed Sun,
New Year–Epiphany & period in
Aug.*

ARQUA PETRARCA
◇ **Villa del Poeta €€**
Via Zane 5. Tel: 0429 777361;
www.villadelpoeta.it.
15 rooms.
Closed Jan & Feb.

VICENZA
◇ **Aries €€€**
Via Leonardo da Vinci 28. Tel:
0444 239239; www.arieshotel.it.
73 rooms.

◇ **Cristina €€**
Corso SS Felice e Fortunato 32.
Tel: 0444 324297;
www.hotelcristinavicenza.it.
33 rooms.

🍽 **Antico Ristorante agli
Schioppi €€**
Contrà del Castello 26.
Tel: 0444 543701.
*Venetian cuisine. Closed Sat
evenings, Sun, mid-Jul to mid-Aug,
Christmas–Epiphany.*

🍽 **Antica Trattoria Tre Visi €€**
Corso Palladio 25. Tel: 0444
324868.
*Traditional and classic Vicentine
cooking. Closed Sun pm & Mon,
2 weeks in Jul.*

MAROSTICA
◇ **Due Mori €€€**
Corso Mazzini 73. Tel: 0424
471777; www.duemori.com.
12 rooms.
Closed period in Aug.

BASSANO DEL GRAPPA
◇ **Villa Ca' Sette €€€**
Via Cunizza da Romano 4. Tel:
0424 383350; www.ca-sette.it.
19 rooms.

PRACTICAL INFORMATION

TOUR INFORMATION
The addresses, telephone numbers and opening times of the attractions mentioned in the tours, including the telephone numbers of the Tourist Information Centres are listed below tour by tour.

TOUR 1

i Piazza Marconi 16, Stresa.
Tel: 0323 30150 or 31308, fax: 0323 31308 or 32561.

i Piazza Dante Alighieri 14, Baveno.
Tel: & fax: 0323 924632.

i Corso Zanitello 6/8, Pallanza (Verbania).
Tel: & fax: 0323 503249 or 556669.
Viale delle Magnolie 1.
Tel: & fax: 0323 557676.

1 Stresa
Villa Ducale, Museo Rosminiano
Tel: 0323 30091.
Open Mon–Fri 9–noon, 3–6.

For children
Villa Pallavicino
Tel: 0323 31533.
Gardens open 28 Feb–2 Nov, daily 9–6.

2 Isole Borromee
Isola Bella
Palace and gardens.
Tel: 0323 30556.
Open mid-Mar to Oct 9–5.30.

Isola Madre
Palace and botanical garden.
Tel: 0323 30556.
Open mid-Mar to Oct 9–5.30.

Back to nature
Fondotoce Special Nature Reserve
Park Office, Via Canale 48, Fondotoce. Tel: 0323 496596.

6 Cicogna
Val Grande National Park
Park Information Centre, Via Pozzolo, Cicogna.
Tel: 0324 36101.

8 Pallanza
Villa Taranto
Via Vittorio Veneto 111.
Tel: 0323 55667.
Open Apr–Oct 8.30–5.30.

Villa San Remigio
Tel: 0323 504401.
Guided tours only by prior appointment (Sat–Sun and Jul–Aug) with tourist office.

Special to...
Verbano Art, Landscape and History Museum
Palazzo Viani Dugnani, Via Ruga 44.
Tel: 0323 542418.
Open Nov–Mar 10–noon, 3–5.30. Closed Mon.

TOUR 2

i Piazzale Duca d'Aosta, Arona.
Tel: & fax: 0322 243601.

i Via Mazzini 12–14, Belgirate. Tel: & fax: 0322 7494.

i Via Ing Viotti 2, Massino Visconti.
Tel: & fax: 0322 219713.

1 Arona
Parco della Rocca
Open 2 Jan–Mar, holidays only 10–5; Apr–May, daily 2–5; Jun–Oct, daily 10–7.30; Nov–1 Jan, holidays only 10–4. No dogs.

Statue of San Carlone
Tel: 0322 249669.
Open Apr–Oct 9–12.30,

2–6.30; Nov–Dec., Mar, Sat–Sun and public hols 10–12.30, 2–4.30. Closed Jan–Feb.

Archaeological Museum
Piazza San Graziano 36.
Tel: 0322 48294.
Open Tue 10–12, Sat–Sun 3.30–6.30. By appointment Thu 10–12.

Special to...
Villa Ponti
Via San Carlo 63.
Tel: 0322 44629 or 240467.
Visits by appointment only or during exhibitions and concerts.

3 Lesa
Villa Stampa & Manzoni Museum
Via alla Fontana 18.
Tel: 0322 76421.
Open Aug, Thu 10–noon, Sat–Sun 5–7.

5 Massino Visconti
Castello Visconti
Tel: 0331 219713.
Privately owned. Can currently only be viewed from outside. Phone for information.

8 Parco Regionale dei Lagoni di Mercurago
Information: Direzione del Parco, Via Gattico, 6, Arona. Tel: 0322 240239.

TOUR 3

i Verbania: see *Tour 1*.

i Via Roma 37, Cànnero Riviera.
Tel: & fax: 0323 788943.

i Via A Giovanola 25, Cannobio.
Tel: & fax: 0323 71212.

i Piazza Risorgimento 10, Santa Maria Maggiore.
Tel: 0323 28857.

i Largo Zorzi, Locarno.
Tel: 0041 91 7910091, fax: 7519070.

Special to...
Ghiffa Hat Museum
Corso Belvedere 279, Ghiffa. Tel: 0323 59174.
Open Apr–Oct, Tue, Sat–Sun 3.30–6.30; Jul & Aug also Thu. Groups daily by appointment.

Back to nature
SS Trinità Special Nature Reserve
Visitor Centre, Via SS Trinità 48, Ghiffa.
Tel: 0323 59870.
Telephone for times first.

3 Santa Maria Maggiore
Rossetti Valentini School
Tel: 0324 98078.
Telephone for times.

Chimneysweep Museum
Piazza del Risorgimento 28. Tel: 0324 95091.
Open Jul–Aug, daily 3.30–6.30, Sun–Mon 10–noon.

4 Locarno
Castle & Archaeological Museum
Via B Rusca 5. Tel: 91 756 31 70/80.
Open Tue–Fri 10–noon, 2–5, Sat–Sun 10–5.

TOUR 4

i Stresa: see *Tour 1*.

i Via Per Nocco 2, Gignese.
Tel: & fax: 0323 208406.

i Via Bossi 11, Orta San Giulio.
Tel: 0322 905614.

i Via Regaldi 4, Varallo.
Tel: 0163 564404.

i Piazza XXIV Aprile 17, Omegna.
Tel: 0323 61930.

1 Gignese
Umbrella & Parasol Museum
Via Golf Panorama 2.
Tel: 0323 202064.
Open Apr–Sep 10–noon, 3–6. Closed Mon, except Jul & Aug.

For children
Alpinia/Alpino
Tel: 0323 20163.
Open Apr–Oct, 9.30–6. Closed Mon.

Back to nature
Sacro Monte Special Nature Reserve
Orta San Giulio.
Tel: 0322 911960.
Open daily 9.30–6.30.

Special to...
Calderara Foundation
Via Bardelli 9, Vacciago, near Ameno.
Tel: 0322 998192.
Open 15 May–15 Oct, 10–noon, 3–6. Closed Mon.

6 Madonna del Sasso
Sanctuary
Tel: 0322 981156.
Hours vary. Call for latest details.

7 Varallo
Picture Gallery
Palazzo dei Musei,
Via Pio Franzani 2.
Tel: 0163 51424
Open Tue–Sun 10–12.30, 2.30–6.30.

8 Quarna Sotto
Ethnographic Museum
Via Roma.
Tel: 0323 826368 or 826134.
Open Jul–Aug, 4–7. Rest of year by appointment.

9 Omegna
Foundation-Forum Museum of Crafts and Industry
Parco Maulini 1.
Tel: 0323 866141.
Open Mon–Sat 9–12.30, 2.30–6, Sun 2.30–6.30

TOUR 5

i Via Carrobbio 2, Varese.
Tel: & fax: 0332 283604.

i Palazzo Municipale, Piazza Italia, Laveno.
Tel: 0332 668785.

i Piazza Garibaldi 10, Angera.
Tel: 0331 960256.

1 Sacro Monte
Baroffio Museum
Tel: 0332 212042.
Open Thu, Sat–Sun 9.30–12.30, 3–6.30.

Villa Pogliaghi
Tel: 0332 283604.
Telephone for visits.

Back to nature
Campo dei Fiori Regional Park
Tel: 0332 436571.

Special to...
Castiglioni Museum
Villa Ioeplitz.
Tel: 0332 281590.
Open Jul only or by request.

2 Casalzuigno
Villa Della Porta Bozzolo
Tel: 0332 624136.
Park and villa open Wed–Sun 10–6.

5 Laveno
Civic Chinaware Collection
Palazzo Perabò, Cerro.
Tel: 0332 666530.
Open Fri–Sun 10–noon, 2.30–5.30, Tue–Thu 2.30–5.30.

For children
Doll Museum
Rocca di Angera.
Via Rocca 10.
Tel: 0331 931300.
Open Mar–Oct, 9–5.30.

Civic Archaeological Museum
Via Marconi 2,
Tel: 0331 931133.
Open Mon, Thu, Sat 5–7pm, or by request.

TOUR 6

i Varese: see *Tour 5*.

i Via Cardinale Branda 14, Castiglione Olona.
Tel: 0331 858301.

1 Castiglione Olona
Collegiate complex (Museum of Sacred Art)
Via Cardinale Branda 1.
Tel: 0331 850903.
Open Apr–Sep, Tue–Sun 10–1, 3–6; Oct–Mar, Tue–Sat 9.30–12.30, 2.30–5.30. Closed Mon.

Civic Museum of Palazzo Branda Castiglioni
Via Mazzini 23, Tel: 0331 858048.
Open Apr–Sep, Tue–Sat 9–1, 3–6, Sun 3–6; Oct–Mar, Tue–Sat 9–noon, 3–6, Sun 3–6.

2 Gornate Olona
Monastery of Torba
Via Stazione 2, near Torba.
Tel: 0331 820301.
Open Wed–Sun 10–6. Closed Mon, Tue & Dec–Jan.

3 Castelseprio
Archaeological Site
Via Castelvecchio 58.
Tel: 0331 820438.
Open Tue–Sat 8.30–7.30, Sun 9.30–6.30.

Recommended walk
Ticino Natural Park
Direzione a Oleggio, Via Garibaldi 4, Varano Borghi.
Tel: 0321 93028, fax: 0321 93029.

7 Biandronno
Museum of Virginia Island
Virginia Island.
Tel: 0332 766268.
Seasonal opening.

TOUR 7

i Piazza Cavour 17, Como.
Tel: 031 269712, fax: 031 240111.

i Palazzo Civico, Lugano, Riva Albertolli.
Tel: 0041 91 9133232, fax: 0041 91 9227653.

i Palazzo Comunale, Lanzo d'Intelvi.
Tel: 031 840143, fax: 031 261152.

For children
Al Maglio Zoo
Magliasco.
Tel: 0041 91 6061493;
www.zooalmaglio.ch.
Open Apr–Oct, daily 9–7; Nov–Mar, daily 10–6.

4 Morcote
Scherrer Park
Tel: 0041 91 9133232.
Open mid-Mar to end Oct, 10–5; Jul & Aug 10–6.

5 Lugano
Cantonal Museum of Art
Via Canova 10.
Tel: 0041 91 9104780;
www.museo-cantonale-arte.ch.
Open 10–5, Tue 2–5, but hours can vary according to exhibitions. Closed Mon.

Museum of Fine Arts
Parco Civico, Villa Ciani.
Tel: 0041 91 8667214.
Open 10–noon, 2–6, but hours can vary according to exhibitions. Closed Mon.

Cantonal Museum of Natural History
Viale Cattaneo 4.
Tel: 0041 91 8154761.
Open 9–noon, 2–5. Closed Sun–Mon.

Special to...
Museum of Extra-European Culture
Via Cortivo 24.
Tel: 0041 5886 6960;
www.mcl.lugano.ch.
Open Mar–Oct, 2–7. Closed Mon.

9 Campione d'Italia
Civic Gallery
Opposite Casino.
Hours can vary according to exhibitions. Closed Mon.

i Tourist Information Centre
🔟 Number on tour

TOUR 8

i Piazza Cavour 17, Como.
Tel & fax: 031 3300111.

4 Tempio Voltiano
Viale Marconi.
Tel: 031 574705.
Open Apr–Oct, 10–noon, 3–6; Nov–Mar 10–12, 2–4. Closed Mon.

5 Villa Olmo
Via Cantoni.
Tel: 031 252443.
Villa hours vary depending on current exhibitions. Gardens Mon–Sat 8am–dusk.

Recommended walk
Castel Baradello
Via Castel Baradello.
Tel: 031 592805.
Open Thu, Sat–Sun 2–6.

8 Civic Museums
Town Museum
Piazza Medaglie d'Oro.
Tel: 031 271343.
Open Tue–Sat 9.30–12.30, 2–5, Sun 10–1. Closed Mon.

Giuseppe Garibaldi
Museum of the
Risorgimento
Palazzo Olginati 1,
Piazza Medaglie d'Oro.
Tel: 031 271343.
Open – see Town Museum.

Special to...
Pinacoteca Palazzo Volpi
Via Diaz 86. Tel: 031 269869.
Open Tue–Sat 9.30–12.30, 2–5, Sun 10–1.

Silk Museum
Via Castelnuovo 1.
Tel: 031 303180.
Open Tue–Fri 9–12, 3–6. Closed Sat–Sun.

Fondazione Ratti Textile Museum
Lungolago Trento 9.
Tel: 031 233224;
www.fondazioneratti.org.
Visits by appointment only.

TOUR 9

i Como: see *Tour 8.*

i Via Regina 33/b, Cernobbio.
Tel: & fax: 031 349730.

i Via Regina 3, Tremezzo.
Tel: 0344 40493.

i Via Statale Regina 1, Cadenabbia.
Tel: & fax: 0344 40393.

i Piazza Venini 1, Varenna. Tel: & fax: 0341 830367.

1 Cernobbio
Villa Pizzo
Via Regina.
Tel: 031 511700.
Visits by appointment only.

Villa Erba
Via Regina.
Tel: 02 4997 7134.
Visit www.villaerba.it for latest details.

Villa d'Este
Via Regina 40.
Tel: 031 3481.
Hotel – open to guests.

2 Moltrasio
Villa Passalacqua
Viale dei Cipressi.
Occasionally open for concerts – check in town.

Special to...
Villa Balbianello
Near Balbianello, Lenno.
Tel: 0344 56110.
Park open Easter–Oct, 10–12.30, 3.30–6.30. Closed Mon & Wed.

6 Tremezzo
Villa Carlotta
Tel: 0344 40405,
fax: 0344 43689;
www.villacarlotta.it.
Open mid-Mar to Apr 9–4.30; Apr–Sep 9–6; Oct to mid-Nov 9–5.

8 Varenna
Villa Cipressi
Tel: 0341 830113.
Open Mar–Oct, daily 9–6

(longer hours in high summer).

Villa Monastero
Tel: 0341 830129,
fax: 0341 831281.
Open: see Villa Cipressi.

9 Civate
Basilica of San Pietro al Monte
Tel: 0341 551576.
Open Jul & Aug, Sun 8.30–5; rest of year by request.

10 Erba
Archaeological Museum
Villa San Giuseppe.
Tel: 031 615262.
Open Tue 9–noon, Wed & Fri 3–6.

TOUR 10

i Via Marconi 1 (corner Piazza Duomo), Milan.
Tel: 02 725 24300.

i Via N Sauro 6, Lecco.
Tel: 0341 295720,
fax: 0341 295730.

i Piazza Mazzini, Bellagio.
Tel: & fax: 031 950204.

1 Lecco
Villa Manzoni
Via Guanella 7.
Tel: 0341 481247,
fax: 0341 369251.
Open 9.30–5.30. Closed Mon.

Visconti tower
Piazza XX Settembre.
Tel: 0341 282396.
Open only for temporary exhibitions.

Museum of the Risorgimento and the Resistance
Palazzo Belgioioso, Corso Matteotti 32.
Tel: 0341 481248.
Open 9.30–2. Closed Mon.

2 Bellagio
Villa Melzi d'Eryl
Tel: 39 3939 457 3838.
Open Apr–Oct, 9–6.

Special to...
Villa Serbelloni
Tel: 031 950216.
Open to non-residents.

8 Merate
Villa Belgioioso
Via Roma.
Tel: 02 8057484.
Visits by appointment.

Astronomical observatory
Tel: 039 999111.
Very limited opening hours. Call tourist office for current details.

9 Monza
Duomo (Cathedral)
Piazza Duomo.
Visits to the Iron Crown 9–noon, 3–5.

Back to nature
Villa Reale
Viale Regina Margherita 2.
Tel: 0393 22086.
Visits by appointment.

TOUR 11

i Lecco: see *Tour 10.*

i Piazza Garibaldi 8, Menaggio.
Tel: & fax: 0344 32924.

i Piazza Garibaldi 9, Barzio.
Tel 0341 996255,
fax: 0341 910103.

1 Mandello del Lario
Museum of Motto-Guzzi Motorcycles
Via Parodi 57.
Tel: 0341 709111.
Guided tour 3–4 except Sat, Sun & holidays. Closed Jan.

Special to...
Larian Boat Museum
Via Statale 139, Pianello del Lario, near Dongo.
Tel: 0344 87235 or 0344 87294.
Open May–Nov, Sat–Sun 10.30–12.30, 2.30–6; Jul–15 Sep, daily 2.30–6.30.

🟦 Abbazia di Piona
Tel: 0341 940331.
Open 9–noon, 2–6.

🟦 Bellano
Orido (gorge)
Tel: 0341 821124.
Open all year round.

🔟 Alessandro Manzoni home
Via A Manzoni 4.
Tel: 0341 996125.
Open Mon–Fri 9–noon, also 3–5.30 Mon & Wed. Library 3–6, except Thu & Sun.

TOUR 12

i̲ Piazza Marconi (railway station), Bergamo.
Tel: 035 210204.
Via Gombito 13, Bergamo.
Tel: 0352 42226,
fax: 0352 42994.

🟦 Angelo Mai Civic Library
Piazza Vecchia 15.
Tel: 035 399430.
Open: lending & reference 8.45–11.45, 2.30–5.30.

🟦 Piazza Duomo
Basilica of Santa Maria Maggiore
Piazza Duomo.
Tel: 0352 23327.
Open Apr–Oct, 8–noon, 3–7; Nov–Mar, 8–noon, 3–6; holidays 8–10.30, 3 7.

Colleoni Chapel
Piazza Duomo.
Tel: 0352 210061.
Open Apr–Oct, 9–12.30, 2–6.30; Nov–Mar, 9–12.30, 2–4.30. Closed Mon.

🟦 Cittadella
Civic Natural Science Museum
Piazza della Cittadella 10.
Tel: 035 399422.
Open Tue–Fri 9–noon, 2–6, Sat–Sun 9–7.30. Closed Mon.

Archaeological Museum
Piazza della Cittadella 12.
Tel: 0352 42389.
Same hours as Civic Natural Science Museum.

🟦 Pinacoteca dell'Accademia Carrara
Piazza Giacomo Carrara.
Tel: 0353 99677;
www.accademiacarrara.
bergamo.it.
Open Tue–Sun 10–1, 2.30–5.30. Closed Mon.

Gallery of Modern Art
Piazza Giacomo Carrara.
Tel: 0353 99527/8.
Visits only during exhibitions

🟦 Il Sentierone
Bergamo Donizetti Theatre
Piazza Cavour 15.
Tel: 035 4160611.
For guided tours contact theatre box office. or go to www.teatrodonizetti.it.

For children
Fantasy World Minitalia
Via Vittorio Veneto 52,
Capriate San Gervasio.
Tel: 0290 90169, fax:
0290 903469;
www.leolandiapark.it.
Open Apr–Jul, Mon–Fri 9.30–6, Sat–Sun 9.30–7.30; Aug. daily 9.30–7.30.

TOUR 13

i̲ Bergamo: see Tour 12.

i̲ Lungolago Marconi 2/c, Iseo.
Tel: 0309 80209,
fax: 0309 81361.

i̲ Via Lungolago Tempini 5, Pisogne.
Tel: 0364 880423.

i̲ Via Briscioli, Capo di Ponte.
Tel: 0364 42080.

i̲ Piazza Einaudi, 2, Boario Terme.
Tel: 0364 531609.

i̲ Piazza 13 Martiri 34, Lóvere.
Tel: 0359 962178
(seasonal).

🟦 Trescore Balneario
Spa establishment
Via Gramsci. Tel: 035 4255511;
www.termeditrescore.it.

Villa Suardi, Church of Santa Barbara
Via Statale 122.
Tel: 0359 40828.
Visits by request.

🟦 Iseo
Sassabanek Centre
Via Colombera 2.
Tel: 0309 80600.

Special to…
Church of Santa Maria della Neve
Pisogne.
Tel: 0364 87032.
Open May–Sep, 9.30–11.30, 3–6; Oct–Apr, Tue–Fri 3–5, Sat–Sun 9.45–11.15, 3–5. Closed Mon.

🟦 Capo di Ponte
Naquane National Park
Near Naquane.
Tel: 0364 42140.
Open 9–one hour before sunset. Closed Mon except holidays.

Museum of the Centre of Camun Prehistoric Studies
Via Marconi, 7.
Tel: 0364 42091.
Open Mon–Fri 9–5.

Parish church of San Siro
Tel: 0364 42080.
Visits by request.

🟦 Boario Terme
Spa establishment
Piazzale Terme 2.
Tel: 0364 525011.

Special to…
Academy of Fine Arts
Palazzo Tadini, Via Tadini.
Tel: 0359 62780.
Open May–Sep Tue–Sat 3–7, Sun 10–noon, 3–7; Oct–Apr by appointment.

TOUR 14

i̲ Brescia: see *Tour 15.*

i̲ Lungolago Marconi 2c, Iseo.
Tel: 0309 80209.

🟦 Provaglio d'Iseo
Monastery of San Pietro in Lamosa
Via Cesare Battisti.
Tel: 0309 83477.
Open Sat 2.30–6, Sun 10–noon.

Back to nature
Torbiere del Sebino Natural Reserve
Information: Consorzio, Via Europa 5, Provaglio d'Iseo Tel: 0309 823141.

🟦 Capriolo
Ricci Curbastro Agricultural and Wine Museum, Villa Evelina
Via Adro 37.
Tel: 0307 36094.
Estate open daily 8.30 12, 2–7. Museum by appointment.

🟦 Nigoline Bonomelli
Franciacorta Golf Club
Via Provinciale 32,
Nigoline di Franca Corta.
Tel: 0309 841167.

For children
Acqua Splash
Via Gen. Della Chiesa 3, Timoline.
Tel: 0309 826441.
Open 1st Sat Jun–last Sun Sep 9.30–7.

🔢 Bornato
Villa Monte Rossa
Tel: 0307 254614.
Visits by request.

Castle
Via Castello, 24.
Tel: & fax: 0307 25006.
Open Easter–Oct, every Sun; rest of year by request.

🔢 Rodengo-Saiano
Abbey of San Nicola
Via Brescia 83.
Tel: 0306 610182.
Open 9–noon, 3–6.

TOUR 15

i Via Musei 32, Brescia.
Tel: 0303 749916.

❶ Piazza Paolo VI
Rotonda and Duomo
Vecchio
Tel: 0304 3418.
*Open Apr–Sep, 9–noon,
3–7; Nov–Mar, Sat–Sun
10–noon, 3–5.*

Duomo Nuovo
Tel: 0304 2714.
Open 8–noon, 4–7.30.

Special to…
Tosio Martinengo
Picture Gallery
Via Martinengo da
Barco 1.
Tel: 0303 774999.
*Open Jun–Sep, Tue–Sun
10–5; Oct–May, Tue–Sun
9.30–1, 2.30–5.*

❺ Via dei Musei
Tempio Capitolino
Via dei Musei 57/a.
Tel: 030 46031.
*Tempio: Tue–Sun 10–1,
2–5.*

❻ Monastero di
Santa Giulia
City Museum
Via dei Musei 81/b.
*Open Jun–Sep, Tue–Sun
10–6; Oct–May, Tue–Sun
9.30–5.30.*

❼ Castello
Museum of the
Risorgimento
Castello.
Tel: 030 44176.
*Castle: daily 8am–dusk.
Museum: Tue–Sun 9.30–1,
2.30–5.*

Specola Cidnea
Castello.
Tel: 030 2978672.
*Call to confirm latest
opening times.*

Special to…
Luigi Marzoli Armoury
Museum
Castello, Mastio Visconteo.
Tel: 030 293292.
*Open Tue–Sun 10–1,
2.30–5.*

TOUR 16

i Brescia: see *Tour 15.*

i Viale Marconi 2,
Sirmione.
Tel: 030 916114 or
916245, fax: 030 916222.

i Via Porto Vecchio 34,
Desenzano. Tel: 030
748726.

i Piazza Sant'Antonio 4,
Salò. Tel: 0365 21423.

i Corso Repubblica 8,
Gardone Riviera. Tel:
0303 748736.

i Via Statale 1,
Toscolano Maderno.
Tel: 0303 748741.

❶ Sirmione
Grotte di Catullo
Tel: 030 916157.
*Open Mar–Oct, 8.30–7;
Nov–Feb, 8.40–4. Closed
Mon, except holidays.*

Rocca Scaligera
Tel: 030 916468.
*Open Apr–Sep, Tue–Sun
9–7; Oct–Mar 9–4.30.*

Spa establishment
Piazza Castello 12.
Tel: 030 916412,
fax: 030 916192,
www.termedisirmione.
com

❷ Desenzano
Giovanni Rambotti Civic
Archaeological Museum
Via T Dal Molin 7/c.
Tel: 030 9144529.
*Open Sun & holidays
10–noon, 3–7; weekdays
3–7. Closed Mon.*

Roman villa
Via Crocefisso 22.
Tel: 030 9143547.
*Open Apr–Sep, 9–6.30
or 7.30; Oct–Mar, 9–5.
Closed Mon.*

❻ Salò
Nastro Azzurro
Museum
Palazzo Fantoni. Via
Fantoni 49.

Tel: 0365 20804.
*Open Sat 10–12, 3–7, Sun
10–12, 3–5.*

❼ Gardone Riviera
Hruska botanical
gardens
Via Roma.
Tel: 0365 521139.
*Open mid-Mar to mid-Oct,
9–7.*

Special to…
Il Vittoriale
Piazza del Vittoriale,
Gardone Sopra.
Tel: 0365 296511,
fax: 0365 296512.
*Open Apr–Sep, Tue–Sun
9.30–7; Oct–Mar, Tue–Sun
9–1, 2–5.*

❽ Toscolano
Maderno
Bogliaco Golf Club
Via Golf.
Tel: 0365 643006.

Back to nature
Alto Garda Bresciano
Park
Via Oliva 32, Gargnano.
Tel: 0365 71449.

❿ Polpenazze
Museo Archeologico
della Valle Sabbia
Piazza San Bernardino 2.
Tel: 0365 31410.
*Open Tue–Fri 9–noon, Sat
9–noon, 2–5.*

⓭ Lonato
Fortress
*Open Sat–Sun 10–noon,
2.30–6.30.*

Ugo da Como
Foundation, Casa della
Podestà
Via Rocca 2.
Tel: 030 9130060.
Open – see Fortress.

TOUR 17

i Largo Medaglie
d'Oro al Valor Militare 5,
Riva del Garda.
Tel: 0464 554444,
fax: 0464 520308.

i Via Trento 15, Idro.
Tel: & fax: 0365 83224.

i Piazza Boldini 2,
Gargnano.
Tel: 0365 71222.

i Piazza Umberto I 18,
Tignale.
Tel: 0365 73462.

i Piazza Marconi 12,
near parish church,
Tremosine.
Tel: 0365 953185;
Via Alessandro Voltino.
Tel: 0365 916012
(seasonal);

i Via Comboni 15,
Limone sul Garda.
Tel: 0365 954265.

❶ Riva del Garda
Riva del Garda Fortress
Picture Gallery
Piazza Cesare Battista 3.
Tel: 0464 573869.
*Open mid-Mar to Jun &
Sep–Oct, Tue–Sun 10–6;
Jul–Aug daily 10–6.*

For children
Molina di Ledro
Lakedwelling Museum
Via Lungolago 1.
Tel: 0464 508182.
*Open mid-Jun to mid-Sep,
Tue–Sun 10–1, 2–6; mid-
Sep to Nov & Mar to mid-
Jun, Tue–Sun 9–1, 2–5.*

TOUR 18

i Riva del Garda: see
Tour 17.

i Via Roma 67, Tenno.
Tel: 0464 502153
(seasonal).

i Viale delle Palme 1,
Arco.
Tel: 0464 532255.

i Via Manci 2, Trento.
Tel: 0461 216000.

i Via Vittorio Emanuele
3, Lèvico Terme.
Tel: 0461 706101.

i Corso Rosmini 6,
Rovereto.
Tel: 0464 430363.

i Lungolago Verona 19,
Torbole Nago.
Tel: 0464 505177.

Special to…
Varone Falls
Tel: 0464 521421.

2 Arco
Castle
Tel: 0464 510156.
*Open Apr–Sep, 10–6,
Oct–Mar, 10–4. (Jan–Feb,
Sat–Sun only 10–4).*

Casinò
Via Magnolie.
Tel: 0464 516830.

For history buffs
Arboreto
Via Lomego.
Tel: 0464 270314.
*Open Apr–Sep, 8–7,
Oct–Mar, 9–4.*

4 Drena
Castle
Tel: 0464 541220.
*Open 10–6 (also 10–7
Jul, Aug, Nov, Dec & Feb).
Closed Mon.*

6 Trento
Buonconsiglio Castle
Via Clesio 5.
Tel: 0461 233770.
*Open Jun–Oct, Tue–Sun
10–6; Nov–May, Tue–Sun
9.30–5. Closed Mon.*

Duomo
Piazza Duomo.
Tel: 0461 234419.
*Open 7.30–12.30,
2.30–7.*

**Museum of Modern and
Contemporary Art**
Palazzo delle Albere,
Via da S. Severino 45.
Tel: 800 397760.
Open 10–6. Closed Mon.

**Tridentine Museum of
Natural Science**
Via Calepina 14.
Tel: 0461 270311.
Open 10–6. Closed Mon.

**Caproni Museum of
Aeronautics**
Via Lidorno 3,
Trento Aeroporto.

Tel: 0461 944888.
*Open Tue–Fri 9–1, 2–5,
Sat–Sun 10–1, 2–6.
Closed Mon.*

Scenic routes
**Giardino Botanico
Alpino**
Near Trento.
Tel: 0461 948050.
*Open Jun–Sep, 9–5;
Jul–Aug, 9–6.*

9 Rovereto
**Fortunato Depero
Museum**
Via della Terra 53.
Tel: 0464 434393.
Open Tue–Sun 10–1, 3–6.

**Italian War History
Museum**
Via Castelbarco 7.
Tel: 0464 438100.
Open Tue–Sun 10–6.

MART
Corso Bettini 43.
Tel: 800 327760.
Open 10–6. Closed Mon.

TOUR 19
---

i Aeroporto Valerio
Catullo, Verona.
Tel & fax: 045 8619163;
Via degli Alpini 9, Verona
Tel: 045 8068680;
fax: 045 8003638;
Piazza XXV Aprile,
Verona.
Tel: 045 8000861.

1 Piazza Bra
**Maffei Stone Tablet
Museum**
Piazza Bra 28.
Tel: 045 590087.
*Open 8–1.30. Occasionally
open pm. Closed Mon.*

Arena
Tel: 045 8003204.
*Open Tue–Sun 8.30–6.30,
Mon 1.45–6.30; during
opera season 9–3.30.*

2 Via Mazzini
Casa di Giulietta
Via Cappello 23.
Tel: 045 8034303.
*Open Tue–Sun 8.30–7.30,
Mon 1.30–7.30.*

4 Piazza dei
Signori
Lamberti tower
Palazzo del Comune.
Tel: 045 8032726.
*Open 9.30–7.30.
Closed Mon.*

6 Teatro Romano
Archaeological area
Regaste Redentore 2.
Tel: 045 8000360.
*Open Tue–Sun 8.30–7.30,
Mon 1.30–7.30.*

8 Castelvecchio
Civic Art Museum
Corso Castelvecchio 2.
Tel: 045 806 2611.
*Open Tue–Sun 8.30–7.30,
Mon 1.45–7.30.*

Back to nature
Giardino Giusti
Via Giardino Giusti 2.
Tel: 045 8034029.
*Open summer 9–8; winter
9–sunset.*

TOUR 20
---

i Verona: see Tour 19.

i Piazzale Betteloni 15,
Peschiera del Garda.
Tel: 045 7551673,
fax: 045 7550381.

i Via F Fontana 14,
Lazise.
Tel: 045 7580114,
fax: 045 7581040.

i Piazzale Aldo Moro 5,
Bardolino.
Tel: 045 7210078,
fax: 045 7210872.

1 Peschiera
del Garda
**Museum of the History
of the Risorgimento**
Piazza Catullo 1.
Tel: 045 7550938.
Currently closed.

2 Gardaland
Near Ronchi di
Castelnuovo del Garda.
Tel: 045 6449777,
www.gardaland.it
*Open Apr to mid-Jun to
mid- to end Sep 10–6; mid-
Jun to mid-Sep*

10am–11pm; Oct, Sat–Sun
10–6; 19 Dec–6 Jan 10–6.

3 CanevaWorld
Via Fossalta 1, Lazise
sul Garda.
Tel: 045 6969700,
www.canevaworld.it

Back to nature
Villa dei Cedri Park
Piazza di Sopra 4, Colà
di Lazise.
Tel: 045 75909881.

Scenic routes
**Consorzio Tutela Vino
Bardolino**
Piazza Matteotti 8.
Tel: 045 7211964,
fax: 045 7210820.

5 Bardolino
**Cantine Fratelli Zeni
Wine Museum**
Via Costabella 9
Tel: 045 6228331.
*Open mid-Mar to Oct,
9–1, 2–7.*

**Cisano Olive Oil
Museum**
Via Peschiera 54, Cisano
Tel: 045 6229047.
*Open Mon–Sat 9–12.30,
2.30–7, Sun and holidays
9–12.30. Closed Wed &
Sun in Jan & Feb.*

For children
Paese di Bengodi
Viale del Lavoro 107,
Ferlina di Bussolengo.
Tel: 045 7156849,
fax: 045 6767092.

Rio Valli Water Park
Near Fosse, Cavaion
Veronese.
Tel: 045 6268392,
www.riovalli.com
*Open Mon–Fri 9.30–7,
Sat–Sun 9–7 from last
Sun in May to first Sun
in Sep.*

6 Parco Natura Viva
di Pastrengo
Loc. Figara 40,
Bussolengo.
Tel: 045 7170113, fax:
045 6770247,
www.parconaturaviva.it.
Open Mar–Nov 9–6.

TOUR 21

ⁱ Verona: see *Tour 19*.

ⁱ Piazza Andrea Mantegna 6, Mantua.
Tel: 0376 432432,
fax: 0376 363292.

ⁱ Via Marta Tana 1,
Castiglione
delle Stiviere.
Tel: 0376 944061,
fax: 0376 948940.

🄵 Villafranca di Verona
Risorgimento Museum
Castello, Corso Vittorio
Emanuele II.
Tel: 045 7902901.
*Open Sat 4–6, Sun 3–7
(6.30 Nov–Feb); second
Sun in month 10–noon,
3–7.*

🄱 Mantua
Palazzo Ducale
Piazza Sordello 40.
Tel: 0376 224832 or
041 241897;
www.mantovaducale.it.
*Guided tours Tue–Sun
8.30–7.*

Palazzo Te
Viale Te.
Tel: 0376 323266 or
365886.
*Open Tue–Sun 9–6,
Mon 1–6.*

**House of Andrea
Mantegna**
Via Acerbi 47.
Tel: 0376 360506 or
326685.
*Open Tue–Sun 10–12.30,
3–6 during exhibitions.
hours may vary.*

**For children
Acquapark Altomincio**
Salionze.
Tel: 045 7945131,
fax: 045 7190147.

Mincio Park Association
Via Marangoni, 36.
Tel: 0376 22831,
fax: 045 362657.

Parco Acquatico Cavour
Near Ariano.
Tel: 045 7950904 or
045 6371139, fax: 045
6370618, www.
parcoacquaticocavour.it
*Open late May–early Sep
9.30–7.*

🄷 Cavriana
**Consorzio Tutela Vini
Mantovani a Doc**
c/o Camera di
Commercio, Via Calvi 28.
Tel: 0376 234220.

**Museo archeologico
dell'Alto Mantovano**
Piazza Castello 8.
Tel: 0376 806330;
www.museocavriana.it.
*Open Tue–Fri 9–noon,
Sat–Sun 9–noon, 3–6.*

🄸 Solferino
**History Museum and
Ossuary, Rocca**
Tel: 0376 854019 or
854068.
*Open Apr–Sep, Tue–Sun
9–12.30, 2.30–6.30.
Special calendar rest of
year. Closed Mon and
16–31 Dec.*

🄹 Castiglione delle Stiviere
**International Red Cross
Museum**
Palazzo Longhi, Via
Garibaldi 50.
Tel: 0376 638505.
*Open Apr–Oct, Tue–Sun
9–12, 3–6; Nov–Feb,
Tue–Sun 9–12, 2–5.*

TOUR 22

ⁱ Verona: see *Tour 19*.

ⁱ Piazza Donatori di
Sangue, Garda.
Tel: 045 6270384,
fax: 045 7256720.

ⁱ Via Fratelli Lavanda 5,
Torri del Benaco.
Tel: 045 7225120
(seasonal).

ⁱ Frazione Porto,
Brenzone.
Tel: 045 7420076
(seasonal).

ⁱ Via Capitanato 6/8,
Malcésine.
Tel: 045 7400044,
fax: 045 7401633.

**For children
Baie delle Sirene Park**
Near San Vigilio.
Tel: 045 7255584;
www.parcobaiadelle
sirene.it.
Open daily in summer.

🄱 Torri del Benaco
Castello
Via Fratelli Lavanda 2.
Tel: 045 6296111;
www.museodelcastello
torridelbenaco.it.
*Open Jun–Sep, daily
9.30–1, 4.30–7.30; Apr,
May, Oct daily 9.30–12.30,
2.30–6; Nov–Mar, Sun only
2.30–5.30.*

**Special to…
Baldo and Garda Natural
History Museum**
Castello, Via Castello 1.
Tel: 045 6570333.
*Open May–Sep, daily
9.30–8; Oct–Apr, Sat–Sun
10–5.*

🄹 Novezzina
**Monte Baldo Botanical
Garden**
Tel: 045 6247288;
www.ortobotanico
montebaldo.org.
Open Mar–Sep, daily 9–6.

TOUR 23

ⁱ Piazza San Marco 71.
Tel: 041 5298711,
fax: 041 5230399;
Santa Lucia railway
station.
Tel: & fax: 041 5298711.

🄵 Grand Canal to Ponte dell' Accademia
**Civic Natural History
Museum**
Salizzada del Fondaco dei
Turchi 1730.
Tel: 041 5240885.
*Open Tue–Fri 9–1,
Sat–Sun 10–4.*

Museum of Modern Art
Fondamenta di Ca'
Pesaro 2076.
Tel: 041 721127; www.
museicivicivenezianii.it.
*Open Apr–Oct, daily 10–6;
Nov–Mar, daily 10–5.*

Museum of Oriental Art
Fondamenta di Ca'
Pesaro 2076.
Tel: 041 721127.
*Open as for Museum of
Modern Art above.*

**Giorgio Franchetti
Gallery**
Calle Ca' d'Oro 3932.
Tel: 041 5222349.
*Open Tue–Sun 8.15–7.15,
Mon 8.15–2.*

**Museum of 18th-
century Venetian Art**
Ca' Rezzonico, Campo
San Barnaba 3136.
Tel: 041 2410100.
*Open Wed–Mon 10–6
(closes at 5 Nov–Mar).
Closed Tue.*

🄱 Gallerie dell'Accademia
Campo della Carità 1050.
Tel: 041 5222247.
*Open Tue–Sun 8.15–7.15,
Mon 8.15–2.*

**Peggy Guggenheim
Collection**
Palazzo Venier dei Leoni,
Fondamenta Venier.
Tel: 041 2405411.
Open 10–6. Closed Tue.

🄱 Piazza San Marco
Basilica di San Marco
Tel: 041 5225205.
*Open Apr–Oct, Mon–Sat
9.30–5, Sun 2–4; Nov–Mar,
Mon–Sat 9.45–4.30, Sun
2–4.*

Campanile di San Marco
Tel: 041 5224064.
*Open Nov–Mar, daily
9.30–3.45; Apr–Jun & Oct,
9–7; Jul–Sep, 9–9. Closed
3 weeks after Christmas.*

Treasure of San Marco
Basilica di San Marco.
Tel: 041 5225697.
Open as for Basilica above.

Correr Museum
Piazza San Marco 52.
Tel: 041 2405211.
*Open Apr–Oct, daily 9–7;
Nov–Mar, daily 9–5.*

Special to...
Fondazione Giorgio Cini
Isola di San Giorgio
Maggiore.
Tel: 041 5240119.
*Open Tue–Sun 10–6.
Closed Mon.*

[4] Palazzo Ducale
Piazzetta San Marco.
Tel: 041 2715911.
*Open Apr–Oct, daily 9–7;
Nov–Mar, daily 9–5.*

Archaeological Museum
Piazza San Marco 52.
Tel: 041 5225978.
*Open Apr–Oct, daily 9–7;
Nov–Mar, daily 9–5.*

**[6] Santa Maria dei
Miracoli**
Campo Santa Maria
Nuova.
Tel: 041 2750462.
*Open Mon–Sat 10–5,
Sun 1–5.*

Special to...
**Jewish Museum and
Synagogue**
Campo dei Ghetto
Novo 2902/B.
Tel: 041 715359.
*Open 10–7, Oct–May
until 5.30. Closed Sat &
Jewish holidays. May also
closes early on Fri.*

[8] Campo San Polo
Church of San Polo
Tel: 041 2750462.
*Open Mon–Sat 10–5,
Sun 1–5.*

**[9] Santa Maria dei
Frari**
Campo dei Frari.
Tel: 041 2750462.
*Open 10–6, Sun & holi-
days 1–6.*

**[10] Scuola Grande di
San Rocco**
Campo di San Rocco
3054.
Tel: 041 5234864.
Open Apr–Oct, daily

*9–5.30: Nov–Mar, daily
10–4.*

Murano
Museum of Glass Art
Fondamenta Marco
Giustinian 8.
Tel: 041 739586.
Open 10–5. Closed Wed.

Torcello
Torcello Museum
Piazza Santa Fosca.
Tel: 041 2702464.
*Open Mar–Oct, Tue–Sun
10.30–6; Nov–Feb, Tue–Sun
10–5. Closed Mon & holi-
days.*

TOUR 24
---

[i] Venice: see *Tour 23*.

[i] Via Francesco Maria
Preti 66, Castelfranco
Veneto.
Tel: 0423 491416.

[i] Piazza Garibaldi 73,
Àsolo.
Tel: 0423 529046.

[i] Piazzetta Trento Trieste
9, Feltre.
Tel: 0439 2540, fax: 0439
2839.

[i] Via XX Settembre 61,
Conegliano.
Tel: 0438 21230, fax: 0438
428777.

[i] Piazza Monte di Pietà
8, Treviso.
Tel: 0422 547632.

[1] Malcontenta
Villa Foscari
Tel: 041 5203966.
*Open Tue and Sat 9–noon,
Apr–Oct only.*

For children
Aquaestate di Noale
Near Mestre.
Tel: 041 5800907.
*Open Jun–Aug, daily
9.30–7.*

[2] Mira
Villa Seriman
Via Nazionale 420.
Tel: 0330 261510.
Visits by appointment.

Villa Valmarana
Via Valmarana 11.
Tel: 041 4266387;
www.villavalmarana.net.
*Open Mar–Oct, daily
10–6; rest of year by
appointment.*

[3] Stra
Villa Pisani
Via Doge Pisani 2.
Tel: 049 502074.
*Open mid-Mar to Apr &
Oct, Tue–Sun 9–6;
Apr–Sep, Tue–Sun 9–8;
Nov–Mar, Tue–Sun 9–5.
Closed Mon.*

**Villa Foscari-
Negrelli-Rossi**
Via Doge Pisani 1–2.
Tel: 019 9800335.
*Open Tue–Fri 9–noon,
2.30–4, Sun 10–6.*

[5] Àsolo
Civic Museum
Loggia del Capitano,
Via Regina Cornaro 74.
Tel: 0423 524637.
*Open Sat–Sun 10–noon,
3–7.*

Rocca
Tel: 049 710977.
*Contact tourist office for
latest hours.*

Special to...
Villa Barbaro
Masèr.
Tel: 0423 923004.
*Open Jan & Feb, Sat
10–5, Sun 11–5; Mar &
Jul–Aug, Tue, Thu, Sat
10–6, Sun 11–6; Apr–Jun
& Sep–Oct, Tue–Sat 10–6,
Sun 11–6; Nov–Dec, Sat
7, Sun 2.30–5.*

[6] Possagno
House of Antonio
Canova
Tel: 0423 544323.
*Open 9–12.30, 3–6.
Closed Mon.*

[7] Feltre
Civic Museum
Via Luzzo 23.
Tel: 0439 885241.
*Open Tue–Sun
10.30–12.30, 3–6.*

Archaeological site
Piazza del Duomo.
Tel: 0439 83879.
*Open Mar–Oct, Sat–Sun
10–1, 4–7; Nov–Feb,
Sat–Sun 10–1, 3–6.*

**Recommended
walk**
Dolomiti Bellunesi
National Park
Piazzale Zancanaro 1.
Tel: 0439 3328.
www.dolomitipark.it

[8] Conegliano
Civic Museum
Piazzale Castelvecchio 8.
Tel: 0438 22871.
*Open Apr–Sep, 10 noon,
3.30–7; Oct–Mar,
10–12.30, 3.30–6.30.
Closed Mon, also week-
days in Nov.*

Scuola dei Battuti
Via XX Settembre
(Duomo).
Tel: 0438 22606.
*Open Sun & holidays
3–6.30.*

[9] Treviso
Santa Caterina
Via Santa Caterina.
Tel: 0422 547632.
*Open Tue–Sun 9–12.30,
2.30–6.*

TOUR 25
---

[i] Venice: see *Tour 23*.

[i] Piazza del Santo,
Padua. Tel: 049 8753087
(seasonal).
Vicolo Pedrocchi, Padua.
Tel: 049 8767927.

[i] Via del Santuario 6,
Monsélice.
Tel: 0429 783026.

[i] Via Negri 9, Este.
Tel: 0429 600462.

[i] Piazza dei Signori 8,
Vicenza.
Tel: 0444 320854/
544122.

[i] Piazza Matteotti 12,
Vicenza. Tel: 0444
3208542.

Practical • Information

i Tourist Information Centre
12 Number on tour

i Piazza Castello 1,
Maròstica.
Tel: 0424 72127.

i Largo Corona d'Italia
35, Bassano del Grappa.
Tel: 0424 524351.

i Porta Bassanesi 2,
Cittadella.
Tel: 0499 404485.

1 Padova (Padua)
Basilica del Santo
Piazza del Santo.
Tel: 049 8242811.
Open sunrise–sunset..

Palazzo della Ragione
Piazza delle Erbe.
Tel: 049 8205006.
*Open Feb–Oct 9–7;
Generally closed early
Nov–Jan.. Closed Mon.*

Eremitani Church
Piazza Eremitani 9.
Tel: 049 8756410.
*Open summer, 8.15–noon,
Sun & holidays 9–noon,
3.30–6.30; winter, Sun &
holidays 9–noon, 3.30–5.*

**Civic Museum and
Scrovegni Chapel**
Piazza Eremitani 8.
Booking essential: tel: 049
2010020 or at www.
cappelladegliscrovegni.it.
*Open Tue–Sun 9–7.
Occasional late opening to
10pm in summer.*

Scuola del Santo
Piazza del Santo. Tel: 049
8755235.
*Open Mar–Oct, 9–12.30,
2.30–7; Nov–Feb, 9–noon,
2.30–5.*

San Antonio Museum
Piazza del Santo.
Tel: 049 8225656.
*Open summer, daily
9–12.30, 2.30–6; winter,
10–1, 2–5.*

Botanical gardens
Via Orto Botanico 15.
Tel: 049 656614.
*Open Apr–Oct, 9–1, 3–6;
Nov–Mar, Mon–Sat 9–1.*

For children
Padua Amusement Park
Via Fogazzaro 8/D, Padua.
Tel: 049 8805025.
Open daily 10–10.

2 Arquà Petrarca
House of Petrarch
Via Valleselle.
Tel: 0429 718294.
*Open Tue–Sun 9–12.30,
3–7. Closed Mon.*

Special to...
Villa Pizzoni Ardemani
Valsanzibio.
Tel: 049 8059224;
www.valsanzibiogiardino.
it.
*Open Mar–Nov, 10–1,
2–sunset.*

Back to nature
Colli Euganesi Nature
Park
Via Rana Ca' Mori 8,
Este.
Tel: 0429 612010.

3 Monsélice
Sanctuary of the Sette
Chiese
Open 10–noon, 2–7.

Castle
Via del Santuario 24.
Tel: 0429 72931.
*Open Apr–Nov, 9–10.30,
3.30–5.
Closed Mon.*

4 Este
National Atestine
Museum
Via Negri 5/C.
Tel: 0429 2085.
Open Tue–Sun 9–8.

5 Montagnana
Rocca degli Alberi
*Open Apr–Oct, every
afternoon until sunset.*

Civic Museum
Castello di San Zeno,
Piazza Trieste.
Tel: 0429 804128.
*Guided visit at 11am Wed,
Thu & Fri in summer; at
11, 12, 4 & 5 Sat–Sun
only in winter.*

**6 Montecchio
Maggiore**
Castles of Romeo and
Juliet
Tel: 0444 696608.
Open by appointment.

**Villa Cordellina
Lombardi**
Via Lovara 36.
Tel: 0444 696085.
*Open Apr–Oct, Tue–Sun
9–1, 3–6. Closed Mon and
winter.*

7 Vicenza
Basilica Palladiana
Piazza dei Signori.
Tel: 0444 323681.
Closed for restoration.

Teatro Olimpico
Piazza Matteotti 11.
Tel: 0444 222800.
*Open Jun–Aug, 9–7; rest of
year, 9–5. Closed Mon.*

**City Picture Gallery and
Palazzo Chiericati**
Piazza Matteotti.
Tel: 0444 321348.
*Open Jun–Aug, 9–7; rest of
year, 9–5.*

Duomo (cathedral)
Piazza Duomo.
Tel: 0444 325007.
Open 10.30–noon, 3.30–7.

Basilica di Monte Berico
Viale X Giugno 87.
Tel: 0444 320999.
*Open 6–12.30, 2.30–7.30
(6pm in winter); Sun &
holidays 6am–8pm (7pm
in winter).*

Villa Valmarana ai Nani
Via dei Nani 2.
Tel: 0444 543976;
www.villavalmarana.com.
*Open 15 Mar–5 Nov,
Tue–Sun, 10–noon, 3–6;
rest of year, Sat–Sun
10–1, 2–4.*

**La Rotonda and Villa
Almerico-Capra**
Via Rotonda 45.
Tel: 0444 321793.
*Open mid-Mar to mid-Nov,
Tue–Thu 10–noon, 3–6;
mid-Nov to mid-Mar,
Tue–Sun 10–noon, 2.30–5;
(exterior); mid-Mar to mid-
Nov, Wed only 10–noon,
3–6 (interior).*

8 Maròstica
Castello Inferiore and
Costume Museum
Piazza Castello 1.
Tel: 0424 72127.
*Open Sun 2.30–6. Other
times by appointment.*

**9 Bassano
del Grappa**
Museum of the
Alpine Soldiers
Ponte degli Alpini 36061.
Tel: 0424 503650.
Open Tue–Sun 9–6.

Grappa Museum
Via Gamba 6
(Ponte Vecchio).
Tel: 0424 524426.
Open daily 10–8.

Ceramic Museum
Palazzo Sturm, Via
Schiavonetti. Tel: 0424
524915.
*Open Apr–Oct, Tue–Sat
9–12.30, Sun 3.30–6.30;
Nov–Mar, Fri 9–12.30,
Sat–Sun 3.30–6.30.*

Scenic routes
Memorial Chapel of
Monte Grappa
Tel: 0424 53101.
*Open summer, 9–noon,
2–5; winter, 10–noon, 1–4.*

10 Cittadella
Palazzo Pretorio
Via Marconi 30.
Tel: 049 9413411.
Open for exhibitions only.

INDEX

Index

Index & Acknowledgements

The Automobile Association

wishes to thank the following libraries and photographers for their assistance in the preparation of this book.

AA PHOTO LIBRARY 14, 30, 39b, 74, 75, 97; ARCHIVI ALINARI/ARCHIVIO SEAT (FOTO ALINARI/TATGE) 26, 31; C CONCINA 111; A DALLE VEDOVE 107b, 119c, 154; FONDAZIONE IL VITTORIALE DEGLI ITALIANI 24a, 99; INTELFOTO 46–7; M. LANFRANCHI 48, 49, 54–5, 55a, 59, 61b, 62a, 65, 66, 68, 69, 89b, 171; M LA TONA 149; E MANGHI 38, 39a, 41b, 42–3, 45, 47b, 55b, 67b; L PESSINA 6, 16, 17, 18, 20, 22, 23, 24b, 32, 35, 36, 107a; M PEZZOTTA 71, 76, 78, 79a, 83, 85, 86, 86–7, 87a, 88b, 90, 92b, 92–3, 104, 105b, 121a, 126–7, 162–3; L PRANOVI 133, 135a, 145, 147b, 157; PRANOVI-DALLE VEDOVE 95b, 100, 119a, 119b, 128, 129, 130–1, 131a; REALY EASY STAR 41a, 98, 113a; REALY EASY STAR/L. ANTON SCATOLA 102; REALY EASY STAR/P BENINI 146–7; REALY EASY STAR/M BRUZZO 134, 138–9, 146b, 153; REALY EASY STAR/E CARPEGNA 148; REALY EASY STAR/C. CONCINA 108, 109b, 114, 115, 120, 142b, 150, REALY EASY STAR/G. FURGHIERI 136; REALY EASY STAR/M MARCHETTI 127a; REALY EASY STAR/L PESSINA aletta, 7, 8, 9a, 10–11, 13, 15, 19, 21a, 27b, 33, 40, 51b, 52a, 60, 64b, 67a, 73b, 81b, 109a; REALY EASY STAR/L PRANOVI 25, 116, 117; REALY EASY STAR/C RICCI 118; REALY EASY STAR/G RODANTE 44; REALY EASY STAR/V ROSSATO 56; REALY EASY STAR/M RUBINO 88a; REALY EASY STAR/L SECHI 70, 79b, 84–5, 89a; REALY EASY STAR/SINTESI/. MENEGHETTI 156; REALY EASY STAR/SONECA 144; REALY EASY STAR/T SPAGONE 11b, 12, 27a, 28, 29, 36–7, 43b, 50, 51a, 53, 61a, 63a, 64a, 72, 73a, 73c, 77, 82, 91, 93b, 94, 105a, 112a, 112–13, 122, 124, 135b, 139a, 140, 142a, 143, 151, 152; REALY EASY STAR/F TANEL 137, 141, 155; REALY EASY STAR/R VALTERZA 5, 9b, 21b, 34, 52b, 57, 58, 62–3, 95a, 103, 110, 121c, 121b, 125, 132, 167; REALY EASY STAR/A ZABERT 123; L SECHI 80b, 80–1; TERME SIRMIONE 96; R VALTERZA 101; D ZENATI 106.

Touring Map
1:500 000

Index to map pages

Legend

Lines of communication

Toll motorway

Toll-free motorway

Single-carriageway motorway

Exit and toll booth, service station, toll barrier

Major 4- and 2-lane roads

Regional 4- and 2-lane roads

Major or local road

Other roads, difficult roads

Motorway and road under construction

Two-, one-track railway, shuttle train

Rack or funicular railway

Cable-car, chair-lift

Other signs

12 Motorway distances in km

12 Partial and total road distances (km)

A1 45 Motorway number, main road number

F70 European road number

2315 Pass, height (in metres), gradients

Civil and tourist airport, ship or ferry, lighthouse

Major tourist port, other tourist ports

All-year and seasonal shipping lines

National, regional or provincial boundary

Tourist attractions

Hotel, refuge hut, holiday village, camping site

Church or abbey, chapel, castle, other fortified buildings

Villa or construction, archaeological and prehistoric remains, ruins

Cave, waterfall, other natural attractions

National park, park or gardens, scenic route

Historical and artistic attractions

Extremely interesting

Very interesting

Interesting

Resorts and natural attractions

Primary importance

Very important

Important

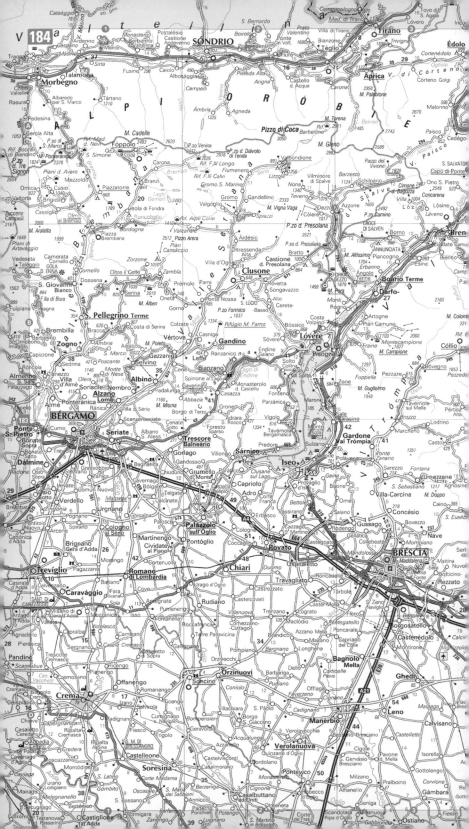

ATLAS INDEX

Atlas Index

Atlas Index

Town Plans

Index to town plans

Legend

Highway and thoroughfare		Monuments and buildings - Exceptional interest	
Main road		Monuments and buildings - Very interesting	
Other roads		Monuments and buildings - Interesting	
Pedestrian zone		Church	
Railway line and station		Tourist information office	
Hospital		Principal parking area	
Gardens and parks		Contour map showing elevation and gradient	

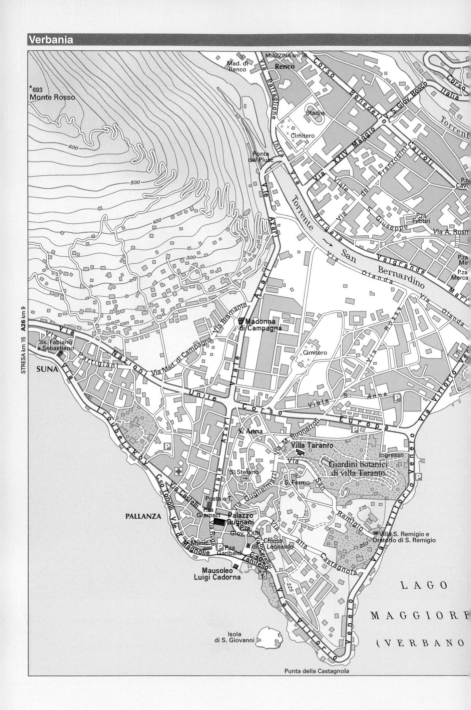

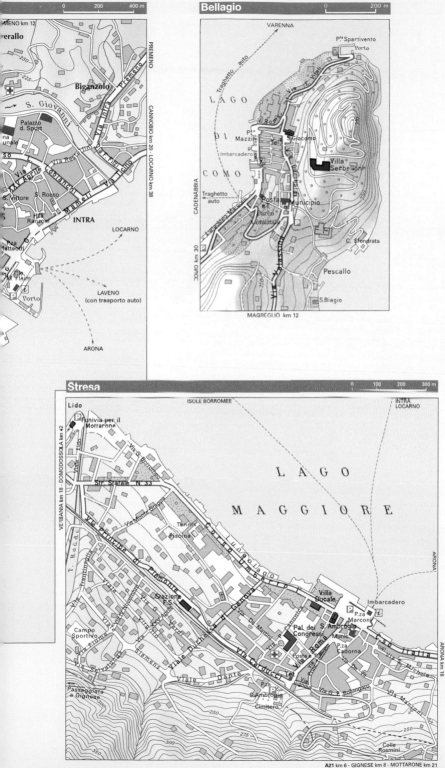

Bellagio

VARENNA

Traghetto auto

P.ta Spartivento
Porto

L A G O

D I

Via E.Vitali

Via Roma

C O M O

P.za
Mazzini
Tel.
S.Giacomo

Imbarcadero

CADENABBIA

Villa
Serbelloni

Traghetto
auto

Lungolago Marconi

COMO km 30

Posta
e
Tel.

Municipio

Via Garibaldi

Parco
Comunale

C. Sfondrata

Pescallo

S.Biagio

MAGREGLIO km 12

---

verallo

MENO km 12

PREMENO

PREMENO

CANNOBIO km 20 - LOCARNO km 38

Biganzolo

S. Giovanni

Palazzo
d. Sport

na
unale

so

Via Intra

Via Premeno

Via Restellini

Via Ticino

XXV Aprile

Cobianchi

Via Mameli

S. Rocco

S. Vittore

Ranzoni

INTRA

Via

P.za G.
Matteotti

P.le

M. Vitim

P

Porto

LOCARNO

LAVENO
(con trasporto auto)

ARONA

Stresa

ISOLE BORROMEE

INTRA
LOCARNO

Lido

Funivia per il
Mottarone

VERBANIA km 18 - DOMODOSSOLA km 42

Via Lido

Viale Lido

Via G. Borghetto

Via Monte Grappa

Str. Statale N. 33

Tennis
Piscina

L A G O

M A G G I O R E

T. Roddo

T. Frontmorta

Via Principe di Piemonte

Viale

Via XXV Aprile

Via Duchessa di Genova

Corso Umberto I

Via Genova

Via De Martini

Villa
Ducale

Imbarcadero

Campo
Sportivo

Via Fiume

Viale Virgilio

Via Siemens

Via Selvalunga

Viale Duchessa di Genova

Via Carducci

Viale Dante

Pal. dei
Congressi

Via De Vit

Via Roma

S.Ambrogio

P.za
Marconi

Munic.

P.za
Cadorna

Cso Italia

ARONA

ARONA km 16

Via Mazzini

Posta e
Tel.

Via G. P. Bolongaro

Via Michelangelo

Via Mantoni

Passeggiata
a Gignese

P.za
S.Ambrogio
Cimitero

Colle
Rosmini

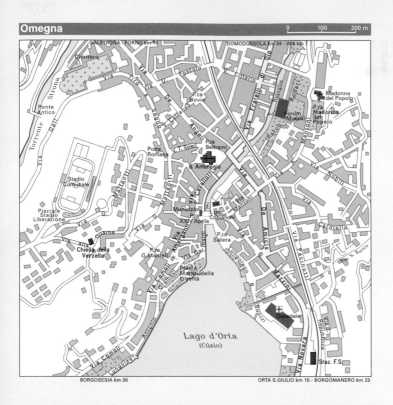

Lago d'Orta
(Cúsio)

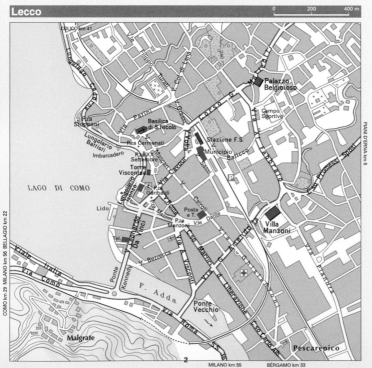

LAGO DI COMO

Gardone Riviera

0   100   200   300 m

RIVA DEL GARDA km 41

S. MICHELE

Strada Panoramica di S. Michele

Vittoriale
degli
Colli
Italiani

FASANO
DI SOTTO

Montecucco

150

100

200

GARDONE
DI SOPRA

P.ta
Vittoriale

Viale

del

Casinó

MORGNAGA

Via Trento

150

Municp.

Villa
Alba

Vittoriale

Torre
S. Marco

Giardino
Botanico
Heuska

200

Corso

Corso Zanardelli

Strada

Besun

Via Zanardelli

Imbarcadero

Staz.
Autolinee

GARDONE
RIVIERA

L A G O

Corso Zanardelli

Viale Trento

DESENZANO km 22 BRESCIA km 34

D I   G A R D A

Barbarano

BARBARANO

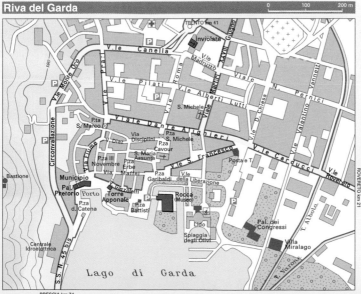

Riva del Garda

0   100   200 m

TRENTO km 41

V.le Canella

Inviolata

Via Madruzzo

XXIII Giugno

Via Montе d'Oro

P

Via Roma

Viale Pilati

Viale Alberti Lutti

Viale N. Pernici

P

S. Michele

Via Manini

Via D. Chiesa

Viale Valentino

P.ta
S. Marco

Viale Dante Alighieri

Via
Diaz

Via
Disciplini

P.ta
S. Michele

P.za
Cavour

Viale Carducci

Via Fiume

Circonvallazione

P

S. Maria
Assunta

P.za III
Novembre

P.za
Erbe

Via
Maffei

Via
S. Francesco

Posta e T.

Viale Roverelo

ROVERETO km 21

Bastione

Municipio

Pal.
Pretorio

Porto

Pazzolelli

Torre
Apponale

P.za
Garibaldi

Rocca
(Museo)

V.le
della Liberazione

P

Pza
d. Catena

P.za
Battisti

T. Albola

Lido

T. Varone

Pal. dei
Congressi

Centrale
Idroelettrica

S.S.N. 45 bis

Spiaggia
degli Olivi

Villa
Miralago

L a g o   d i   G a r d a

BRESCIA km 74

201

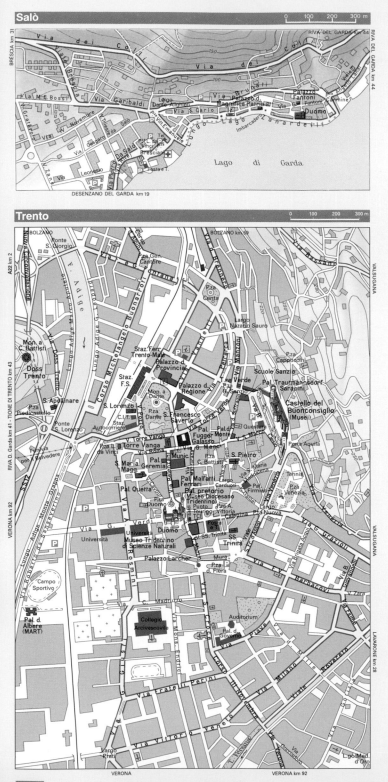

Salò

0 100 200 300 m

BRESCIA km 31

RIVA DEL GARDA km 44

RIVA DEL GARDA km 44

Via dei Colli

Viale Brescia

Via dei

Via Brunati

Via M.E. Bossi

Via Garibaldi

Largo Dante Alighieri

P Via Fantoni

Palazzo Fantoni

Fontoni

Via IV Novembre

V. Thiene

V. Trieste

V. Thiene Balla Sala

Via Gasparo da Salò

Via

Largo

Via Pietro da Salò

Union Lago

P Palazzo d. Magnifica Patria

Via S. Carlo

Palazzo d. Magnifica Patria

Duomo

Via Zanardelli

Camine

Tel. da Posta Bresciana

Pasla I.T.

Imbarcadero Zanardelli

Leonesio

Via Zana

Via

P

DESENZANO DEL GARDA km 19

Lago   di   Garda

Trento

0 100 200 300 m

BOLZANO

A22 km 2

Nuova Ricavalesana

Ponte S. Giorgio

Via G. Grazioli

Corso

Pza Gen. Cantore

BOLZANO km 69

VALSUGANA

F. Adige

Corso Michelangelo Buonarroti

Pza Centa

Pza

Largo Nazario Sauro

P

Mon. a C. Battisti

Doss Trento

Corso Alpini Adige

Staz. Terr. Trento-Male

i

P

Palazzo d. Provincia

P.za Cappuccini

Scuole Sanzio

P.za

S. Apollinare

Staz. F.S.

S. Lorenzo

Mon. a Dante

Palazzo d. Regione

Te Verde

P.za Sanzio

Pal. Traumannsdorf Saragini

VALSUGANA

P.za Piedicastello

Ponte S. Lorenzo

C.I.T.

Staz. Autocorriere

S. Francesco Saverio

Via Torre Verde

Castello del Buonconsiglio (Musei)

RIVA D. Garda km 41 - TIONE DI TRENTO km 43

Nuova per il Belvedere

V. Torre Vanga

da Vinci

Torre Vanga

P.za d. Vela

Via Roma

Pal. Fugger Monte Galasso

Pal. d.

P Questura

Via Manzoni

Porta Aquila

VERONA km 92

Lungo Adige Adige

S. Maria Magg.

Pal. Geremia

Via Mazzini

Munic.

Largo C. Battisti

S. Pietro

S. Maria Maddalena

Tennis

Lungo Adige S. Severino

P

Pal Quetta

Via S. Croce

Piazza Duomo

Pal Malfatti Ferrari

Pal. pretorio

Largo Carducci

Pal. Firmian

P.za Venezia

Via

Via G. Verdi

Università

Duomo

Museo Diocesano Tridentino

Punto i Touring

Via A. Gazzoletti

Via Nuova

Via G. Grazioli

P

Università

Museo Tridentino di Scienze Naturali

SS. Trinità

Posta e T.

Via Travai

Via Cavour

Via V. F.

Via B. Barbacovi

VALSUGANA

Campo Sportivo

Palazzo Larcher

Mura

P.za d. Fiera

Via Orsomson

V. Zara

Pal. d. Albere (MART)

C. Madruzzo

Collegio Arcivescovile

Via Monte Baldo

Auditorium

Pal. d. Governo

Largo

Via Piave

Via Mirano

Via Rosmini

Via Roveretto

LAVARONE km 28

Via Grazie

Viale Perini

Via Vittorio Veneto

Via R. Zandonai

V. Verona

Via Crocioni

Largo Prati

VERONA

VERONA km 92

L.go Med. d'Oro

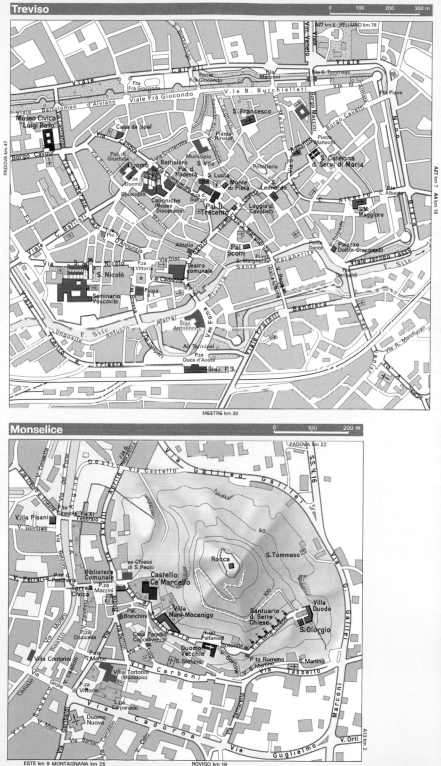

Treviso

0   100   200   300 m

A27 km 8 - BELLUND km 78

Vll. Venero

Canoli

Ponte
Frà Giocondo

P.ta
Frà Giocondo

Viale

Viale Barlomeo d'Alviano

Viale Frà Giocondo

V.le B. Burchiellati

Rta
Manzoni

Via S. Tommaso

V.le III

Pnt Piave

Museo Civico
"Luigi Bailo"

Casa da Noal

S. Francesco

S. Caterina
d. Servi di Maria

PADOVA km 47

BORGO CAVOUR

Piazza
Rinaldi

Municipio

S. Vito

Piazza
Matteotti

A27 km 7   A4 km 19

Duomo

Battistero

S. Lucia

Pescheria

Pal. d.
Podestà

Monte
di Pietà

Canova

Pal. di
Giustizia

P.za d.
Duomo

Pal. B.
Trecento

P.za d.
Signori

S. Leonardo

Loggia d.
Cavalieri

C. Albega

S. Alberto

S.M.
Maggiore

Episcopio

Canoniche
Museo
Diocesano

S. Pio X

Alitalia

Pal.
Scotti

Ponte
Dante

Palazzo
Dolfin-Giacomelli

Viale Iacopo Tasso

F. Sile

C. Bailo

D'Annunzio

Via Diaz

S. Margherita

P.za
d'Vittoria

Teatro
comunale

S. Margherita
Santa

Ponte
Garibaldi

S. Nicolò

V.le Cadorna

S. Nicolò

Seminario
Vescovile

Alì Terminal

Staz.
Antoinne

Lungozile   F. Sile

Trieste

P.za
Duca d'Aosta

Staz. F.S.

MESTRE km 20

Monselice

0   100   200 m

Via Castello

Galileo Galilei

PADOVA km 22

S.S. N.16

Villa Pisani

V. Giurinelli

Rocca

S. Tommaso

50

Biblioteca
Comunale

ex Chiesa
di S. Paolo

Castello
Ca' Marcello

Torre
Civica

Pal.
Mazzini

Villa
Nani-Mocenigo

Santuario
d. Sette
Chiese

Villa
Duodo

100

S. Giorgio

Pal.
Branchini

Casa Paradiso
Capodivacca

Lgo
Paltanien

Rotonda

P.za
Ossicella

Duomo
Vecchio

S. Stefano

P.ta Romana

S. Martino

S. Martino

Villa Contarini

P.za
S. Marco

Villa Tortorini
(Municipio)

Via Carboni

Via Tasselto

P.za
d'Vittoria

Lgo
Carpanedo

Duomo
Nuovo

Via Cadorna

Via Guglielmo

V. Orti

A13 km 2

ESTE km 9 MONTAGNANA km 25

ROVIGO km 19

Desenzano del Garda

0   150   300 m

RIVA DEL GARDA km 64

LAGO DI GARDA

Lungolago C. Battisti

Via A. Gramsci

Via Roma

Via Romana

Posta e T.

Cappelletti

Via Mazzini

Duomo

Cat. d. Turismo

Via Castello

Imbarcadero

P.za Matteotti

Via Anelli

Via Garibaldi

P.za Maggiore

Castello

Via dei Molini

Cast.

Museo Archeologico

Guglielmo Marconi

A4 km 3 - BRESCIA km 28

VERONA km 37

ALLA STAZIONE F.S.

Sirmione

0   100   200 m

P.ta di Sirmione

Grotte di Catullo

Antiquarium

Fonte Termale Boiola

Via Catullo

S. Pietro in Mavino

Lido

L A G O

Via Cennari

Via

S. Staffalo

Stab. Termale

Via G. Piana

Via Vitt. Eman.

S. M. Maggiore

Mura

Posta e T.

Carducci

Rocca Scaligera

Imbarcadero

P.le Porto

D I

G A R D A

Lungolago A. Diaz

Viale Marconi

Pal. Congressi

Tennis

Montebaldo

XXV Aprile

Via

DESENZANO km 10 - PESCHIERA km 11

Vicenza

ASIAGO km 56 - TRENTO km 96

Viale Aldo Ferrarin

F. Baracca

Viale Trento

P.le Tiro a Segno

Viale Ortigara

S. Croce

Via d. Monte Zovetto

Cappuccini

Via d. Monte Cimone

Via Batt. Framarin

Cairoli

S. Felice

Ss. Felice e Fortunato

Corso Ss. Felice

Via Torino

Via G. Maganza

Strada di Gogna

A4 km 6 - VERONA km 51

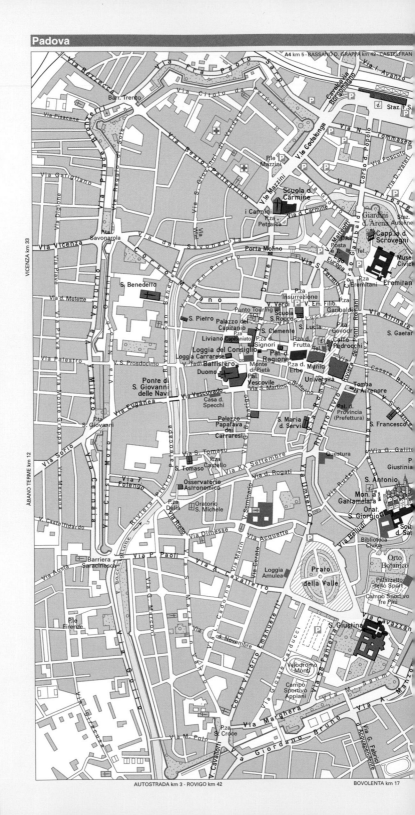

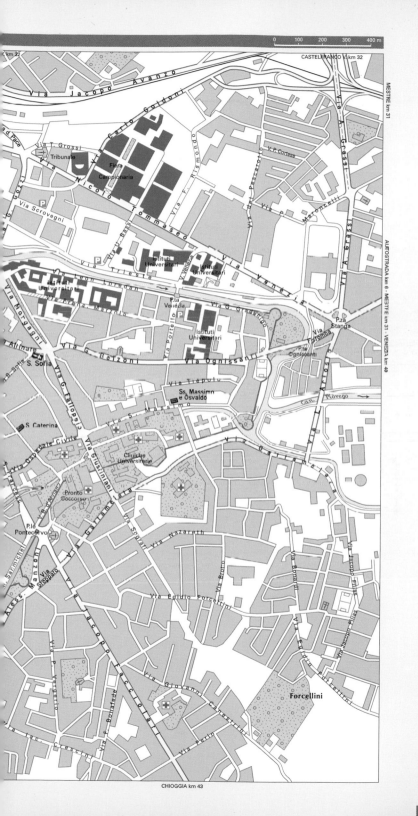

Via Jacopo Avanzo

Via T. Grossi
Tribunale

Via Nicolo Tommaseo

Via Carlo Guidoni

Fiera Campionaria

V. P. Cortese

Via P. Maroncelli

Via Scrovegni

P

Via Trieste

Istituti Universitari

Via Leon Latedan

Istituti Universitari

Istituti Universitari

Istituti Universitari

Via Venezia

Via Fusinato

Via Morgagni

Via G. Belzoni

Via Proato Marzola

P.ta Venezia

P

Istituti Universitari

Via G. Gradenigo

P.za Stanga

Via Pistombra

S. Sofia

Via Altinare

Via S. Sofia

Via G. Fallopio

Via Ognissanti

P.ta Ognissanti

Can. Piovego

Via Tiepolo

S. Caterina

Ss. Massimo e Osvaldo

Via S. Massimo

Via Giustiniani

Cliniche Universitarie

Via dell'Ospedale Civile

Via Garibaldi

Pronto Soccorso

P.le Pontecorvo

Via S. Sanmichel

Via Stoppato

Via Manon

Via Soplari

Via Nazareth

Via Bronzetti

Via Bonardi

Via Jacopo Filias

Via Egidio Forcellini

Via Jacopo Facciola

Via Giovanni Canestrini

Via Forcellini

Forcellini

Via Bonarde

Via Pietro